Northwest Vista College
Learning Resource Center
3535 North Ellison Drive
San Antonio, Texas 78251

D1520893

The Japanese Family in Transition

ASIA/PACIFIC/PERSPECTIVES
Series Editor: Mark Selden

The Japanese Family in Transition

From the Professional Housewife Ideal to the Dilemmas of Choice

Suzanne Hall Vogel

with Steven K. Vogel

ROWMAN & LITTLEFIELD PUBLISHERS, INC.
Lanham • Boulder • New York • Toronto • Plymouth, UK

Published by Rowman & Littlefield Publishers, Inc.
A wholly owned subsidiary of The Rowman & Littlefield Publishing Group, Inc.
4501 Forbes Boulevard, Suite 200, Lanham, Maryland 20706
www.rowman.com

10 Thornbury Road, Plymouth PL6 7PP, United Kingdom

British Library Cataloguing in Publication Information Available

Library of Congress Cataloging-in-Publication Data

Vogel, Suzanne Hall, 1931–2012.
The Japanese family in transition : from the professional housewife ideal to the dilemmas of choice / Suzanne Hall Vogel with Steven K. Vogel.
pages cm. — (Asia/Pacific/perspectives)
Includes bibliographical references and index.
ISBN 978-1-4422-2171-0 (cloth : alk. paper) — ISBN 978-1-4422-2172-7 (electronic)
1. Families—Japan—Case studies. 2. Housewives—Japan—Case studies. 3. Women—Japan—Case studies. 4. Japan—Social conditions—1945– I. Vogel, Steven Kent. II. Title.
HQ682.V65 2013
306.850952—dc23
2012048484

The paper used in this publication meets the minimum requirements of American National Standard for Information Sciences Permanence of Paper for Printed Library Materials, ANSI/NISO Z39.48-1992.

Printed in the United States of America

Contents

Preface

My mother, Suzanne Hall Vogel, first traveled to Japan in 1958–1960 with my father on the field research trip that produced *Japan's New Middle Class* (1963). My parents were introduced to six families in a Tokyo suburb they called "Mamachi" through an elementary school parent-teacher association. They moved to Mamachi just before the school year began, and my older brother attended the local nursery school. In culturally appropriate fashion, my mother generally interviewed the wives, while my father spoke with the husbands. Needless to say, as we shall see in this volume, she often got the fuller picture of family life. My father was more the scholar and writer, however, so he wrote the book.

My parents have kept up with these families ever since, four of the six families in particular. My mother forged a deep and lasting friendship with the mothers, and this book represents an honest but loving testament to them. This is not the work of a detached observer but rather someone who was deeply embedded in the lives of her research subjects. My mother was only able to portray the intimate details of Japanese family life over a period of more than five decades because she knew these women so well. And as you will see, she wields the analytical lens of the psychotherapist and sociological researcher along the way.

Our family has remained close to these four Mamachi families over the years, and the friendships now extend down for three generations. I was actually closest to the fourth mother, the one not chosen for this book. My mother did not use the real names of these women to protect their privacy, so I will follow this practice and call this fourth mother "Mrs. Kimura." The Kimura family was my host family on weekends in 1978–1979, when I was attending a Japanese high school with weekday boarding. Mrs. Kimura embodied for me the best of the professional housewife ideal: total devotion to family, empathy for her children, resilience, warmth, and support. She was not as ingeniously strategic as Mrs. Suzuki or as feisty as Mrs. Itou, but she was a perfect host mother for me.

My mother had no trouble choosing the first two cases for this book: Mrs. Itou and Mrs. Suzuki had such amazing life stories, filled with dramatic twists of plot. They confided in my mother the most fully, and they had a remarkable ability to articulate their impressions and to analyze the dynamics of their families. Mrs. Tanaka and Mrs. Kimura had less dramatic and perhaps more typical life stories. The book would need one such case but perhaps not two, so Mrs. Tanaka was selected.

I also got to know the three leading ladies of this book quite well over the years. I worked as an English tutor at Mrs. Itou's after-school school (*juku*) during high school, as we shall see in chapter 3. I would bike over to the Itou family home on Saturday evenings, join the family for a leisurely dinner, and then proceed to the school with elder son Ken. Mrs. Tanaka lived with us in Cambridge for several months in 1977, so I experienced how she combined formality in speech with warm informality in person. I occasionally visited Mrs. Suzuki and witnessed firsthand how she would hold court from her own kitchen.

For my mother, this book represented a labor of love—a love for these three friends and for Japanese women more broadly. She thoroughly enjoyed talking to these women and analyzing their lives, but she was less keen on the arduous task of writing and editing. I worked closely with her during the later stages of revision. Meanwhile, Misato Nishijima, who had been one of my mother's social work trainees at Hasegawa Hospital, devoted herself to the Japanese translation. Misato outdid me by a clear margin, as the Japanese edition, *Kawariyuku nihon no kazoku*, came out in June 2012. My mother passed away only days before the book arrived in Cambridge, but she took great satisfaction in knowing that it was done and the English edition would soon follow.

Our Japanese friends insisted on a combined event to celebrate the book and to mourn her passing, so my brother David and sister Eve and I, two spouses, and two children set off on a bittersweet journey to Tokyo in August. The Mamachi families were well represented at the event, as well as many of my mother's professional friends. We had a follow-up gathering with Mrs. Itou and family a few days later. Mrs. Itou was her usual self, delightfully devoid of the usual Japanese housewife reticence, freely offering opinions on a wide range of topics and liberally embellishing some old stories. Ken joined us as well, but I sensed that the tension with his mother documented in chapter 3 had not completely dissipated. My wife and I followed this gathering with a J-Pop (Japanese popular music) concert and fireworks with two of the Itou grandchildren. If only my mother could have joined the festivities.

My mother and I discussed the acknowledgments over Mother's Day weekend, but we did not manage to write them out in full. She reported that her greatest debt was to the six families who agreed to participate in the original field research from 1958 to 1960, and especially to the three house-wives of this book. The Mamachi families opened their homes and their lives to her and became lifelong friends. The late Dr. Takeo Doi was her first and greatest teacher in the field of Japanese psychology, and his wife Yachiyo was second only to him. Countless other Japanese scholars, mental health professionals, and friends helped to support the research over the years in myriad ways, from making introductions to providing fresh insights. The staff at St. Luke's and Hasegawa Hospitals offered clinical expertise, case experience, and personal support. The Fulbright Foundation provided finan-cial support for a research year in 1988–1989. Pat Murray helped with edit-ing, and Kenneth Haig and Yuko Hara offered critical research assistance. Mark Selden and an anonymous reviewer provided helpful comments, and Susan McEachern, Carrie Broadwell-Tkach, and Jehanne Schweitzer guided the manuscript from review through production.

Steven K. Vogel
Berkeley, California

Chapter One

The Postwar Ideal

"Would YOU want to be a Japanese housewife?!?"

Some Japanese feminists shot this question at me during the 1978 Tokyo Symposium on Women, where I presented a paper on the Japanese *sengyou shufu*, or "professional housewife."[1] I had written the paper for an American audience to challenge American stereotypes of Japanese women and to present Japanese middle-class suburban housewives in their own terms. I had developed friendships with a group of such housewives from 1958 to 1960, and they had impressed me with their personal strength and their mothering skills. Trying to be a good anthropologist, I was more descriptive than evaluative in my account, but my overview was generally positive. The women who came together at that symposium, however, had a very different mission. They strongly criticized the traditional Japanese housewife role as confining and oppressive. I suddenly found myself confronting a major challenge from Japanese women themselves! I realized that there were within Japan two contradictory images of the professional housewife: a strong and intelligent woman, confident in the central importance of her role as a nurturer, admirably guiding her family; and a weak and pitiful woman, confined to servitude in the house, submissive to men and obedient to her mother-in-law. "Which was more true?" I wondered.

I have wrestled with these conflicting images over the years. I have witnessed the tension between those who insist that concern for family welfare demands that mothers be full-time homemakers and those who believe that women must be encouraged to develop their full potential in all areas. As this struggle continued, women's roles have steadily evolved, resolving old problems and generating new ones. Over the postwar decades, the multigenerational family gave way to the nuclear family. Women married later and bore fewer children, and more women chose not to marry at all. They became better educated, and gained better prospects for employment. Then since the 1990s, they confronted greater economic uncertainty with slower economic growth, rising unemployment, a decline of lifetime employment, and an increase in part-time and temporary work. Yet the overarching ideal of the professional housewife persists amidst this constant social change and a growing diversity of activities and opportunities for Japanese women. Much of the ongoing resistance, compromise, and accommodation can be seen as forms of reaction to that persistent ideal. This ideal provides a powerful lens through which to understand the contested nature of the feminine role in Japan since 1945.

In this book, I argue that the role of the professional housewife both constrained and empowered Japanese women. That is, Japanese housewives had considerable autonomy and authority within their designated realm precisely because of fixed gender roles, with women centered on the home and children while men focused on work. The professional housewife ideal had enormous costs: it locked women into specified roles regardless of their preferences or abilities; it impeded women from pursuing other dreams and from contributing to society in other ways; and it made women feel unworthy if they were not living up to the ideal. Yet it also delivered some real benefits: Japan's postwar professional housewives were the true masters of their home and family; they garnered great confidence and security from having a clear role and mission; and they were exceptional mothers to generations of Japanese.

Moreover, I suggest that the professional housewife ideal continues to cast a shadow over Japanese society today, even as it fades. Current-day wives and mothers have more options than their mothers and grandmothers did, and yet they find themselves unprepared to cope with this new era of choice. Government policies and social services remain designed primarily for male breadwinner families, not for working mothers. Many women still feel that they must choose between full-time mothering and full-time work because they cannot possibly fulfill the expectations of a Japanese wife and mother unless they do so full-time. Their own professional housewife mothers and grandmothers taught these women to conform within an orderly society, not to make choices in a fluid one. Japanese women today have less pride and confidence in their housewife/mother roles, and many of them worry about their inability to duplicate the "professional" model of their mothers and grandmothers. Japanese mothers are less authoritative within the family than their predecessors, and arguably less effective.

Furthermore, the decline of the professional housewife ideal has had *psychological* effects. It has contributed to a shift in the nature of social and psychological disorders in Japan, and possibly to the increase in these disorders overall. Japanese women are now less bound by constraints or tormented by mothers-in-law or husbands, but more anxious over choices. Social change and economic uncertainly have fueled a surge in new types of psychological disorders, including school refusal, withdrawal from society (*hikikomori*), and sexless couples.

While I studied Japanese women's roles, my vantage point was always that of an American woman, a mental health clinician by profession, with a sociological/anthropological perspective. I wanted to know how different societies produce different patterns of mental health issues. While all societies have mental health problems, and there is no evidence that either Japanese women or American women are any sicker than most, I wondered how the issues facing Japanese women compared to those facing American women. In Japan, I learned how the pattern of mental health problems at any given time reflects the particular social, cultural, and historical context, and how the prevalent patterns of psychiatric symptoms shift as society changes. Women's social role in a given society conditions women's overall well-being, both positively and negatively.

This book draws on insights into the changing character and self-perception of Japanese women gained in three periods of research. This makes it possible to trace major changes and continuities in the position of middle-class women over half a century. In 1958–1960, my first trip, I appreciated the strengths of the Japanese housewives I encountered. In the 1970s, I became aware of the feminist arguments behind a rising and critical opposition to traditional women's roles as I repeatedly returned to Japan. And after 1988, I learned more about changing social patterns and associated psychiatric problems through my annual six-week visit to a mental health hospital in Tokyo where I supervised social workers and sometimes worked directly with patients. While this clinical work gave me the most insight into the stresses of the changing women's role, it was the early suburban housewives who taught me how "normal" women dealt with the traditional *sengyou shufu* role. Chapters 2 through 4 examine the lives of three of these women who have lived through the entire postwar period to examine in depth how the positives and negatives of the professional housewife role played out in their own life stories and in the lives of their families. Chapter 5 then addresses the many changes from the 1960s through the present, with special attention to the more dramatic changes since the 1990s, including major new challenges to the family and the employment system.

TRADITIONAL HOUSEWIVES

The Japanese professional housewife was a well-defined role, idealized since the 1880s as the epitome of the "good wife and wise mother" (*ryousai kem-*

bo). In this view, reinforced by community and social pressures, all women should be mothers, married, devoting themselves full-time to their families. They should be nurturing, able to raise healthy and successful children, and willing to provide total care for a husband and parents as well as children. They typically met their husbands through an arranged marriage (*omiai*), and their relationship with their children took precedence over their relationship with their husbands. In 1958, the middle-class suburban women I knew universally accepted this role. I realized that most Americans would find it intolerably restrictive. Indeed, my gut feeling from the time I first went to Japan was that I would *not* want to be a Japanese housewife. That role did not include the kind of relationship I wanted in my marriage. At the same time, I greatly admired the housewives I met, and I was aware that my own feelings reflected my own cultural predispositions. I wanted to observe their world from their point of view, and to understand as realistically and deeply as possible the contradictions and complexities of their lives. I wanted to know how they reconciled conflicts and how they coped with challenges over their lifetimes. What enabled them to be so competent and so satisfied in roles that seemed to preclude dimensions that were central to me?

I first encountered Japanese families when Ezra Vogel, my former husband, our toddler son, and I lived in the Tokyo area from 1958 to 1960 doing research on Japanese family life. We focused on middle-class suburban families, six of which had been selected for us by principals of schools in the community and had agreed to meet with us for the duration of our research period in Japan. The husbands were not farmers or small merchants, whose wives would be expected to help with the business. They were mostly professionals, or "salarymen," who worked in the offices of large companies. Their wives were *sengyou shufu*, the full-time "professional" housewives. Most of the husbands had college degrees while the wives had graduated from girls' high schools (*jogakkou*). We called them our "well" families, comparing them with another set of families whose members were in psychiatric treatment centering on a child's symptoms. They were indeed quite normal families with healthy children, reasonably good intra-familial relationships, and no serious psychiatric issues. The Japanese women I came to know well were housewives participating in our research, plus a few friends and neighbors. All were full-time housewives, whose lifestyle indicated that they aspired to be "good wives and wise mothers." I later learned that this ideal filtered into the values of the middle class from the gender roles of the samurai classes in pre-Meiji Japan. The Meiji elite promulgated it purposefully to dignify Japanese women in the eyes of Westerners, while also keeping them at home and preventing them from competing with men. [2]

Japan's New Middle Class gives an account of what we learned about family life in the suburban town where we lived and did much of our interviewing. [3] Now fifty years later, I realize that we conducted our research at the heyday of the professional housewife ideal, for the patterns we observed relied on historically contingent socioeconomic conditions. Farmers were declining as a percentage of the population, while salarymen were increasing. Economic prosperity allowed more middle-class wives to afford to stay home with children full-time. As we shall see in the concluding chapter, the professional housewife ideal has gradually faded over the past fifty years as women gained better education and improved job prospects, family structure evolved, and then economic stagnation since the 1990s undermined employment protection and economic security. Meanwhile, I have discovered that this ideal has impeded Japanese society's transition to a new era characterized by more options for women, and contributed to the emergence of new social problems.

Our living situation taught me much about the realities of daily family life in our Tokyo suburb of Mamachi. Our small house was comparatively new, but it retained features of a more traditional style. Its central area was two *tatami* rooms with *shouji* sliding screens that opened wide to the outdoors during the day and were closed at night after heavy outer wooden doors were pulled shut. The approach to our house, via neatly swept dirt pathways alongside six-foot wooden fences, reminded us of the privacy and security the neighbors valued and of the cooperative responsibility they assumed for common space. During the day, guests entered our house through the entryway, calling out "*gomen kudasai*" (excuse me) to announce their presence. They would take off their shoes, step up into the house, and slide into a pair of waiting slippers. Children playing in the yard could come in through almost any room just by climbing up onto the veranda and entering through the open *shouji*, leaving their shoes outside. A smaller, Western-style room with a wooden floor contained chairs, a TV, a small table, and a gas heater, which provided the only heat in the house except for the *kotatsu*.[4] In the evenings we sat and studied Japanese there, but during the day everyone was busy working, sometimes sitting Japanese style on the *tatami*, or else warming in the *kotatsu*. One *tatami* room was more formal, aesthetically simple and elegant with a *tokonoma* (alcove), while the other was more like a family room, made warm and comfortable by the presence of the *kotatsu* in the center.

Few families used beds. Together with our two-year-old, we slept on *futon*, the soft thick mats that we laid out on the *tatami* every night. I longed for a crib for our young one, something that seemed not to exist in Japan at that time, but I had no choice but to adopt the Japanese style of putting a small child to sleep by lying down with him until he fell asleep, and then groggily rousing myself to get through the rest of the evening. The kitchen was spare: there was a two-burner gas range set on a square wooden cabinet, no oven, a small refrigerator, and a sink set so low I had to bend over it. The toilet was a well-cleaned, no-flush hole in the floor. The *kumitoriyasan* (night-soil collector) came weekly to take away the contents in his barrel. I had little trouble learning to sleep on the floor and to squat over the toilet. Now, in my later years, I am grateful to find beds in most places and high-tech toilets in Japan that make ours in the United States seem positively primitive by comparison.

I was grateful to experience ordinary Japanese living conditions, but the best thing about our Mamachi lifestyle was our maid. We were fortunate to have in our house a small maid's room. In just a few years the practice would largely disappear, but at that time live-in maids, who were treated as part of the family, were still commonly found in middle-class households and they were easy to find. Our maid, Mitsuko-san, was a vital part of our family. She cleaned, shopped, heated our Japanese bath (*ofuro*), and used the still-warm bathwater the next day to wash clothes. She instructed the grocery delivery boy that we foreigners need lots of milk; while most families had one half-pint bottle delivered daily, we had at least ten. She happily took care of our two-year-old, freeing me to ride my bicycle through small, car-free lanes to do my interviewing. My daily conversations with her enlightened me about many aspects of ordinary life and accustomed me to the style and vocabulary of daily conversation.

Most of our neighbors remained secluded behind their fences, often with guard dogs loose in the yard for added protection, but a couple of families were friendly and helpful. One five-year-old boy became our son's playmate and led him into a fun-filled year at a nearby preschool. When the time came to return to Boston, our son David, by then three, was still hanging onto his preschool backpack when he boarded the plane.

The families we visited lived in houses with the same kind of facilities that I was learning to use. Some were not much bigger, while others, with larger families, had more space. Whether they had maids or not, the women were all busy from morning to night tending to the house and keeping their families going. They kept their homes and the streets outside them immaculately clean, and I was often impressed by other little things, like how neatly and efficiently they could fold garments and linens and fit the maximum number of items into a small cabinet or drawer. I admired the simplicity of the décor in their houses, the small gardens they tended, and the way they presented meals. The wives were responsible for everything within the house and inside the fences. It was not necessary to call ahead to make sure someone was home before going to visit. The wife was almost always at home. And if she went out briefly to shop, there would always be someone else there watching the house until she got back. For the most part, these women did not have much time to cultivate outside hobbies or to participate in civic affairs in their child-raising years. To the extent they did so, however, they chose activities that would complement rather than conflict with their housewife role, such as flower arrangement or the PTA.

FULL-TIME YET INDEPENDENT

I admired my Japanese women friends' well-organized lives and their commitment to their families. Yet I knew I would not want to take on their role. I could see at work the internalized values of a patriarchal system that still held some sway, even though it had been ebbing since the war. Those values decreed that a woman must obey a man throughout her life: as a child, her father; as a wife, her husband; as an old woman, her eldest son. To live forever under the dictates of one man or another would stir an American revolution in my soul. Such a relationship would not provide me, or most American wives, with the strong marital bond based on mutual affection and emotional support that I needed. It took me longer to realize that in many ways these Japanese wives were actually much more independent than I was. The very separation of roles gave the women a level of responsibility for their lives at home that promised little interference from their husbands. They made their own decisions. Their status was secure, and they did not worry about approval from their husbands.

The emotional independence of these wives was brought home to me by two specific incidents. Many had expressed envy of my freedom to go out socially with my husband, but I gradually realized that these comments were mostly flattery and did not represent their true feelings. When one wife had to travel to Hong Kong with her husband, her friends were not envious—rather they commiserated with her. Why? Because they agreed that once the couple had exhausted the subject of the children, she and her husband would have little to talk about. In short, they assumed emotional and social distance between wife and husband as their reality.

The most striking incident came when we invited all the families cooperating with our research project to an open house. We asked everyone to come from all three generations. The response was interesting: the wives got together beforehand and decided that the husbands should not be included. They later explained that if the husbands came, then the wives and children would have no fun. The husbands would do all the talking, and the rest of the family would have to be quiet. So grandparents, mothers, and children came but no fathers. (I thought to myself that these wives were actually far from weak. It took some nerve for them to decide who was to be invited to *our* party!)

What I came to understand about the Japanese family, especially in Mamachi, is discussed at greater length in *Japan's New Middle Class.*[5] Much of what caught my attention at that time has been articulated and analyzed in studies by sociologists of Japan. Chie Nakane, for example, gave clear definition to what she called Japan's vertical society (*tateshakai*), where relations with one's superiors and inferiors are more important than horizontal peer relationships.[6] In Japan, a group-focused rather than an individualistic society, the welfare of the family and maintaining its structure took priority over the individual needs of any one member. Fifty years later, I now see more clearly how the focus on the group actually sustained the psychic needs of individuals in the high-growth era by providing the security of stable codes of behavior plus the satisfaction derived from collective achievement. Several decades later, however, this group ethic left many Japanese unprepared for a new era characterized by more uncertainty and choice.

Takie Sugiyama Lebra described Japanese society as sociocentric rather than egocentric.[7] Fitting into and supporting one's group, especially family or work groups, was fostered ahead of individual fulfillment. "What is ruled out as an unacceptable motive is *wagamama*, selfishness."[8] I observed such attitudes in the Mamachi families, but I have come to see them as a matter of emphasis within a hierarchy of values. In East and West alike there are both group-centered and individualistic values; the difference lies in which is ascendant. Americans favor the idea that if the individual prospers, the group will benefit and therefore the welfare of the individual should not be sacrificed for the group. Japanese assume that if the group prospers the individual benefits from the security and status conferred by this. They do not condone individual inclinations that undermine group welfare but rather look on behavior of that sort as selfishness.

The subordination of individuals to families was attested by the way births were registered. Each new baby was not issued an individual birth certificate but was entered in the father's family register. When the mother married into the family as a bride, her name was first removed from her own father's family register and then added to that of her husband. Apparently it was possible by this system to enter into a state of legal anomie, as in cases in which a divorced woman might end up being registered nowhere, having been removed from her birth family's register upon marriage and expunged from her husband's, and yet not reentered on her original family registry when she was divorced. She would then, among other things, have no claim to a place in any cemetery when she died. This particular problem has gradually disappeared since the 1980s, when divorced women started to get together to find cemetery space for themselves.

While I saw the rigid male-dominated family and the group emphasis as confining, the Japanese I knew more often experienced it as secure, stable, and predictable. A firm structure gave protection. Responsibilities on all sides were clear. The division of labor, at least in 1960, was almost universally accepted. The roles of men and women were separate but parallel. The husband had overall responsibility to provide for the family and authority over family decisions, but the salaryman jobs held by so many Mamachi men took virtually all of a man's time and energy six days a week or more, usually until late at night.[9] There were few restrictions on the demands made on Japan's salarymen. The woman's job of home and family care demanded equally all-consuming devotion. In her case, too, she put in long hours, day and night, answerable to unrestricted demands on her own time and energy. The husband's work supported Japan's push for national economic productivity and progress, and the wife's work enabled the husband to do his job, a point stressed by the government. Both jobs had a high degree of permanence and stability: divorce, layoffs, and resignations were rare. Marriage was called "lifetime employment" for the wife, complementing the lifetime employment system for the husband-salaryman. Lebra notes that there was a lower incidence of wife abuse in well-structured families that gave women security and comfort. Family caretaking was, and to a considerable extent continued to be, what gave women status and standing in society. [10]

In extended families at that time, a young wife was placed under the tutelage and supervision of her mother-in-law, who oversaw the household. The young wife's work was childcare, food preparation and serving, house cleaning, shopping, monitoring schoolwork, caring for elders in the household, and attending to all her husband's needs. The wives I met routinely prepared beautiful box lunches for all children going off to school and for their husbands or other men going to work, greeted them on their return home, and had ready slippers, perhaps a change of clothes, a hot bath, and a meal. The wives were there to serve dinner to their late-returning husbands, no matter how late the hour, long after others had eaten and gone to bed. Husbands were allowed to relax and rest from their work at the office, coddled, soothed, and affirmed. They were certainly not to be criticized or expected to help with household chores. We often heard about a husband who did not even know how to make a cup of tea or boil an egg and rarely ventured into the kitchen. Wives took care of everything related to the house, including gardening and house repairs. In most cases they also managed the family finances. The husband handed over his paycheck and the wife then divided it up to pay bills and cover children's expenses, and she then handed her husband money for his daily or weekly expenses. She oversaw savings and did the bookkeeping.

All this, as I came to see, gave wives (or at least the senior wife in extended families) considerable power within the household. Many wives in fact had almost complete control over household affairs and child-rearing, despite the nominal authority of the husband. Within that limited sphere of operation, they seemed to have more control than most American wives did. I heard stories of young brides who were miserable under the stern direction of exacting mothers-in-law, who were worked from dawn until late at night caring for house and family, but I did not encounter such women. Mostly because they were not living with their in-laws, the women I talked with were in complete charge of their own households. [11] They seemed to accept the status quo: men, devoted to their jobs, worked long and hard and used their pay to provide financial support, while women put in equally long hours caring for the family. Socially women were subordinated to men, but I also sensed that men's and women's responsibilities were complementary, and that men and women each had strength in his or her sphere.

Families where the husband/son-in-law had been adopted into the wife's family were the exception that supported the norm of patriarchal families. Although the *ie* system had been legally abolished by the postwar Civil Code in 1948, it remained customary in Mamachi and elsewhere to consider the senior male in a household—not the female—as its head. When there were no male heirs, not infrequently a family would marry one daughter to a man who agreed to be removed from his own family register, be registered and thereby adopted into the bride's family, and become a legal heir. He was called a *mukoyoushi* or adopted son-in-law. Succeeding his father-in-law, he assumed the authority and responsibility to maintain the family's well-being by providing financial support, upholding discipline within the family, and managing the family's relations with the outside world. Just as a young father respected and looked after his own father, a *mukoyoushi* was expected to defer to his father-in-law until the latter retired. The *mukoyoushi* pattern has almost disappeared in recent times, with fewer sons to spare in smaller families. Also, fewer men are willing to give up their own name, and more families will allow a branch family line to die. But in 1958 the pattern was still relatively common.

AMAE

As I struggled to make sense of this society and its patriarchal legacies, particularly the strong mother-child relationship, Takeo Doi, the preeminent psychoanalyst, was invaluable to me. His two best-known books, *The Anatomy of Dependence* and *The Anatomy of Self*, illuminate basic Japanese psychology and the crucial function of *amae* (initially translated as "dependence") for the development of children and healthy relationships. [12]

Years before the publication of these books, however, my family and I experienced *amae* directly. Through a fortunate introduction, soon after our arrival in Tokyo in 1958 we rented a house next door to the Doi home and soon found ourselves indulging in the benevolence of the family. We shamelessly depended on Takeo and his wife Yachiyo for help concerning countless daily needs, including how and where to shop, how to find a live-in maid, and even how to plant a Western-style lawn in the front of the house. (As we discovered soon enough, our lawn was an immensely silly idea for a Japanese setting.) Takeo, who had a talent for teaching meaningful Japanese expressions, suggested in his straightforward manner that the most natural way to express gratitude was often not "*arigatou*" (thank you) but "*osewa ni narimasu*" (I am indebted to you).

Doi used different English translations at different times for *amae*, since there is no best English gloss for this term, but in my understanding the essence of Doi's *amae* is seen in the mother-child relationship, how a baby seeks and receives nurturance from its mother. A baby whose most important needs are fulfilled through this intimate, interactive relationship is more likely to develop in a healthy way. A child who has not been nurtured by a truly caring and understanding mother might be more likely to develop psychological problems. Such an empathic connection is basic to all healthy and helpful relationships.

In retrospect, I recognize that Doi not only valued the professional housewife ideal, but that he viewed the intimate relationship between a full-time mother and her small child as the essential *amae* relationship. Japan's devoted mothers epitomize *amae* with their close physical bond and nonverbal understanding with the child. Yet the potential for *amae* is universal, transcending the Japanese context and the mother-child relationship. In fact, I have come to understand Doi somewhat differently over the years, particularly through my clinical practice. I now believe that Doi was stressing the importance of a particular kind of empathy (even though he does not use that term): the nonverbal understanding of another person. And he felt that such empathy was critical to professional therapeutic relationships as well as to family relationships.

The close relationship between Japanese mothers and babies was sometimes referred to as "skinship," describing comforting physical contact. In that day, babies were almost always in physical contact with their mothers. Nursing generally went on for a year or longer, any time the baby wanted to nurse. Babies and toddlers, and even somewhat older children, slept with their mothers, or with their fathers when a new baby was born. Many Japanese mothers have commented that they feel sorry for the poor lonely American infants put to bed in rooms by themselves and sometimes allowed to cry themselves to sleep. An infant or small child in 1960s Japan was carried on the mother's back, whether she was working in the field, in a store, or around the house. Young children typically bathed with their mothers, sometimes until puberty, although growing boys would begin bathing with their fathers.

A Japanese mother would consider a baby's cry as signaling the need for immediate attention, if not as a sign of inadequate maternal care. I remember being mildly annoyed when a Japanese mother quickly came over to comfort my two-year-old who was crying because I had told him sharply, "No." She clearly felt sorry for him, and I felt chastised.

The constant physical contact of skinship let the mother and child be constantly, wordlessly, aware of each other's feelings. The mother, sensing the baby's needs, took care of them before they became a problem. She learned to sense when the baby needed to urinate or defecate and would hold him while he performed. Toilet training was early, although American doctors consider this behavior as training for the mother more than the child. Babies and children were indulged and their needs met as fully as possible, usually until the child started school and other types of training began.

This type of close relationship described as *amae*, in which the child naturally expected and received caring responsiveness from the mother, was also the basis for social training. The baby was soothed, not stimulated like American babies, and encouraged to be quiet and gentle. In teaching social behavior like bowing, the mother would move the child's body into the right position with a minimum of explanation. The maternal intimacy led the child to sense and to follow the mother's wishes, thus avoiding the need for authoritarian commands. From all I had seen, read, and heard, Japanese children thus raised were considerably less prone to what American parents refer to as the "terrible twos." During the 1980s and 1990s whenever Japanese parents came into my Boston-area therapy office with a toddler in tow, the child would sit quietly on the parent's lap for a whole hour. I have seldom seen an American child do that. I marveled at the effects of this closeness and soothing.

Dependence on mother was used for social control in other ways. I once watched a mother walking with her two-year-old to the grocery store. The child dawdled and wandered from time to time, as children do. While an American mother might grab the child's hand and insist that the child stay with her, the Japanese mother instead quietly ran a bit ahead, immediately causing the child to hurry and catch up so as to not lose the mother: no scolding, no commands. One evening, when a child next door could be heard crying, our maid explained to us that he was being punished by being shut out of the house. Now he was crying and banging on the gate to be let in again. An American mother would never use that type of punishment, I thought; rather she would lock the child *in* the house, or send him to his room, depriving him of his independence, not his dependence.

Communication among family members also involves a great deal of silent, nonverbal communication, often bodily cues, compared with Western societies where families rely more on verbal communication. The Japanese verb *sassuru* means to sense the other person's feeling without words, and *isshin denshin* refers to unspoken mutual understanding. This silent communication has been particularly valued between spouses, though it was more often the woman who was called upon to do the sensing. "According to the Japanese traditional ideal," notes Sumiko Iwao, "the most manly of men was a man of few words."[13] Silent understanding was valued for both sexes. "Understanding attained without words is more precious than that attained through precise articulation."[14] Yet it was the men who expected their wives to grasp their needs without an explicit request, all the more because it was the wife's job to serve her husband. Wives might wish for similar silent understanding from their husbands, but even when it was there from time to time, they did not expect it.

With roles segregated and feelings often communicated silently or unvoiced, for many couples this was enough to ensure minimal conflict between them. For them, their ability to understand each other became stronger after living together for years. I often heard it said that for couples in middle age, a good relationship is like the air: "It is vital for both sides but its presence is hardly felt." In the Tokyo of 1960, I was occasionally told that romantic love was much too fickle to be the basis for anything as important as marriage.

THE HIDDEN STRENGTH OF JAPANESE HOUSEWIVES

By 1960, when we said goodbye and returned to the United States, I understood better how the husband-wife separation of roles and the marital lack of what I thought of as intimacy fit the pattern of family life. Even though I did not wish for that pattern myself, I admired my Japanese friends' child-rearing skills and devotion to family, and I accepted that they were generally comfortable and content. Their clear division of labor with little overlap in roles minimized arguments. Little sharing meant few conflicts. I was astonished by the wives' minimal involvement with anything outside the house or interests of their own. They occasionally expressed envy, that my husband helped with our son and did the dishes on the maid's day off, and that we traveled and socialized together. Over time, however, I recognized that they liked being in charge at home without interference from their husbands. They knew their role was important and the family depended on their care; they preferred the company of children or female relatives. They were stiffer when husbands were around. There was a familiar saying: "A good husband is healthy and absent" (*teishu wa joubu de rusu ga ii*). Above all, their relationships with their children were their greatest satisfaction, their purpose in life (*ikigai*).

These were not weak and dependent women, contrary to the stereotype in the West. They had emotional strength and independence and did not seek emotional support or comfort from their husbands, even while extending to them physical comforts and emotional affirmation. But to whom, I wondered, did they turn for emotional sustenance, for a response to their own need for *amae*? They seemed to be always giving, but seldom receiving. The best answer I could come up with at that time was that they received emotional gratification from the close relationship with their children; they turned to their own mothers or sisters for comfort if they lived near enough; and some turned to the quiet and solace of nature.

After I had lived in Tokyo for two years and several subsequent summers, these women had become good friends, and I was grateful to them for sharing their world with me. Realizing that I had seen the "good wife, wise mother" in action, I wrote the article "Professional Housewife" as seen through my anthropological lens, to help correct American stereotypes of Japanese women.[15] Without consciously intending to, I had made Japanese women's roles an ongoing focus of interest. I could see their strengths, their skills, and the importance of their mothering role. I had wondered if they saw themselves as inferior to men, but a couple of them had spontaneously spoken about their role as mother as being important and valuable, as much as any job in the world. It remained a source of wonder to me that they did not seem to need what I needed, namely a closer, sharing marital relationship and equal participation in the outside world. Even knowing my own preferences, I was able to accept a largely positive view of their role as manifested in the lives of these happy and healthy women.

THE WOMEN'S MOVEMENT

Quite the opposite view confronted me at the 1978 symposium when I presented my glowing view of the housewife role. This was not a surprise. For some years, American-style feminist groups had been forming in Japan. Furthermore, I had spent 1975–1976 in Tokyo talking with career women, including feminists, in order to broaden my understanding of Japanese women and to understand the changes taking place at that time. I had set up an interviewing project with the encouragement of the Radcliffe Institute at Harvard to compare full-time unmarried career women and women who combined family and career with the full-time housewives I had met earlier and continued to see as friends. I also met with some feminist groups and/or their leaders, including Yayoi Aoki, Sachiko Ide, and Chizuko Ueno.

Basically, the feminists saw women as being unduly restricted and oppressed within the family, and discriminated against in the workplace. I heard of and spoke with wives who had been exploited by their husband's family and wives locked in an everlasting struggle with their stronger mothers-in-law. Trying to combat this kind of oppression and exploitation, the women's movement rejected the ideals of the good wife–wise mother and the professional housewife.

An increasing number of women in Japan sought meaningful outside employment, but they were encountering severe difficulty in launching and maintaining careers. They complained that career paths open to women were few and hard to enter. Successful unmarried professional women were accepted but stigmatized as unfeminine. The married career women I interviewed often had a mother or mother-in-law willing to help with childcare.

Married women who worked simply because they wanted to were considered selfish. And they had to carry out all their family duties as well as their job with no help from their husbands. By 1975, I could see that the live-in maids, common in middle-class families in the 1950s, had pretty much disappeared, many of them going to work in newly booming factories. What remained was the traditional reluctance to have outsiders come into the home, so that cleaning ladies or baby-sitters were considered unacceptable intruders. Paradoxically, this meant that young wives in the growing numbers of nuclear families, while liberated from domineering mothers-in-law, were often more burdened by housework and childcare than the older generation of mothers had been in the extended families, even with their new electric appliances.

I was especially impressed by the story of one woman researcher, a graduate of an elite university married to a scientist from that university. Her husband was broad-minded enough to recognize her need to do work of her own choosing and agreed that she could pursue her own career, so long as she also carried out all her duties at home. With three children and a full day teaching, she got up at 5:30 every morning, straightened the house, did the laundry, fixed breakfast and lunches, and took two children to school and another to day care before going to work. On returning home, she picked up the children and shopped for groceries, and then cooked the family's dinner. She never argued with her husband about chores. He had made it clear that he would spend full-time on his research. Besides, she told me, her daily struggles were all over by the time he came home at night. She often wondered why she put herself through such stress by working, but at the same time she was grateful that she had been able to continue.

Another professional woman active in a women's group felt such anger and alienation from her husband that she moved into an apartment two blocks away. There she pursued a totally independent life during the day, including a career and an affair, but went back to the family house every morning to cook breakfast, make lunches, clean up, and usually leave something for her husband and teenage child to eat at supper. She did not seek a divorce and neither did he. He reputedly said that he had no cause for divorce, evidently because she was still doing her duties, even though spousal communication and affection were nil.

These women astounded me with their energy and perseverance. They refused to be confined by their housewife role but continued to fulfill the responsibilities that went with it because it was their job and their moral duty. I was also struck by the paramount importance given to maintaining the structure of the family. Among those I talked with, more than a few were completely alienated from their spouses, emotionally and sexually, and led separate social lives but did not divorce. Most often they continued to live in the same house and keep the family intact. There was a name for this situation: *kateinai rikon,* or "divorce inside the family."

My impression of Japan's new women's movement at that time was that apart from a few flamboyant women—the *Chupiren* or Pink Helmet Brigade, for example—and a few women seeking public office, most of their efforts were not nearly as aggressive or confrontational as those of many American feminists. They sought to part with the notion that women were always secondary, the family's needs coming first. The movement backed rights for women not only to have an education equal to men's, but also to work and to receive equal treatment in the working world. Yet not until 1985 was the equal employment law passed, and even then it lacked penalties for noncompliance.

The first annual International Women's Conference (*Kokusai Josei Gakkai*) took place in 1978 and yearly after that. Kiyomi Kawano, a social worker trained in the United States, launched a series of "feminist therapy" clinics in Tokyo, and later in Osaka.[16] These clinics, somewhat similar to American consciousness-raising groups, provided group support and individual counseling to help women become aware of their own feelings and needs, express themselves effectively, and take action when needed on their own behalf. They also provided training for counselors. Yoriko Madoka had already organized *Nikoniko Rikon* (Smiling Divorce), a group formed to support women who wanted to divorce.[17] The feminist magazine *Agora* started coming out. Then and subsequently, much of the political effort on women's behalf was toward making day care more available and more affordable so that married women could work. Some elite tracks (medicine, law, some government ministries) opened up to women, but even many years later I found that most women felt pressure to resign from their jobs when they became mothers. Maternity leave or the opportunity to work at the same job part-time after a maternity leave was the exception rather than the rule. In the 1970s and even the 1990s, a woman who wanted to return to work after her children started school could usually get only lower-status so-called part-time work, often with full-time hours and no benefits.

One meeting in 1976 of a relatively militant feminist group advanced a message that seemed creatively Japanese. The strongest speaker did not suggest political demonstrations or angry attacks on husbands or other men, which I would have expected as an American. Rather, she suggested simply "cutting the umbilical cord," that is, ceasing to respond to the needs of men. To me, this indicated an inclination to avoid direct confrontation and at the same time an awareness of women's strength and how to use it. These women knew how fully their husbands depended on them for daily care, and they realized that their most effective protest strategy would be to withdraw that care. It was interesting to reflect that in the midst of a group of strong-minded feminists, I was being reminded of the strengths I had discovered earlier in the traditional housewife role.

In fact, most feminists at that time were pushing for greater recognition of the value of women in their caretaking role. They wanted their contribution to society to be considered as important as men's. The fervor of some was fed by remarks in the press—made by men—about women's supposed intellectual inferiority, but on the whole they sought to utilize strengths acquired in the home to empower women to speak for themselves and to broaden participation in society. They encouraged political activities that arose out of family concerns, such as consumer unions and community service. While they favored equality in the workforce, they more often lobbied for good day care, menstrual and maternal leave, and other supports for women who worked to help their families financially. In other words, they were not seeking to change women's caretaking role in the home, but wanted to strengthen it, expand it, and acquire for it attention and appreciation equal to that given men's work.

Sumiko Iwao argues that women have generally viewed politics as something unrelated to their lives and values, so they "have exercised power mainly in their personal or local spheres."[18] Robin LeBlanc suggests that women are involved in the political world differently than men. Through ethnographic fieldwork in suburban Tokyo in the 1990s, she found that Japanese housewives were engaged in politics primarily through community activism such as welfare volunteer work or consumer groups. LeBlanc characterized women's relationship with politics as one more caring, personal, and egalitarian than that of men.[19]

Yayoi Aoki, one of the early feminist writers after the war, heralded the "feminine principle" and "eco-feminism." In our 1976 interview, she remarked, "In contemporary society, where a woman's role is essentially limited to reproduction and even that is given no value as labor, women seek a means of enhancing their status in whatever way possible, striving to achieve some positive recognition of their existence." In a 1989 follow-up interview, she explained that her eco-feminism placed emphasis on what is natural, considering women as biologically distinct but not inferior, and arguing against today's movement toward more and more technology, away from nature.

For Chizuko Ueno, a well-known feminist cultural theorist, eco-feminism ignored the realities of capitalist industrial society and the influence of the class structure. She argued in our 1976 interview that the *sengyou shufu* model applied only to the middle class and only since the Meiji period. Poorer women always worked beside their men. And in this industrial age, women's fulfillment and equality would require basic changes in society and could only be achieved when the men "come home," that is, when they value the home as much as their work and participate in caring for home and children. She put forth a view that has become more prominent over time, and has gone on to publish many articles and books.[20]

The feminist movements in Japan and the United States are similar in many ways, but the American movement has been more confrontational and more insistent on equality in the working world. That is, the assumption that men's roles define successful lives is stronger. The Japanese movement has been less combative, more strongly characterized by efforts toward gradual but steady changes in women's lives and in Japanese family life, while pushing for stronger recognition of the social and economic value of housewives and other women. In both countries, feminist movements have evolved and become less strident since the 1970s, perhaps because they have, after all, had an impact on the changing society.

A PSYCHOTHERAPIST'S PERSPECTIVE

My psychosocial perspective stems from my professional training as a clinical caseworker/psychotherapist. Our early work in Japan, from 1958 to 1960, was sociological research on Japanese family life. Although we focused mostly on normal, healthy families, our connection with the Japanese National Institute of Mental Health brought us in contact with symptomatic families and their treatment. After 1988, however, I was directly involved with clinical work and teaching, first during a Fulbright research year at St. Luke's Hospital in Tokyo and subsequently during yearly periods of four to six weeks at Hasegawa Hospital, a large private psychiatric hospital in suburban Tokyo. All during these years, I continued to learn from Takeo Doi and the psychiatrists, psychologists, and social workers to whom he introduced me. Quite literally, I continued to *amaeru* on his benevolence and his wisdom. I could learn from my Japanese colleagues about psychiatric problems and compare them with the kinds of problems exhibited by the American patients I saw the rest of the year in Cambridge, Massachusetts. For twenty years I also worked with wives of Japanese scholars at Harvard University, both as individuals and in groups. I was able to observe how the problems changed over the years, and how they compared to what I had observed in Japan. This gave me an added cultural and historical perspective.

Through this clinical work and observation over several decades, I discovered how the cultural context affects the manifestations of psychological stress. Japan's troubled youth, for example, are more likely to "act in," withdrawing into their homes, whereas their American counterparts are more likely to "act out," engaging in mischief or violence in the streets. Japanese married couples in distress are more likely to resort to an emotional divorce, or "divorce within the household," whereas Americans are more prone to make a formal break. Likewise, the social changes over the past fifty years within Japan have altered the manifestations of psychological distress, and may have even contributed to an increase in the overall level of psychological disorders. In the early postwar years, for example, young mothers were more likely to be tormented by authoritarian husbands or mothers-in-law, whereas in recent years they are more likely to be traumatized or even abused by their children. In chapter 5, we shall examine these broader social and economic developments from the 1960s to the present. In particular, we will view the traditional postwar patterns and subsequent changes through the lens of social problems and psychiatric symptoms, giving us clues to the dynamics of the society over time.

The following three chapters present the life stories of three ordinary and yet extraordinary professional housewives: three of the six housewives from our original research sample from 1958–1960. All three were part of the "new middle class," although they varied somewhat in wealth and status: the wives of a doctor (Tanaka-san), an accountant (Itou-san), and a family business owner (Suzuki-san), respectively. They were all full-time housewives at the time, and they exercised considerable autonomy and authority within their prescribed realm of the household and child-rearing. And yet, as we shall see, they were also very different. By examining these three lives over a period of fifty years, we not only gain insight into the strengths and vulnerabilities of Japan's postwar professional housewives; we also see how their roles shifted as they grew older and as Japanese society evolved. We gain further insight into social change by comparing their life experiences to those of their daughters and granddaughters.

NOTES

1. Suzanne H. Vogel, "Some Reflections on Changing Strains in the Housewife/Mother Role," *Kokoro to Shakai* 57 (1989).

2. Joanna Liddle and Sachiko Nakajima, *Rising Suns, Rising Daughters: Gender, Class and Power in Japan* (London: Zed Books, 2000).

3. Ezra F. Vogel, *Japan>'s New Middle Class: The Salary Man and His Family in a Tokyo Suburb* (Berkeley and Los Angeles: University of California Press, 1963).

4. A *kotatsu* is a low table covered with a blanket. A heating system is attached underneath the table for people to get warmth during the winter.

5. Vogel, *Japan's New Middle Class*.

6. Chie Nakane, *Tate shakai no ningen kankei* [Human Relations in a Vertical Society] (Tokyo: Kodansha, 1967).

7. Takie Sugiyama Lebra, *Japanese Women: Constraint and Fulfillment* (Honolulu: University of Hawaii Press, 1984), 127.

8. Lebra, *Japanese Women*, 297.

9. Vogel, *Japan's New Middle Class*, 32–34.

10. Lebra, *Japanese Women*, 296, 305.

11. As noted above, the local elementary school principal helped us to recruit our six "well" research families. Among these, four had adopted sons-in-law (*mukoyoushi*) and none lived with the husband's parents. Families with a mother living with her in-laws may have been more reluctant to participate in our study because they would have more difficulty speaking freely.

12. Takeo Doi, *The Anatomy of Dependence: The Key Analysis of Japanese Behavior* (Tokyo: Kodansha International, 1973); and *The Anatomy of Self: The Individual Versus Society* (Tokyo: Kodansha International, 1986).

13. Sumiko Iwao, *The Japanese Woman: Traditional Image and Changing Reality* (Cambridge, MA: Harvard University Press, 1993), 98.

14. Iwao, *The Japanese Woman*, 98.

15. Suzanne Vogel, "Professional Housewife: The Career of Urban Middle Class Japanese Women," *The Japan Interpreter* 12, no. 1 (1978): 17–43.

16. Kiyomi Kawano, *Feminisuto Kaunseringu* [Feminist Counseling] (Tokyo: Shinsuisha, 1991).

17. Madoka is a Japanese politician who has actively supported divorced women in Japan.

18. Iwao, *The Japanese Woman*, 215.

19. Robin M. LeBlanc, *Bicycle Citizens: The Political World of the Japanese Housewife* (Berkeley and Los Angeles: University of California Press, 1999).

20. For example, Chizuko Ueno, *The Modern Family in Japan* (Melbourne, Australia: Trans Pacific Press, 2009).

Chapter Two

Mrs. Tanaka

Embracing the Role

Among the many Japanese women I have known, Mrs. Hanae Tanaka is the most content and successful with her lifetime role of housewife, mother, grandmother, and great-grandmother. She has continued to thrive into her nineties thanks to her natural fit with her core role, the richness of her relationships, her passion for her hobbies, and her flexibility and ingenuity in dealing with the different stages of her life. Indeed, she has lived through several historical periods, covering most of the twentieth century. She was born, educated, and married before World War II; struggled through the war to care for her family of newborns and small children; experienced the new middle-class lifestyle after the war; confronted widowhood in 1965; and has now seen both her family and her artwork grow and thrive into the twenty-first century. Her story is one of a model professional housewife, with extraordinary homemaking and family care skills complemented by cultural and artistic talents.

Hanae may have been near-perfect as a professional housewife, yet she was quite a challenge for me as a researcher.[1] In contrast to Mrs. Itou and Mrs. Suzuki (chapters 3 and 4), who openly shared with me their innermost conflicts and contradictions, Hanae not only had a more happy and harmonious life, but she also tended to present a more manicured façade and to avoid speaking about her own feelings. She employed the most ornate and polite Japanese phrasing. She preferred talking about others rather than herself, and she discussed social issues in the abstract. Yet over time, I felt that I got to know the real Hanae, perhaps in a distinctively Japanese way. That is, I learned about her less from direct verbal communication than from observing her living situation, her behavior, and her relationships, from the stories she told about others, and from our shared experiences.

At age ninety-two when I last saw her in 2006, Hanae was still much the same lively, friendly, chatty, positive-thinking devotee of family and flowers whom I had known for forty-eight years. Still healthy except for severe arthritis in her knees that prevented her from walking without support, she maintained her independence with a walker to get around her apartment, a wheelchair when outside, and with the telephone to keep her in constant contact with her many friends and family. She was also busy with her dried-flower designs, which she occasionally showed at exhibitions, both locally and in a Ginza gallery. She told me she was still having a good life; she was very blessed or fortunate (*megumaremashita*). At every visit, I was greeted by her smiling, happy face and her warm interest in the people and the beauty around her.

Hanae would not often express frustration or negative reactions, or delve into her psyche. She never wanted to pour her heart out to me or to use me as a confidante to clarify some issue she might have. She has not suffered from the conflicts or restrictions common to many of her contemporaries, which modern-day women decry as inherent in the housewife role. I have heard about many happy and unhappy events in her life over the years, and I have noted her ready tears, for instance, when she related that her middle-aged daughter was seriously ill. But she has had few complaints or conflicts. She dealt with problematic situations realistically, and came through with an accepting attitude. She always talked of other people's strengths, omitting or deemphasizing any discussion of their lacks or her disappointment or anger with them. In recent years, she has explained her way of dealing with life as being *maemuki*, that is, looking forward and accentuating the positive. I have come to trust that this is genuine. Perhaps she has most wanted me to share in her joys and her successes.

In contrast to many women, she has never shown any sign of a wish to be a man, nor even any jealousy or competitiveness with men. Although she saw her husband and other men as superior to her in knowledge of the world, she was not envious of them. She occasionally compared herself with other women; she felt competitive with her older sister in her childhood. She clearly liked men, very much enjoying their company. Even today her eyes twinkle when she talks with a man friend, or when she hears of a couple enjoying each other. Her description of traditional Japanese marriage, certainly her own, is that the arranged marriage (*omiai*) is followed by love marriage (*renai*). She undoubtedly had a good marriage, and enjoyed her husband's company. And though widowed in 1965 at age fifty, she made herself a full life without thought of remarrying.

Hanae has maintained an underlying self-confidence and a gentle asser-tiveness, even while her language is politely humble and deferent. She trusted her own judgment about the everyday matters that concerned her, and she was capable of disagreeing with her husband. In our relationship, I have found she is certainly not a pushover. Even though she agreed to my writing about her life, she never really enjoyed focusing on herself, always preferred having others join us in a fun conversation, and sometimes frustrated my plans for a one-on-one conversation by arranging group entertainment when I came to visit. She was always the model of politeness, but never passive or helpless. Through her love of beauty and of joyful sociability, she actively drew others into her world. Perhaps she channeled those aspects of her femi-ninity to give her control or influence in her realm.

THE NEW MIDDLE CLASS

The Tanakas agreed to see us almost weekly to teach us about family life in Japan. Ezra usually talked with Dr. Takao Tanaka while I talked with Hanae, although we also got to know the children, and on occasion met with various groupings of parents, children, other relatives, and friends.

The Tanakas were members of Japan's "new middle class" after the war: professional and salaryman families, moving ahead in the world. They were ambitious for their own betterment, emphasizing the education of their chil-dren for successful careers and marriages, and eager to show the world the economic, social, and cultural achievements of the Japanese nation. The Tanakas readily took on the role of our teachers, with Takao talking at length about his struggle to educate himself and move upscale from the ignorant farm boy of his birth to the successful suburban family doctor he had be-come. Hanae was eager to teach us about Japan's highly developed arts such as flower arranging, tea ceremony, and cooking. We were eager and grateful learners, visiting them weekly for a year and a half, learning much about daily life along the way.

Takao, at fifty-two in 1958, was well established in his community as a family doctor with his own clinic attached to the house, widely respected within his professional association and an active supporter of the local public schools. Hanae, at forty-four, with five children aged twelve to nineteen, was an officer in the PTA, and was well known and liked via the neighborhood association and her participation in various women's activities. Like most professional housewives of the day, she was eager to improve her skills by taking lessons in cooking, flower arranging, and tea ceremony. The flower arranging and tea ceremony lessons often continued indefinitely, with the student becoming a teacher after many years of study and experience. The Tanaka children were all thriving, academically and socially, with the youngest boy in sixth grade at the local public school, the oldest boy in the first year of medical school (which begins in the first year of college), and three girls in between in good private junior and senior high schools suitable for girls.

Although Hanae and Takao had both moved up in living standards from their families of origin, Takao had come the farthest, since his birth family had suffered impoverishment and many losses. And it was his professional status that set the stage for the status of the Tanaka family. Takao was born in 1906 in a poor rural family. His mother and five of the seven children died of dysentery when Takao was twelve. This farm family worked all day every day, with no vacations, no recreation, no hobbies. At times food was scarce. His mother worked on the farm as well as in the house, and never had the opportunity for a hobby like flower arranging. Takao's memories of his childhood were few, but he was loved and valued as the oldest son, and he was clear that his parents were kind, though strict. Children were expected to be obedient to parents and teachers in those days, and physical punishment was accepted as *ai no muchi*, or love-spanking. After he graduated from sixth grade, the end of compulsory schooling at the time, Takao determined to leave the farm and to make a life and career for himself in the city. His father was upset that his eldest son was deserting the family, and told him that if he left he could never come back home to live. The father and the one remaining sibling, a younger brother, still remained in the country in 1958. Takao had visited them a few times in the ensuing years, and occasionally sent them money. At age thirteen Takao went to a nearby city, where an uncle and some cousins lived. Staying in a room in a relative's house, he worked at various odd jobs while trying to continue his education, and then moved in with the uncle to help him with his medical practice. He fondly remembers an aunt, who was very strict with him, but also loving. While helping as a general errand boy, he also learned about medical practice and put himself through high school. He worked and then studied at a medical college in Tokyo until he was able to obtain his doctor's license. At age twenty-one, he was rejected by the army for health reasons. He continued his study and research as well as his practice during the war, and attained an added degree, a doctorate, in 1955.

Hanae, born in 1914, had grown up with less deprivation but hardly luxurious circumstances in downtown Tokyo where her father owned a kimono shop. Her mother and the children helped out in the shop, as was typical of shopkeeper families. Hanae remembers her mother working hard all day in the shop and into the night on bookkeeping, while two maids cared for the children and did housework. Her mother had no time for play or for hobbies, but she did take time to get her hair professionally done every week, Hanae recounted with a giggle. Hanae, the second of eight children, attended a *jogakkou* (girls' high school), a middle-class achievement in those days.

Her school did not permit its students to go to movies, to read novels or women's magazines, or to have male friends. Hanae describes herself as serious and studious. She would believe her teachers when they threatened that mischief would lead to "climbing needle mountain" or "swimming blood river." Her father died during her high school years, and a few years later, her younger brother, the eldest son who was expected to take over for the father, tragically died at age eighteen in cadet training. Hanae still treasures the family book of memories with pictures of this brother. The family, which had been reasonably comfortable, then faced difficult times, and the mother was forced to give up the kimono shop. Nevertheless, the three younger sisters, just like Hanae and her older sister, were able to graduate from *jogakkou*. The two younger twin brothers graduated from a prestigious private college in Tokyo.

Hanae described her mother as warm and loving, well liked by customers and neighbors. She talked more about her older sister, however, with whom she was close and competitive. Although Hanae did well enough in school, and was even class representative one year, her sister was an excellent student and was the one that their mother depended on to help with bookkeeping, planning, and purchasing in the store. Hanae, in contrast, was *otonashii* (quiet and docile). She followed her sister around, walking behind her, as her sister would cover for her. She also envied her sister, and hated her own shyness. She would frequently argue with her sister, resenting what she felt was her mother's favoring the sister. Hanae spent much time in the store, helping out in ways she defined as less difficult than the sister's tasks. She can now appreciate that she was freer than her busy sister to enjoy taking care of the younger children or socializing with the store staff. In fact, the store people protected her and preferred her to her sister, as the sister's assertiveness aroused resentment. Hanae discovered that shyness appeals to Japanese people. She learned to take pride in her reputation for friendliness and her popularity with the staff and customers. In these softer and more feminine ways, I noted, she held her own in this underlying competition.

Hanae's three years as a kindergarten teacher, after graduating from *jogakkou*, gave her more confidence and contact with people. Some of her friends commented that she became a different person—less *otonashii*, more outgoing and lively. Her marriage to Takao Tanaka in 1938 ended her career as a kindergarten teacher. She was twenty-three and he was thirty-one. Takao's teacher, who clearly saw Takao as an up-and-coming young man, arranged the marriage. His good friend, whose child was in Hanae's kindergarten class, recommended Hanae as a popular teacher, very good with children. Since they both had great trust in this *nakoudosan* (go-between), they felt no need for an extensive investigation of each other's background, as occurred before many marriages in those days. They married quickly, as the wisdom of the day dictated, to enjoy the novelty and not to dig up each other's faults and spoil their enthusiasm. Takao went to work the next day, without any honeymoon, and soon the new couple settled in the middle-class suburb of Tokyo where they lived thereafter. Their home adjoined the family medical clinic and its small hospital. (In those days, and often even now, doctors typically had their own small hospital for caring for their patients.) The house was in the style most common at that time: a two-story wooden structure with sliding glass doors that opened wide during the day to the verandah and a small garden; *tatami* rooms with futon sleeping, one Western-style room with a piano, and a kitchen with a dining table, an oven (an exceptionally modern and unusual item at that time), a toilet serviced by the "night-soil" man, and the typical bathtub that could hold one or two people.

During her years between high school and marriage, Hanae became involved in the Christian religion, specifically the *mukyoukai*, the "no-church" church founded by Kanzou Uchimura.[2] Her older sister's friend had introduced her to it. She remembers it as teaching the importance of love and love of others, which has remained a part of her approach to life. Takao was a Buddhist, not interested in religion. Hanae continued to attend church after marriage, but gave it up after her first baby was born.

The Tanaka's eldest son, Masami, was born in 1939, one year after the wedding, as the China war was gathering momentum. Three girls, Masako, Yoshiko, and Michiko, followed during the main war years, and the second boy, Mamoru, appeared two years after the war ended. I was puzzled in 1959 that Hanae expressed embarrassment about having so many children. I figured she was just being humble for the sake of politeness, but perhaps she was comparing herself to the young couples of the day who were starting to limit the number of children. Both Takao and Hanae made it clear that they wanted two boys, since both their families had suffered from losing the first son. And sure enough, the Tanakas had no more children after the second boy was born. Contraception was not unknown to them.

Although many families suffered greater losses, the Tanakas had difficult times during the war. Takao did not have to go into the army, but he was told to stay where he was and care for anyone needing medical attention, especially after the air raids. He was not allowed to evacuate to the country for safety as many others did. Hanae often referred to the hard times during those years. Even though she usually had a maid to help, she was always working her hardest, getting up early to make breakfast for everyone, giving birth to babies and caring for them, going out in search of food to buy, washing loads of laundry by hand. The air raids were frightening: lights out, getting everyone into the shelter quickly, having to get dressed and gather emergency equipment in the dark. She particularly remembers the last year of the war, when she and the three younger children evacuated to the country where her mother had moved after the Tokyo house burned down. Takao and six-year-old Masami stayed at home so Takao could take care of medical needs there;

but they occasionally took the long train ride into the country, bringing money or goods from the city for Hanae to exchange for food with the farmers. Hanae also made the reverse trip into the city suburbs to check on her husband and son, bringing them groceries. The train trip was strenuous, as she had to carry one-year-old Michiko on her back and groceries in her hands, while making several transfers, occasionally onto freight trains, and fighting her way through crowds. Once they were stopped en route due to fires in Tokyo that could be seen in the night sky. At times they had nothing to eat but a little rice gruel cooked with a bit of vegetable. Nevertheless, they survived without major loss, as their house was not damaged. They usually had something to eat, thanks to Hanae's mother who had made friends with the farmers, who were sometimes not eager to share their supplies with city folk. Hanae says she did not suffer from unnecessary anxiety during this period, as she did not have time to worry. As she told us later, she did not think much about proper discipline or child-rearing techniques during the wartime. She and the children just did what was necessary day by day.

Neighborhood relations were always helpful and cooperative, especially with the next-door housewife with whom she daily conversed, kitchen window to kitchen window, and with whom she shared everything. Both Takao and Hanae commented that the neighborhood returned to normal after the war, but a bit less cooperative and a bit more competitive and private.

INITIAL IMPRESSIONS

From the first meeting, Takao and Hanae were quite cordial, generous with their knowledge and their time, eager to teach us about the cultured life they and other middle-class Japanese had achieved. Takao took time out from his clinical work in the middle of the day to talk with us in an unhurried manner. He adopted the role of teacher, telling us in detail about Japanese society, about professional, business, and educational developments, and how the urban and suburban family life differed from patterns in the countryside. Hanae, always wearing a demure yet beautiful kimono, welcomed us with her warm smile and easy laugh, although in the beginning she sat in respectful silence while her husband did most of the talking. A few weeks later, she began to come into her own as she described the various beautifully crafted Japanese sweets she served with our tea, all exquisitely designed to fit the season, the occasion, or some special sentiment. With Japanese food, she emphasized, attractiveness to the eye is as important as taste to the mouth. She told us about the flower arranging lessons and tea ceremony lessons she and other mothers were enjoying. Her pleasure in having the time, the money, and the leisure to enjoy such hobbies was apparent, especially as she told us she had never had the opportunity to take up any hobby as a girl at home.

She invited us to a tea ceremony so we could experience the beauty and grace that required so much time and practice to achieve. Since she regretted that she knew very little about music, she had made a point of arranging music lessons for her three daughters. Takao also told us of his pleasure in his hobby, fishing: He often went with a small group of colleagues on Sunday, from very early morning to late at night. The Tanakas seemed to enjoy socializing with a group of close friends, he with male colleagues and she with other mothers. They each respected the achievements of the other. While she demonstrated tea ceremony, she bragged about the prize Takao had won for catching the biggest trout.

At first Ezra and I had moments of frustration because we were more interested in learning about child rearing, husband-wife relationships, family dynamics or conflicts, and their feelings about everyday life, but we were being feted with a somewhat formal, impersonal discourse about Japanese society. Of course, we always felt an enormous gratitude to them for taking time to talk with us and for putting up with our rather minimal ability with the Japanese language. Hanae was quite patient with me even though she often had to repeat herself for me to understand. Her eloquent use of polite phrasing accentuated my difficulties. Gradually Ezra and I came to realize that Hanae and Takao were making a conscientious effort to teach us what we really needed to know about Japanese society: the pride of the new middle-class husbands in the achievement of a comfortable lifestyle after the war and the satisfaction of the professional housewives in their homemaking and artistic accomplishments. I learned proper women's polite language from Hanae's beautiful phrasing. Hanae once explained to me very carefully that it would be coarse and impolite to follow my suggestion of simply dividing the cost of gasoline between the four of us who took a trip together to Mashiko, the famous pottery-making town. Rather, since the owner of the car had offered us the use of the car out of the kindness of her heart, we should show our appreciation via a very thoughtful gift. This was also a lesson in how the Japanese saw Westerners as too "dry" (rational) while Japanese were "wet" (sentimental).

After some weeks of rather formal discussions, we decided to spend more time one-on-one, with Ezra talking with Takao and me with Hanae. With just us two mothers, Hanae talked more freely about her daily schedule, the children and education, and other relatives and friends. She also asked about me and family life in America. She seemed to relax more after experiencing an informal party at our house. We had fun sharing and comparing. For instance, we laughed as I told her of my first experience with a Japanese toilet, and as she told me of her experience with a Western bathtub in a Kyoto hotel, where she had unknowingly washed herself outside the tub as one would with a Japanese bath.

I noticed, however, that Hanae resisted talking about herself. That was true then, and it is still true today. She admitted to feeling uncomfortable when Ezra had used a tape recorder for our initial interviews, as she imagined that we would laugh at her awkward comments when we listened to the tapes. She also conceded a preference for not talking about herself, but she never refused a question or a discussion. Instead, she laughed and skirted around topics. Although she must have felt some underlying tension, she never seemed tense or unfriendly, as other women have at times. Her easy smile and frequent giggle always felt warm and soft and friendly. She often talked more easily about how most Japanese women handled things, or about other women she knew.

FAMILY LIFE

The Tanaka household functioned rather smoothly, in terms of both activities and relationships. Unlike most households, the father was almost always at home since he worked in the medical clinic attached to the house. The patients did not go into the house, however, or affect its functioning. The nurse and other clinic workers often ate lunch with Takao and the family, and were available in case of a family emergency. Takao's presence meant that he was much more aware of family affairs than most salarymen. The latter were routinely gone all day, not returning until 10:00 or 11:00 p.m. six days a week, and sleeping most of Sunday. In such families, the women's world and the men's world were almost totally separate. Such a wife might have complete control over her household, or she might be subjected to her mother-in-law's supervision.

So what was the division of responsibility and the pattern of family relationships in this family? Of course, Takao had total authority over the clinic and his professional responsibilities. Hanae had responsibility over the household, and generally Takao did not interfere with how she handled the kitchen, the chores, or the children. However, they were both interested in schooling, health, and the larger issues of how the children were developing. As a doctor, he felt strongly about having nutritious food and not breast-feeding too long, not much more than one year. (At that time some mothers breast-fed their babies for two or more years.) Hanae concurred with his opinion. She had some difficulty during the war when she weaned the babies after their first year, as her husband recommended. She sometimes had trouble finding the appropriate food or cooking it for the desired length of time for a toddler's digestion, so she occasionally had to supplement with breast milk.

When Hanae stressed the importance of husband and wife talking and understanding each other, I guessed that she wanted such communication for herself as reassurance from arbitrary authority, even though Takao was less authoritarian than most husbands. She and Takao were generally able to discuss things, and then either agree or simply accept the other's decision. They argued strenuously a few times, and did not speak for two or three days. But soon the necessities of daily life would get them talking again, and the angry feelings would dissipate. Neither would apologize. Hanae's daughters sometimes told her that she should be the first to apologize, but then again they have remarked that she showed strength by not apologizing. When Hanae was annoyed at Takao's behavior, she reminded herself that he had grown up during difficult times, losing his mother early and getting little support from his father. In 1959 they disagreed about his wish for her to always be at home, a common notion for the "*okusan*" role. She felt that she should be able to go out for her hobbies or meetings once the children were all of school age, because their father and the clinic personnel were always available if there was a problem. She laughingly commented that if he were away at his office all day, then he would not know that she went out.

So for Hanae, her husband's working at home had its benefits and its drawbacks. He was more available, so they had greater closeness and a more integrated family life. But he was also there to disapprove, and to control the household money. In contrast to the typical salaryman who would turn over his salary to his wife, who then dispensed money where it was needed, including giving the husband his allowance, Takao received money directly from patients, kept tabs on what he had, and made the decisions about disbursements. He gave money regularly for household expenses and paid for specific needs that arose. His overall income was quite good, so Hanae was not lacking what she needed for the household, the children, or herself. In 1959, however, she expressed the wish to have some money of her own that she could control as she wished. With her husband's agreement, therefore, she took some of the family money and bought a piece of land in the country-side with the hope that it would appreciate and bring her money. Meanwhile, she was proud that Takao had bought four pieces of land, which, added to the land the house and clinic were on, meant that each of the five children would have land when they came of age and needed it.

Beyond all this, of course, Hanae enjoyed relative independence and comfortable freedom because she lacked in-laws. Not only did she not have a live-in mother-in-law telling her how to do everything according to Tanaka family customs and rules; she seldom saw her in-laws, so they had no influence whatsoever. Meanwhile, close relations with her own family—her mother, her siblings, and their children—added social enrichment and support to her life. Although her family mostly lived together in a Tokyo compound while she lived in the suburbs, there was much visiting back and forth. Every year they had a large three-generation New Year's celebration together at the compound.

Hanae was busy in her daily life in 1959, but freer than in the past. As the children were older, she felt she could do without a maid. Until 1957, they had always had a live-in maid, usually a teenage girl from the country who worked for a few years to learn about proper household management so she could marry well. The Tanaka children had become teenage contemporaries of the maid. Masami would occasionally insult the maid, and the maid became jealous of the Tanaka daughters and wanted the same advantages they had. With the maid gone, the girls began helping more. They straightened their own bedding and clothes, and helped clean up after dinner. During school vacation times, they took over major household chores, taking turns with the laundry, cleaning the tub and preparing the bath, and helping with food preparation. The boys were not expected to do housework or even kitchen cleanup.

Hanae always had a busy morning, with breakfast preparation, lunch preparation, kitchen cleanup, straightening up the house, including the boys' futons, and laundry. She did not have to get up as early in the morning as previously because she had purchased an automatic rice cooker. Although everyone in the house, including clinic workers, ate lunch there, they did not all eat together. Hanae was typically through with morning chores and lunch by about 2:00 p.m. and then had two to three hours when she might go out to a school meeting, an *okeiko* (a lesson in flowers or tea), or other of her own activities. She would then return home in time to cook dinner. The family, including Takao, ate together in the evening. Hanae usually joined the girls in the kitchen cleanup, or sometimes helped Mamoru with his studies, or had a few minutes to relax before bedtime.

We had felt from the beginning that Takao and Hanae had a good marriage, and longer acquaintance reinforced that impression. They liked and respected each other. Like most Japanese, they did not use the word "love." They did not show physical affection to each other in front of us or anyone else, as was the Japanese custom. The Tanakas were typical for their time in that they socialized mostly separately from one another, with same-sex groups. Hanae was something of a romantic, however, talking of how love marriage came after arranged marriage, and she was not timid about saying that she would like to do more things together with Takao. She had fond memories of earlier years when they occasionally went dancing together after work hours in Tokyo, while Takao was still doing his research there. They would sometimes take a walk together after dinner, and had known the neighbors to comment on what a nice couple they were. The children chimed in, always in support of their doing things together, and they were angry one year on Mother's Day when their father went fishing. (They had a bit of a Mother's Day celebration the next day.) And Hanae expressed disappointment when Takao went to visit a couple who were mutual friends without her, although she presumed it was because he had medical business to discuss with the husband.

I was not surprised that Hanae talked of being envious that Ezra and I went out together. But I was really amused once when Ezra was away for a few days, and Hanae expressed a wish to see us the instant when he first returned. Her fantasy was of our great joy and great affection at being reunited.

Neither Takao nor Hanae ever discussed their sex life with us, yet it was clear that they both enjoyed their sexual relationship. Takao talked of how most young women at marriage knew nothing about sex and were a bit scared or tense about it, but that a knowledgeable and considerate husband who knew how to approach a woman gently and playfully could make it pleasant. During a different conversation, while talking of his occasional difficulty sleeping, he commented that his wife never had trouble sleeping: She had readily and comfortably gone to sleep even on their wedding night. He also once commented to Ezra that a sexually compatible couple would never separate, even if there were other problems. He once recommended greater sex education for young people, but thought it well to maintain some mystery about the sexual experience.

I was impressed how freely and joyfully Hanae discussed sex in general. I sparked this conversation when I mentioned our visit to a fertility shrine at Shimoda. Hanae asked me right away if I meant the shrine with all the statues of penises, to which I said yes, and we both giggled. In fact, we giggled our way through most of the ensuing conversation, which included discussion about similarly shaped tools made for the pleasure of women. Hanae said she never used such things, but she presumed they were mostly used by court ladies. She also discussed that court ladies or other older women without partners might take a young man for a lover in order fulfill their sexual needs. I noted that she assumed women also had sexual needs and did not see women simply as passive playthings for men, as some women seemed to assume. She also mentioned that men in a group would occasionally visit "pleasure houses," and reluctant group members would feel pressured by others to participate fully. She did not say whether her husband and his fishing group ever included such additional pleasures in their weekends together.

Although I found Japanese reluctant to talk about sex, even with spouses or children, they were less prudish than Americans about bathing together. In fact, bathing was a major recreation and social activity. At hot springs, same-sex groups traveling together would luxuriate in a bath together, laughing and talking. Hanae and her friends would wait until dark and then get in the bath together, naked, to relax and chat. Families bathed together. Sometimes if Hanae wanted to have a good heart-to-heart talk with one of the children, they would bathe together, even in the smaller bath inside the house. She only recently had quit bathing with Mamoru, thinking that he was getting too old for that at age twelve. And yes, she thoroughly enjoyed bathing with her husband at times.

Although Hanae showed no resentment of the higher status of men, she occasionally revealed her consciousness of it. For instance, when Ezra apologized for forgetting to bring a tape, she commented humorously that Japanese husbands would never apologize for anything. She noted that while her mother was always working and had no time for play, her father took time for his own recreation. And as she talked of being thankful for her own religious training and wishing she had given it to her daughters, she explained that men can make their own way in the world but women have to follow their husbands and need inner strength to cope with the external demands placed on them. Overall, Hanae was satisfied with her married life, but might have been even more pleased with more closeness and togetherness, and perhaps more say in some decision making.

THE TANAKA CHILDREN

Although we were introduced to all the children on our first visit to the Tanaka house, we were surprised that neither father nor mother talked about them in our first weeks. Most often when we came, the five were all at school, but even when they were in the house, they were "seen but not heard." The parents said they were *uchibenkei*, meaning quiet and shy with outsiders but loud and talkative within the family. The oldest son seemed to make a point of absenting himself if we were coming. After some months, however, he joined in a conversation with Ezra and then studied English with him for much of our time in Japan.

Although Hanae initiated few discussions about the children, she did talk freely when asked. She volunteered that she had been concerned about her oldest son Masami ever since his middle school days. Despite the academic pressures that all parents and most children felt about passing examinations to get into good high schools and colleges, Masami had studied very little when in middle school and had rejected the tutor his mother had found for him. He had even hidden in the closet or climbed onto the roof to avoid the tutor when he came. Hanae was so alarmed by his disappearance that she felt more relief than anger when he finally reappeared. He seemed to hate women, and particularly mistreated the maid. He would reject water that she brought him, saying it was dirty and he wanted Mother to bring the water. Mother could not understand why he was so cruel to the maid. His sisters complained that he was a tyrant, snobbish and bossy, ordering them around.

His studying changed after he failed the entrance exam to the private junior high school where his friends were going. He talked to Ezra about feeling humiliated by this experience, and withdrew from his friends. For the next several years he was not the sociable, fun-loving boy he had been. He started studying very hard, however, on his own initiative. He seemed to stay away from his mother, but he did at times have long talks with his father. During his high school years, his father explained to him about various lines of work, the pros and cons of careers he might pursue, including business and the professions, and the required education for each. He told his son about his own life experiences, the value of friendships, and the importance of getting along with others, a skill he felt Masami needed to develop. Takao did not pressure him to follow in his footsteps but he did describe the advantages of a good independent professional income, being one's own boss, and possibly taking over the medical practice someday. He was pleased when Masami later decided on his own to enter medical college.

Hanae was also happy with Masami's decision, and she no longer worried about his studying. She was shocked, however, when his independent, stubborn nature led him to keep secret from his parents the fact that he had received an award for being the top student in his first-year college class. They only found out much later, somewhat accidentally. Hanae still fretted because he was careless about grooming and he refused to pick up his own room. Although the younger children shined their shoes every day, Masami refused to polish his shoes, and was angry with his mother when she secretly polished them for him. She worried about him when he went on long mountain hikes with his friends, and was annoyed that he would not give her peace of mind by telling her when he would be coming home. Masami was difficult with his mother, but he seemed to be confidential with his father.

The three girls in the middle were close to each other, and close to their mother. It seemed that the same-sex persons within the family were closer and more comfortable. Also, the educational goal for the girls was different from that of the boys. Girls did not need to experience competition, explained Hanae, and had less need to go to the most prestigious schools, less need to plan for a career. All three went to the same girls' school, private but not far away, with a respectable entrance exam for the middle school but no exam to go on to high school. Since they had been pleased with the school when Masako went there, they sent the other girls as well. Frequently such schools were preferred as better education for girls than coed schools, perhaps better for future professional housewives?

Takao, with his rather modern thinking, thought that even girls should think about how they might earn a living if circumstances forced that on them. He was pleased with Masako's choice for college. She had perceived her father's interest in health and had entered a two-to-three-year nutrition school. Takao thought that would be good training, for either marriage or a career or both. Both Takao and Hanae were a bit more concerned the following year when Yoshiko decided she wanted to study piano and go to a music college. Hanae had been pleased with the girls' studying piano, but she had thought of it only as a hobby. Could Yoshiko take care of herself financially if she had to? Yoshiko said she could teach piano, and she set about practicing very diligently every day and studying with a teacher so she could pass the test for her desired music school. Hanae recalled, humorously, how Yoshiko had wanted to quit taking piano lessons when she was in middle school, and had continued only because her mother persuaded her that it was worthwhile to keep going when she had come so far. As for Michiko, she did not have to think about college yet, but she loved her ballet lessons and going to Takarazuka shows in her spare time.[3]

At that time, Masako, although doing well socially and academically, was described as slightly immature, not showing any interest in boys or marriage, and undoubtedly would need to have a husband chosen for her via *omiai.* She had taken piano and dance lessons, but her interest had turned to nutrition school. Yoshiko was more strong-willed, as seen in her determination with piano, and her father thought her more likely to want to pick her own husband. All three girls shied away from us for some months, but when we really had a chance to play games or to talk with them, they seemed quite personable and friendly. Michiko, like many younger siblings, seemed the most spontaneously fun-loving.

Although the oldest boy kept to himself, the younger four children played together much of the time, especially during summer vacation when they had more time. Masami had his own room, with a bed and desk, no *tatami,* whereas the others slept on *tatami* with futons, which gave them the flexibility to sleep together or separately. Two girls usually slept together. Mamoru sometimes slept in a separate room, sometimes shared a room with a sister or with his mother. There was very little fighting, although the parents explained that sometimes the girls argued about clothes, particularly with the younger two expressing envy that Masako had prettier clothes. Hanae explained that this was because Masako had graduated from high school and now had to wear regular clothes every day instead of a school uniform.

We could not help noting how different these Japanese adolescents were from American ones. While American high school girls were concerned about clothes and hairdos, striving to be cheerleaders or beauty queens, and to catch the most popular boy for a date, comparably aged Japanese girls, like the Tanaka girls, were wearing quite sexless school uniforms, not allowed to wear makeup, and had almost no contact with boys. Hanae, noting that Masako and Yoshiko were maturing, thought it might be well to have a party and invite some boys so they could begin to see what boys were like. I was surprised that Hanae and her friends were usually more attractively dressed and made-up than their teenage daughters—again very much in contrast to the situation in the United States.

The parents faced a critical decision for Mamoru, a sixth grader at the local public school. Where would he go for middle school? He could just proceed to the local public middle school with no exam and no worry, but Mamoru wanted to go to a school in Tokyo as all his friends were feeling grown up and talking about taking the train into the city school. His mother, however, hated to send her youngest boy so far away so early. The more ambitious families often wanted their children to go to a more demanding school, probably one with an entrance exam, which would make it easier to enter a prestigious high school. Mamoru wanted to join his friends, who wanted to go to a particular private school in Tokyo with a difficult entrance exam. Hanae was doubtful that he could pass the exam since he had been always more interested in playing than studying. For some months the whole family debated this issue, while Hanae consulted with Mamoru's teacher and other mothers. Takao said to let him go into Tokyo if he wanted. Masami advised that he should stay at the local public school where he would not be pressured.

Meanwhile, Hanae set about making arrangements for him to enter a Tokyo public school if he did not pass the exam, which is exactly what Masami had done. This school was considered to be superior and more desirable than many other public schools. If such a school had a few empty spaces, they could accept out-of-area students. A suburban family with good connections might arrange this, or they might set up a Tokyo residence, with the boy and his mother listing themselves as living at a local address if they could enlist the cooperation of the true residents of that address. Since Hanae had a cordial friendship with a teacher and a PTA officer there, a few consultation trips into Tokyo bringing *omiyage* (presents) was enough to guarantee Mamoru a place in that school. Giving such presents was officially forbidden, but Hanae found a way to discreetly send presents to the PTA member and to the teacher's wife.

During this time of entrance exam anxiety, the class teacher also put in extra effort, staying until 8:00 p.m. daily to help the students study. Diligent mothers like Hanae brought them their suppers. And Mamoru readily accepted a tutor for more hours. He was much more agreeable and compliant than Masami had been, ready to take parents' or teachers' advice.

This examination hell (*shiken jigoku*), we soon realized, was a widespread phenomenon among ambitious middle-class Japanese. Children were not allowed to play for months, including summer vacations, but had to spend all their time studying. Mothers spent all night waiting in front of the school gate to be the first to present a child's application to take the exam.[4] Families went to the greatest extremes for the college entrance exams; college determined status and associations for the rest of one's life. Some students gave up all hobbies and recreation for the full three years of high school while they studied for the college entrance exam. But the earlier exams were also important, to get into a good middle school and thus into a good high school. Good "escalator" schools, such as the one the Tanaka girls attended, were highly valued because they allowed students to pass to the next level (such as from middle school into high school) within the same school without an exam.

The Tanakas were not the most extreme in their ardor or their pressure for the examination success of their children. Their general approach to child rearing was one of explaining things and talking with the children rather than coercing them. Hanae had learned early from Masami that too much pressure only produced rebellion. Both she and Takao had the clear expectation that all the children would be good students: listen to their teachers, do their homework. And they provided the children with the necessary structure and environment: good schools, a desk for study, help from parents or tutors if needed. They recognized that the children studied more and excelled in the exams when their own motivation propelled them. Takao valued education, but rated health as an even more important factor. Hanae also wanted the children to be happy and to pursue their own interests, while recognizing the need for exam success. The Tanakas believed in allowing their children to choose their own careers, even though many Japanese parents would force one child (most often the eldest son) to take over the family business, and Takao's own father had disowned him for leaving the farm.

So when Mamoru failed the private school exam, he was duly entered into the Tokyo public school. While disappointed for him, his parents were not particularly upset, and even Mamoru seemed to adjust rather easily to his second-choice school, not feeling like a failure as much as Masami had in his time. Hanae attributed his failure to the fact that he did not study on Sundays as many did, that he did not have the same steady tutor, and perhaps he still was not all that interested in study.

The Tanakas were probably not as frantic as some other families about getting their children into the very best schools because they were better established socially and financially than some of the other middle-class families. Their children could more readily fall back on family resources, financial reserves, or social connections, as they did when they arranged for both boys to attend the Tokyo public middle school. Many salaryman families without independent incomes had to work harder to save money for private schools, and hence were determined that their children had to enter the low-tuition but high-prestige national universities, which would then assure them of an elite track career for life. Some salaryman families put the same kind of competitive pressure on their girls, but the more socially established families, like the Tanakas, generally preferred that their girls not be the most competitive students. A girl who performed well but not tops was better for a good marriage. A cultured woman, a good candidate for a professional housewife, was more often skilled at homemaking arts and/or a hobby.

Even though the new constitution after the war changed the rules of inheritance, erasing the rule of primogeniture, the oldest son generally continued to inherit the family business, the house, and the care of parents. As this was no longer mandated, however, families engaged in much discussion over where and with whom older parents should live. Many of Hanae's friends were saying it was better to live separately from children; some claimed it was better to live with one's own daughter; and others clung to the traditional tie with the oldest son. Hanae toyed with all these ideas in her head, but then concluded that she would prefer to live together with the eldest son and his wife if they could all get along well. She mentioned Takao's teacher and his wife, their *nakoudosan* (matchmakers), who were living quite successfully with their son and his new wife. Hanae's mother and three of her siblings with families were all living together in separate houses in a compound in a nice area of Tokyo. All the women—mother, daughters, and daughters-in-law—stuck together and got along well. The brothers were too busy to be involved. Then when I mentioned living with a daughter, Hanae said yes, but what if the daughter's husband was a difficult person? All in all, she thought she would prefer living with her oldest son, as she could get along with a daughter-in-law and did not think her son would be as difficult as a son-in-law.

Hanae's distinctive style of relating to others continued to intrigue me. While seeming to be noncompetitive, she frequently compared herself with others, especially with other women. Sometimes it was just good fun, as when she laughed about the contrast between my height and her shortness. She would put the other person up high and herself down, even though this sometimes felt to me like unrealistic and empty flattery. The word *tateru* struck me as especially appropriate for this style of flattery, as it means to build up someone. Japanese women evidently employed this type of flattery to make others feel good and to make themselves unthreatening. I wondered whether this was Hanae's polite way of handling the underlying competitive nature of these relationships. And was this related to her reluctance to talk about herself, a reluctance to come out from behind her older sister (metaphorically speaking) and show herself where she might be criticized (as her sister was criticized)?

Hanae described herself as somewhat shy, at least reticent about talking in front of groups or singing. She wished she could talk in front of a group, like the PTA, but she just could not do it. Talking with just one or two people presented no problem. She could talk freely, and even assert herself at times. She often took the initiative to organize a group get-together, and her daughters told of being impressed once that she had the nerve to ask a store clerk for two of the gifts being offered at the store, one for her friend as well as one for herself. She would never hesitate to start a conversation or suggest a social event, and hence made friends easily. She once organized her women friends to learn something about American cooking from me. She was eager to have certain friends meet us Americans, particularly a psychiatrist friend and several students interested in studying abroad. The kindergarten children she had taught, all now grown up, still remembered her and came to visit her—a real tribute to her warm heart and social skills.

She often compared herself to a particular woman in her PTA group. At first she noted how the other woman was so young and modern, talking freely and assertively, wearing Western clothes while Hanae always wore a kimono. While she implied that such modernity was good, it was clear that underneath she considered that woman somewhat brash. On a later occasion, her evaluation seemed rather balanced. She expressed admiration for the woman's intelligence and her skill in speaking clearly, but noted that she was not as aware of the feelings of those around her as Hanae would want to be.

Perhaps I learned more from that cooking lesson in 1959 than Hanae and her friends did, by seeing my cooking from their point of view. Although everyone was polite and appreciative, they were clearly disappointed in my sandwiches because they were no comparison with the dainty Japanese sandwiches in aesthetic design. I learned again of the Japanese saying that food should be attractive to the eye as well as to the taste. Then again, after a fairly typical meal we cooked under my instruction, Hanae commented quietly that there was butter in everything. That gave me food for thought, recalling that Westerners had been labeled "*bataa kusai*" (stinks like butter) in times past. Maybe this foretold the time to come when I, along with most Americans, would reduce butter consumption for reasons of health.

A NEW LIFESTYLE

When I visited Hanae in 1969, I learned that she was now a widow and a grandmother. Her husband had died of stomach cancer in 1965. He had tried to treat himself, but finally consulted a surgeon due to pressure from the family. He had undergone surgery, but died a few months afterward. She had also lost her mother just the previous year. I mourned for her as she talked of missing the good times she and her husband could have had together, traveling in their later years as he gradually retired. Yet she was very much the same person in widowed middle age that she had been in her younger years, cheerful and forward-looking. Her children had all grown up and finished school, and four of them were married. After his father's death, Masami had taken a year to finish his medical training and then took over his father's clinical practice, but he gave up his hopes for the extra research that would have earned him a doctorate like his father had. During the year before he could take over the practice, his brother-in-law, Masako's husband, had taken part-time from his own work to cover the medical needs at the Tanaka clinic. Masami had married a classmate in 1969, and now had two preschool children, both boys. He and his family lived with his mother in the same house that I had known years earlier, but they were planning to build a more modern building in the same location, housing both clinic and family quarters, with a separate apartment for Hanae, now the grandmother. Hanae had been busy taking care of all household matters until Masami and his wife could take over some.

Out of five children, the two boys became doctors like their father, and two of the daughters married doctors. What struck me was just how much Takao and Hanae's wishes for the family were coming true—just about everything except for his early death. Not only had Masami chosen to follow his father's profession, but two of the three daughters had married, by *omiai*, men in the same profession, and Mamoru was following suit, just this year graduating from medical school. I knew that Japanese fathers wanted their oldest sons to take over their businesses, but the Tanakas seemed to have extraordinary success. Partly, I speculated, having the clinic and the house in one building gave the boys the chance to be close to their father, to see him working, to listen to his explanation of his job, and to imagine themselves doing the same. His obvious satisfaction with his work, plus neither parent pressuring the children, seemed to be the best motivator. With four out of five children being doctors or married to doctors, they all had much in common and maintained a comfortable closeness. Although Yoshiko did not marry a doctor, she lived near Masako on a plot of land among those that Takao had bought for each of them, and she stayed in touch with the family. And Hanae happily told me about how well she got along with her daughter-in-law.

Hanae and her friends talked about how to grow old beautifully (*utsuku-shiku oeru*). Several women talked about how they now had responsibility toward the older generation as well as their children. They could not even take a plane trip until the parents died. One very assertive and progressive woman talked about wanting to help the community and those less well off via social and political activities. Hanae differentiated herself by saying that her existence was not essential to anyone these days. She was not responsible for elders or children, and she was not interested in helping the community. Being a full-time caretaker was no longer her goal in life (*ikigai*). She felt that assisting the younger mothers would likely be more interference than help. She wanted to travel, continue with tea and flowers, and contribute to her family's enjoyment. She had already traveled to Europe and to Los Angeles to study more about flowers. Her immediate plan was to buy or build a vacation house where all could go to relax, enjoy the outdoors, and play with the children. Within a few months she bought a place in the woods outside a northern resort town.

Most of the women reported getting along well with their daughters-in-law, and said that mothers-in-law were much less bossy and critical of their daughters-in-law than the previous generation had been. Hanae expanded on how much she liked her daughter-in-law and how well they got along. She laughed that the two of them agreed that Masami was the grumpy and difficult person in the household. She explained that she and the younger family had separate quarters within the house. Both she and they could do their own thing, except that she did baby-sit at times and ate supper with them. Hanae kept herself busy with her hobbies, her travels, and her many friends and extended family.

THE YOUNGER GENERATION

In 1975–1976, I was pursuing an interest in the changing roles of Japanese women, so I requested to interview the second generation of women in the Tanaka family. At that time, this included the three Tanaka daughters, all of whom were married, and the eldest son's wife. Mamoru was not yet married. I immediately discovered how houses and relationships had modernized and Westernized. Three of the five lived in newly built, modern houses, mostly Western style, sleeping in beds more often than on *tatami*. The other two were planning similar housing. *Ombu* (the traditional way of carrying babies on the back) was out; baby carriages were in. Beds had replaced futons, except sometimes children continued to sleep on futons on *tatami*. Breast-feeding months had been reduced, or at times replaced with bottle-feeding. Mothers continued to be focused on child rearing, although more mothers were working, including Kazuko and Michiko. Parents were increasingly indulgent, not strict like the prewar days, but the pressures of the examination system were getting stronger. The marital relationship seemed more companionable than typical of earlier generations with two of the couples, but not so with the other two. Strangely the one "love marriage" was not the most loving. And all the wives complained that their husbands did not help with housework or childcare, and did not understand the wives' pressures. (I have found this complaint to be almost universal since the division of labor between the sexes became less rigid.)

Masako, the oldest daughter, told me that children in the smaller families of the 1970s were more self-centered, only concerned about their own success, whereas children in the larger families of the older generation were taught to think of others and to be cooperative. Parents were most concerned about their children's academic success, as that was the key to their future occupational success. They had become more indulgent about everything except studying. Children's freedom was limited not by parents but by external circumstances such as exams.

Masako explained that it was really boys who were pressured about exams, though allowed to be free. Girls were taught to have good manners and be ladylike, and they were compensated by not having to go through exam hell. (I noted to myself that families no longer felt the need for *hanayome shugyou*: intensive training for girls in the domestic arts to prepare them for marriage.)

Masako talked of her own history and her family. After finishing her two-year nutrition schooling, she had stayed on for an extra year of study, and then married a physician highly recommended by her father. Takao, who had anticipated her suitability for an *omiai*, had picked out a young but established doctor with an outgoing personality as well as professional competence. Masako had opted to go with her father's choice rather than marry a young man she had met. Masako was as influenced by her respect for her father's opinion about her marital partner as Masami had been about his career.

By 1976, Masako and her husband, Kentarou, had a daughter in sixth grade, a son in fourth, and another daughter in kindergarten. They had recently built their own house, with an attached clinic, in a neighboring suburb. It was a very well built and elegant house, completely in Western style. They all slept on beds, not on *tatami*. The oldest two children had their own rooms. The youngest one had her own bed in the parents' room, and sometimes crawled in bed with them. Her husband did not mind. In fact, he was very gentle with this youngest daughter and spent time teaching her things. Sometimes all five family members crawled into the same bed and had fun together. Masako had the children by Caesarian section, so she had not breast-fed the babies.

Her family, husband and children, were her *ikigai*. She said in later years she might want to take up her own hobby, such as tea ceremony or calligraphy, but for now her time was totally consumed with household matters. Previously when Kentarou was employed at a hospital, she had some free time because his hours were more like a salaryman's. But now he was always home, working long hours and frequently entertaining professional colleagues. He was an officer in his professional association. Masako found it a great deal of work to do so much entertaining, even with a maid, particularly when the guests stayed overnight; but she enjoyed meeting people, and sometimes ordered food brought in so she could join in the conversation. Then when she was feeling too tied to the house, she would invite her friends over for a relaxed fun time of their own. I noted that they were doing much entertaining at home, somewhat Western style, rather than always taking guests to a restaurant as was the style for the earlier generation.

The daily schedule was TV and dinnertime from 5:00–8:00 p.m., with Father joining at least for dinner. From 8:00–10:00 p.m., everyone studied. Kentarou loved to study. Masako mostly watched the children to see that they were doing their homework, but she did not help them. Weekends were family time, with occasional two-day vacations, or at least Sundays for doing something together. Kentarou enjoyed having his office and clinic at home, and both he and Masako were happy that the children saw a lot of their father.

Their son wanted to be a doctor like his father. That pleased Kentarou but he told the boy he could pursue whatever he wanted, just as Takao had told Masami. At this fourth-grade stage, the son liked sports. In the fifth grade, however, he would have to go to *juku* (after-school school) to study for the entrance exam to a good junior high school, and might not have as much time for sports. The daughter, in sixth grade, had been going to *juku* since the fourth grade; she also had an entrance exam for a good private junior high for girls. That school was an "escalator" school, so she would have no more entrance exams until college. Masako expressed pride in her daughter's cooking, which told me that this daughter was not so pressured to study that she had time for nothing else, as had become common among some families.

Masako's life reflected the modern ways: caesarian birth, bottle-feeding, bed sleeping, and baby carriages instead of *ombu*. Unlike Hanae, Masako helped her husband in his office, and they had a bit more time together and entertained more. In many ways, however, the similarity to Hanae's life was striking: a scholarly physician husband with a clinic at home, close to wife and children, with a boy talking of following in his father's footsteps and a girl going to an escalator school. The basic home- and child-centered pattern of the professional housewife remained.

Yoshiko, the second daughter, also lived out her father's predictions, though not his preferences. She chose her own career and her own marriage. As she had wished, she graduated in piano from the music college of her choice. She met her husband in a choral group, dated him for seven years, and married in 1969. After finishing school, she worked for Yamaha Music Company for four years, teaching piano and organ. She was an independent soul and did not like that job so well, because she could not teach according to her style but had to follow the company's methods. Her husband was a Tokyo University graduate and a salaryman in a large Tokyo firm. They had two children, a son age six and a daughter, five.

Yoshiko immediately told me in a serious tone, however, that she was different from the others (*kawatteiru*). Four years earlier she had converted to a new Christian sect that had become the center of her life. Although she had dated her husband for a long time, she was still surprised after marriage to find that he was a typical Japanese husband (*teishu kampaku*), wanting service and obedience, and salaryman, away all day six days a week, not home till 11:00 at night, and sleeping all Sunday morning. A missionary approached her in her loneliness, asking her if she would like to read the Bible.

Ever since, she had spent a great deal of time reading the Bible and now sometimes taught it at church and made house calls in the area.

Her church involvement had changed her relationship with her husband and children. The church taught obedience, wife to husband and children to parents. She had come to obey her husband, except about her church participation. Previously she had been more permissive with herself and with the children. She had never expressed anger at her husband, but she did not always obey him. She used to let the children do as they wished, thinking they would just grow up naturally. Now she had learned to be strict, and even to punish them with a hand or stick. In practice she seldom spanked them since she was not used to doing so, she reported, so she would have to get used to it gradually.

In obedience to her husband's wishes, she now greeted him warmly at the door when he returned home, picked up his clothes as he undressed, and cooked dinner any time he wanted it, even at midnight. She wondered what he did in the evening: Was he out drinking with colleagues? Was he playing golf on Saturdays? Even her mother thought this was strange behavior, but Yoshiko did not complain even though she never knew where to find him if she needed him.

Her husband loved the children, even though he never saw them except Sunday afternoon, when all four, parents and children, would go on an outing together. Yoshiko took the children somewhere for fun on Saturday afternoons. On weekday afternoons after school, they played together or with a music student, while Yoshiko taught piano, mostly responding to requests from church members. Both children loved school and were doing well. Yoshiko was gradually teaching both children to help with household chores. Her biggest wish was that her husband would join the church and participate in church activities. Of course he wished she would leave the church and live in his style. He did not believe in God, opposed her church, and felt left out because she and the children were so involved in Bible reading and churchgoing. She mentioned being envious of me because my husband helped in the house and we did things together as a family. Yet she was shocked that American children went away to camp for two weeks at a time. No Japanese mother, she thought, could tolerate being away from her children that long.

The children were confused by the contradiction between the parents. Yoshiko would not let them watch TV, for example, but their father would. Her discussions about child rearing with church groups had taught her to protect the children from bad influences.

While Yoshiko was very much taken up with child rearing and caring for house and husband like her mother had been, she stated that her religion was much more important to her than music. She had felt different from her siblings since childhood: quiet, talking little, but doing what she wanted in her own way. She told me in later years that she always quietly walked behind Masako, as though Masako was the leader but she was protected while being different. Her religious studies had come to sanctify her difference and her own way, while giving her strict rules of right and wrong and the support of church discussions about everyday morals. Confusion and ambivalence had been replaced by clear-cut standards. She no longer needed to feel bad about being different from others in her family of origin. She continued to love them and respect them, but refused to do things their way or to participate in any of the traditional Buddhist ceremonies, even family funerals. She no longer felt guilty about opposing her husband in clearly defined ways. She had delineated when she obeyed and when she did not. Her religion helped her navigate contradictions in her housewife role, but did not keep her from wishing, just like other wives, for greater understanding and closeness from her husband.

Michiko, the youngest of the daughters, described her life much like the others, as being centered on her two boys, aged three and one and one-half. Like Yoshiko, she complained of her husband's absence due to his work and recreation. Her nostalgia was palpable as she talked about the best years of her life being the five years, from age eighteen to twenty-three, when she was a ballet dancer with Takarazuka, the famous women's theater group. She was moving ahead, however, making efforts to find interests for herself by starting a bakery business in the building where they lived.

While all the Tanaka daughters were friendly and talkative, Michiko was the most vivacious. She radiated enthusiasm as she reminisced about Takarazuka, where she had done what she loved most and had fun with lots of talented, attractive girls her age. She was proud that she had been accepted into the company on her first try, right after finishing high school. She had married a doctor introduced to her by Kazuko, Masami's wife, via an *omiai*. She knew she would have to quit the theater group sometime, as she could not stay there till old age, and her mother had been urging her to quit at the appropriate age for marriage, which at that time was about twenty-three, in any case, before twenty-five.

Michiko complained, with a humorous laugh, that she was a "golf widow." When her husband was not involved with clinical work, he was playing golf: all day Sunday, often Saturday too, and sometimes he traveled to Osaka for tournaments. He had even thought of playing golf professionally. He won tournaments and was on TV recently. He had set up the kind of medical practice where he worked only by appointment, so he could go golfing by not scheduling appointments. She was resentful and envious that he could do as he wished, while she was totally tied down. She complained to him and they did argue, she laughingly reported. She did not hire a baby-sitter, for several reasons. She and her husband were trying to save money to buy a house; it was better for a child to be raised by the mother; and she would feel sorry for kids locked in a small apartment all day with a baby-sitter. Besides, a baby-sitter would not want the responsibility for two small children on a dangerous street. Michiko sometimes took the children to visit her mother or her friends, or she left them with her mother for a short time. Michiko was following the traditional marital pattern of separation of roles, in work and nonwork spheres, even more than her parents. She was not satisfied with it, but she was developing independent activities. She was more clear spoken than her mother would have been at that age.

Her husband looked forward to taking the kids to the golf course, as his father who also loved golf had taken him. His father, who was visiting at the time of my visit, explained that Japanese usually preferred boys. He was thankful for his son, the only son, amidst four daughters. Michiko, however, would very much have liked a daughter, presumably to replicate the closeness she had with her mother and her sisters.

Michiko was thankful she had found another outlet. She had set up a bread store on the first floor of the apartment building that housed their apartment and her husband's clinic (owned by her husband's parents). She hired others, including her younger sister-in-law, to take care of customers, but she supervised and did the bookkeeping. Michiko enjoyed the business and it made money for the family. She joked that her husband was spending money all the time, while she was making it and saving it and had no chance to spend.

Her in-laws were nearby in the building, and her mother-in-law and a sister-in-law occasionally helped out as receptionists in the clinic. Michiko seemed quite comfortable talking with them. She did not talk about socializing with them, but rather of seeing her own mother and her friends. The father asked me whether Americans take care of their older generation and their ancestors, and then told me that they were still taking care of his mother, age ninety-four, and had someone stay with her at all times.

As the children were getting older, Michiko asked my opinion about discipline, whether it was more effective to criticize children or praise them. She accepted my preference for praise, but commented that it was easier to criticize. She was concerned about future exam hell for her boys. She thought she would not pressure them so hard, but let them decide for themselves whether they would be "bakers or doctors." She pushed the baby in a carriage rather than using an *ombu*, and gave the baby a bottle. The children slept late in the morning, the baby took a nap, and the whole family went to bed together in the same room at night at the same time, about 11:00 p.m. or midnight. The baby slept in a crib, the parents in a bed, and the older boy on a futon on the floor. This preference for nighttime togetherness has continued with many families into the twenty-first century, as I repeatedly hear how they feel sorry for American children who have to go to bed alone.

Of course, the second-generation woman most central to Hanae's daily life was her daughter-in-law Kazuko, oldest son Masami's wife. She had realized her 1960 stated preference for living with her son and his wife, if they could all get along well. They lived in the same house, but with different quarters, and all reported contentment with that arrangement.

Kazuko, however, expressed regret about not living with and taking care of her own parents. She was the oldest of three daughters in a doctor's family living in a different prefecture, had gone to college, and decided on medicine to please her parents, since she had no other special interests. She had planned to return home after medical school to help with her father's practice and probably marry a man who could agree to take her name and live with her family (*mukoyoushi*, or adopted son-in-law). When she met Masami in medical school and decided to marry him, taking his name and living in his parental home, her parents were disappointed and a bit angry, but accepted that she had found someone with whom she would be happy. Her two younger sisters, already married and living at some distance, had not studied medicine. At times when she felt sorry for her parents, she complained to Masami that it was not fair that she took care of his mother but he did nothing for her parents. She pressured him to buy them a house. He sympathized, but said he could not afford it. She did not stay angry for long, because she knew that no one was being selfish. Sometimes she thought that Masami might be envious of her because she still had her father, whereas he did not have his.

She had seen that when a son went into practice with his father, there was often conflict because the son had more up-to-date knowledge, not accepted by the father. In this sense, she and her husband got along better in terms of working together. They often consulted with each other, which was very helpful. She could consult with him on the spot; she could understand his struggles and admire his skill.

Kazuko, unlike the Tanaka daughters, represented a small but growing group of young women in the 1970s who were as interested in their professional work as they were in their children. Like most of these working mothers, she was finding it hard to do both. She never thought it would be so hard to care for children and have a job at the same time. Their two boys, aged five and three in 1976, were cared for by a baby-sitter while Kazuko worked, but she took off several afternoons to be with the children. In contrast to most Japanese mothers, she did not feel guilty for leaving the children with the baby-sitter. She said the baby-sitter was good for the children, because she really played with them, and the boys had a good time. When they were younger, they had occasionally cried for their mother, but by this age they looked forward to the baby-sitter's arrival. Kazuko reported more regrets about lack of work time, because she did not have time to study and keep up, as Masami did. So she found herself leaning on him for new information. Occasionally she wished she were a man or that she had not married, so she could keep up with her profession better. She said she was her father's son, and rather like a man in some ways. Yet she never really considered not marrying, and she knew it was helpful for Masami to have her working with him. She could understand his job, and they had more time together than most young couples. But she wished that he understood her better, wished he would help her with housework and understand the pressures of her dual duties. When I commented that he must appreciate that she took care of the house and children so he did not have to, she smiled with pleasure at my understanding her feelings without saying whether he appreciated it or not.

She was glad she had her work. She would probably be bored and lonely if she did not work. Her profession gave her self-confidence. Her greatest pleasure and her greatest worry were in her work. She was pleased when something went well, but she worried and could not sleep at night if she had a problematic patient. Her children were in between, steady, small pleasures and no real worries. And as the children got older, she could look forward to having more time for work and study.

To my surprise, Kazuko did her own housework, rather than having the baby-sitter do it; she thought it was good for the children to see her in the housewife role. In the evening, she put the children to bed with a story, the children sleeping on futons or on the *tatami*, and she and her husband sleeping in beds. Sometimes the parents crawled in bed with the children to play with them, as they were at such a cute age. When they were infants, they slept in cribs for safety. Kazuko nursed them until they were about six to seven months old, and then fed them from a bottle. They were toilet-trained between one and two years of age. After the boys' bedtime, she and Masami had their own time. Masami either studied or went out to professional meetings. He liked to speak up at those meetings and was becoming a real leader. Kazuko was not interested in being a leader; she used her evenings to sew or watch TV. Once a month she did the bills on a Saturday or Sunday night. Usually on Sundays, they all four went out together. They did not go out as a couple, except to weddings or funerals, but they had time together at home or in the clinic. Although Kazuko mentions being her father's son, I never thought her to be masculine in looks or personality, although perhaps she was more thoughtful and less frivolous than some young Japanese women.

While Kazuko and I were talking, grandmother Hanae was upstairs playing with the boys. When they came down, the boys were full of fun: friendly, outgoing, spontaneous. Kazuko explained that *Obaasan* (Grandmother) played with the children occasionally, but generally did not help out much. Kazuko did not depend on her for help, so Obaasan was free to go out anytime. She was not like some grandmothers who needed to be needed. Obaasan liked to go out with her friends. Mamoru, still single, also lived in the house and ate dinner with Obaasan when he was home. If he was gone, however, Obaasan ate with Kazuko and Masami and the boys. Kazuko did the cooking. Obaasan did not like to cook: she washed her own dishes but not the family dishes, and she prepared and ate breakfast and lunch in her own apartment.

Just as she had hoped, Hanae was living with and getting along with the younger family, enjoying her own life, and causing no trouble. She was not the demanding, controlling mother-in-law of many stories, intent on teaching the "proper" way of doing things. She respected her daughter-in-law, appreciated her helpfulness, and enjoyed her company. Perhaps it was easier for Hanae to refrain from interfering than for some at-home grandmothers because she was less interested in housework and more interested in outside activities.

ONGOING CONVERSATIONS ABOUT MARRIAGE

When I next visited Hanae, she immediately hugged me and shed sentimental tears as she told me how much it had meant to her to be able to visit us in our home in Cambridge in the fall of 1977. I responded with another big hug. But then more tears followed as she responded to the news of our divorce. Her sorrow touched me deeply. It did not surprise me, however, because I knew how important togetherness was to her, and I remembered how impressed and envious she had been of Ezra's and my closeness in 1960. She had thought we had such a good relationship that she found it hard to believe our divorce now. She did not blame either of us, and was prepared to accept the sad reality and move on into the future. She hoped I would remarry, and declared that she would welcome the two of us.

She had enjoyed a good marriage, and if she remarried she would want the same kind of husband. She still felt sad that they could not share their elder years together. She then switched to ask me about American couples sleeping in double beds and enjoying sexual relations. She found that in Japan even though husband and wife were separated during the day, or that there might be arguments, bedtime and lovemaking brought them together again. If the feelings between them were not good, then the sex would not be so good; but if the feelings between them were good, then the sex would be good. When she looked to me for a response, I readily agreed. "Living with a man is the most natural way to live," she added. On another occasion, she told me that she did not want to take on another marriage, but that she could enjoy a "man friend."

I wondered whether she was asking me about American couples because she was puzzling in her head about what went wrong with my marriage. She kept on talking about marriage, this time about the problematic marriages of various friends and acquaintances. She mentioned a good friend of hers, eighty-five years old with an eighty-seven-year-old husband. The wife complained that her husband was getting so difficult and stubborn in his old age that she could no longer tolerate it, and called her son to announce she wanted a divorce. But then she died abruptly just one week later. In another case, a high-ranking husband found his wife in bed with another man, but never told her what he saw and knew. He simply never slept in the same room with her again. The wife also said nothing, even though she may have felt guilty. Hanae talked of the total lack of relationship in that marriage that was being maintained only to maintain their high status in society. I recognized this as a Japanese "*kateinai rikon*," or an emotional divorce while maintaining the family intact. I was surprised, however, by the total silence and avoidance of confrontation between the spouses.

She returned to a more positive note on marriage, with pictures of her youngest son Mamoru's wedding a few months earlier. He had refused two marriage introductions (*omiai*) with women physicians. He did not want such a strong career woman, and he wanted to make his own choice. He did not want to emulate his older brother. Then he met a doctor's daughter and decided to marry her within a few months. She was twenty-three and he thirty. Hanae did not investigate the woman's family, as was often done prior to a marriage agreement. But she did meet the prospective bride and her family, and Hanae also had friends who knew them. She liked the young woman but was a bit put off by her mother, who kept talking about having the couple live near them. Hanae considered whether she should oppose the marriage, but decided not to since Mamoru seemed happy about it. Subsequently the couple did not move to be near her family, but found a house with space for an attached clinic just one train stop from the Tanakas. Mamoru consulted often with his father-in-law, who seemed very happy with the relationship. Mamoru was working shorter hours than many, perhaps because he was just starting out on his own. Hanae did not visit them often. She thought it better to stay away. Her purpose in life continued to be to stay healthy and happy, and to cause her children no trouble.

Meanwhile, the other change in the family was that the new building had been built: a very modern one at the same location on the main street, with the clinic on the first floor, Obaasan on the second floor, and Masami and family on the third floor.

THE FLOWER YEARS

I was surprised to find in 1990 that Hanae, whom I always thought of as proper and formal, defied the traditional picture of an elderly Japanese grandmother. The stereotypical Japanese grandmother quietly sat at home in the background, perhaps doing some needlework, and dressed in modest colors, mostly grays or blacks. The tradition was bright colors for children and young unmarried women, and more quiet and subdued colors the older one became. But Hanae was wearing reds, pinks, blues, and purples in her late seventies, eighties, and even into her nineties. Somewhere along the line, she had given up wearing kimonos and shifted to Western-style dresses. I had not seen her for some years before I started going to Japan for a few weeks every year in the 1990s. I had wondered what kind of lifestyle would befit a professional housewife who lived on into this modern era as a widow.

Far from retiring quietly into the background, Hanae stood out more and more. Yes, she was sometimes called *oshare* or *hade* (a loud dresser), but she liked colors and felt that social rules had become more flexible. She seemed unconcerned about possible criticism. She also stood out by developing her hobby of flowers into a real career, albeit not to earn money. She had moved from the usual flower arranging to making designs with dried flowers, of varying size and style, including framed designs to hang on the wall. She received honors for her designs, and a book was made about her and her work. Indeed, her love of flowers, her ability to design, brought her considerable recognition even as she entered her nineties.

While some widows might spend their days helping with grandchildren or housekeeping, Hanae was not that interested in childcare or in competition with her daughter-in-law for control. She lived all these years with her son and his family, just as she had hoped to, but she saw herself as essentially alone. Although she knew she could always ask for help if she really needed it, she wanted to be independent.

She had thought out her plans for herself. She bought an apartment building with money her husband had left her, and she had income from the rent. She knew she needed something to keep her busy and interested. Though she had much experience with tea ceremony, she decided that it was too static. Flowers offered more opportunities for creativity. She found herself noticing flowers and flower designs wherever she went, freely asking questions about them, making new friends along the way, and learning a lot about what could be done with flowers. On a trip to Thailand with friends, she happened to get into a conversation with a man who told her about dried-flower design. Subsequently she spent some weeks in Los Angeles and San Francisco at workshops learning about it. After she developed some skill, she realized that she could duplicate the same design many times over, sell them, and make money. She chose not to turn her work into a business, however, but to make varying designs that pleased her and those around her.

While shopping on the Ginza one day, her eye picked up flowers in an art gallery. As she stopped in to see the gallery and to ask about the flowers, the conversation developed into a friendship that led the gallery owner to suggest that Hanae exhibit her work there. That was the first of many Ginza exhibits. When she tired of that location, she even had an exhibit at the Imperial Hotel.

Hearing of her skill in starting up friendly conversations, I recalled a small incident in Cambridge in 1977 that amazed me at the time. Hanae, speaking no English of course, went by herself to see the flowers in a neighborhood flower shop. I was worried that she might have gotten lost when a car drove up and a gentleman helped Hanae out of the car. Evidently Hanae and the owner of the flower shop had been involved in a lengthy interaction where he showed her many things that were not on display. The lack of a common language seemed to be no hindrance to communication about something of mutual interest. The driver was a flower shop customer who had joined in the discussion, and then offered to bring Hanae home.

Even severe arthritis of the knees, which she had since her fifties, did not hold her back. A more typical elderly Japanese woman would probably be bashful about her disability and would retire inside her house to take care of herself. The doctors had told Hanae there was nothing they could do for her aging knees, which pained her because bone was rubbing upon bone. But Hanae kept going as much as she could, tolerating the pain. She walked to the train station using a cane or took a cab to the station when she went into Tokyo. When she felt a bit unsteady stepping onto the train from the platform, she would ask a nearby gentleman for a hand to steady herself. She had a manner of asking that was pleasantly appealing: polite, appreciative, humorous, but not obsequious. I am sure she was never refused, and she often continued to converse after boarding the train and sometimes made a lasting friendship. In Takeo Doi's language of *amae*, I would say that she was very skilled at relying on others (*amaekata wa jouzu*), in a natural and sincere way. And of course, she was at least as good at giving as she was at receiving.

As the years went by, her knees became more painful. She began to use a walker both outside and within her apartment. But she continued to care for herself, only eating with the younger couple at night and washing her own dishes. Within the apartment, she could put things in the basket attached to the walker, and transport things from room to room. When I visited, she insisted on making me tea herself, but she ordered a sushi lunch for us. For some years she had been going to her summer house for a month or two to avoid the worst of Tokyo heat. Even there she was often by herself and able to care for herself. For extra safety she kept a telephone near her at all times. She even did her own cleaning, sitting in one spot and vacuuming all around her. She did have a caretaker who cared for the place when no one was staying there, and who did grocery shopping or other errands. She became rather ingenious in devising methods of getting things done with her limited mobility.

Her children and grandchildren were free to make use of the summer house at any time, whether she was there or not. She had built it for them. The rule was that they should leave the place in the same condition in which they found it. So all cleaned up after themselves, and they came frequently and thoroughly enjoyed the beautiful hills and many recreational facilities nearby. They even came in the winter to be near ski slopes.

Sometime in the late 1970s, Hanae discreetly inquired if it might be possible to show some of her work near my home in Cambridge. I initially declined, saying I knew nothing about gallery shows and had no time since I was working a full-time job plus private practice. After I retired from the full-time job, however, I thought perhaps I could manage it. With the collaboration of Dr. Kenneth Reich of the Psychoanalytic Couple and Family Institute of New England, we rented a gallery in the basement of the Unitarian Church at Harvard Square and invited all our friends and colleagues to come to see Hanae's work. Hanae sent over enough of her work to fill the gallery, and she declared she did not want to take any home. She wanted to give some to me and to members of my family as gifts, but then she very generously agreed to give the proceeds from the sale of other items to the institute for its work with children.

So in June 2001, in a gallery in the basement of the Unitarian Church in Harvard Square, we had a three-day grand showing of Hanae's dried-flower designs. Three of her daughters and one granddaughter (Yoshiko's twenty-nine-year-old daughter Yasuko) came along with her for a week's stay. They arrived in Boston at midnight after an eighteen-hour plane ride plus a four-hour delay, looking beautiful, well-dressed, ready to go, not at all tired. They kept it up for the week, enjoying breakfast outdoors on my deck, sightseeing in Boston, and supervising the workers who put up the pictures.

Hanae was thrilled to be in Cambridge; she spoke of this show capping her career. She was sentimental about the long years of our friendship, remembering her visit twenty years earlier, going through the house remembering the rooms, our longtime baby-sitter, and the Japanese friend who was living here at the time. She enjoyed my wearing an elegant dress made some years ago out of a kimono she had given me, and reminisced while looking at a video that Ezra had made of our visits with the Tanakas in 1959. And on the show days, we were all there welcoming and introducing visitors, translating conversations, with Hanae very much the center of the show, standing despite her sore knees to greet each person with a bow. She was radiant.

The daughters and granddaughter were very much part of the show. Masako welcomed guests and flattered them, laughing as she tried out her English words and put her arm around each man. Michiko danced and twirled around the room, reminding me of her Takarazuka past. Yasuko, Yoshiko's daughter, busied herself recording the sales. Yoshiko was quiet and demure, but also made herself helpful. I remember her taking care of my plants in the house on her own initiative, watering them and cutting off the stems with the skill of a professional. The daughters were all very solicitous of me, carrying things for me, asking if I was tired while insisting they were not. Of course, they took good care of Hanae, being her support as she walked. She had promised to pay airfare for all four if they would promise that two of them would always stay close to her for help and support. The other two could go off as they might wish. During the show, one or two of them would leave the group and go shopping. They had to buy their *omiyage* (souvenirs). All enjoyed the show, Japanese and American guests, Tanaka family, and Vogel family.

During some of our informal meals, the daughters quizzed me again about why Ezra and I had divorced. They still found it hard to understand, I think, because they liked both of us and they could not conceive of divorce for any but extreme reasons. They laughed, saying they continually complain about their husbands but still could not imagine divorce. Both Masako and Michiko did office work for their physician husbands. They needed to get back home soon; they were needed there.

INTERVIEW STRUGGLES

After I had decided to write Hanae's life history and she had agreed with the project, I thought I should accept her invitation to visit her summer house so we could talk at greater length and greater leisure. So three times in different years, I spent two or three days there with Hanae. But rather than long, leisurely talks, we had a push-pull experience with each other that rather baffled me and made me question whether she really wanted to talk with me about her life. When so many people love talking about themselves and reviewing their lives, why didn't she? Why did she keep telling me she could not remember the past when I had never pushed her to remember anything that did not come easily? At one point, I even wrote her a letter in polite Japanese, with a friend's help, saying that if she would prefer we discontinue these discussions, that would not endanger our friendship. She responded that she was honored that I wanted to write about her. After taking some time to think this over, I concluded that our priorities were a bit different. I wanted one-on-one conversations with her, occasionally including other family members, while she was looking forward to entertaining me or having others join us while I was there. She sometimes seemed more preoccupied with serving me than having a conversation. She did not particularly enjoy talking about her life history, although she was not really opposed to it. After we talked for a couple of hours in the morning, for instance, she wanted to take me for a ride to see sights and then to take me out to dinner with a widower friend. I managed to forgo the afternoon ride in favor of more discussion, but we went to dinner with her friend and had a delightful time.

Another year, she had arranged to have a kind of conference with six to eight of her women friends, where we all talked about our experiences and took walks in the woods. A couple of the women had fun dressing me up in a

beautiful kimono and taking my picture. Some of Hanae's friends had
wanted to meet her *gaijin* (foreigner) friend and she wanted to share me with
them. I was less enthusiastic about this meeting since I had previously had
enough of being the *gaijin* about whom everyone was curious. In the end, our
push-pull meant we both got some of what we wanted: she made an effort to
cooperate, and I learned to enjoy her inclusive sociability.

I would have liked to explore more with her the problems she might have
faced and the way she dealt with them. She did not respond well to theoreti-
cal questions, as her thinking was more concrete, and she did not enjoy
talking about challenges. As I thought about it, however, I realized that in the
course of my long friendship with her, I had heard something about her
problems and sensed others.

Hanae always said she had never had a real fight with anyone, but she did
recount some conflicts among her siblings. During the 1980s, one group was
not speaking to the other for about a ten-year period due to a battle over
inheritance. The sisters and their husbands were furious at the brother, who
was winning the fight and inheriting most of the mother's money. This was
the younger brother who was officially now the *chounan* (the oldest son, with
all the prerogatives of the eldest) since the older brother had died in training
camp at the beginning of the war. Hanae was unhappy about this intra-
familial fight, but stated that it could not be changed as long as everyone was
angry and thinking irrationally. She would visit with all of her siblings, listen
to their complaints, and then act as though she had not heard the angry words
of the other side. Her opinion or judgment was neither asked nor given. One
sister, a widow, was the most rigid, the most critical, the most stubborn.
Finally, when Hanae began to feel that the anger was cooling down, she
decided to have a picnic and invited all her brothers and sisters, their spouses,
and children. They gradually talked with each other there, and that broke the
ice. Hanae was the quiet peacemaker.

This kind of sibling battle over inheritance seems to have occurred rather
frequently among families, particularly during the bubble of the 1980s, evidently because of the confusion and mixed feelings about the changed inheritance laws after the war. Before the war, it was clear that the eldest son
inherited all the family property and the responsibility of caring for any
family business and for the elder parents. The equal inheritance law passed
after the war, and yet this made things much less clear in practice. And while
all siblings were equal, the eldest son continued to be the "most equal." In
Hanae's family of origin, the eldest son did not inherit everything but he
inherited the most, with the result that the sisters and their husbands were
resentful. Although Hanae did not take sides at the time, she now felt that the
eldest son and his wife deserved the largest slice because they had taken care
of the elderly mother for many years. The brother's wife had been a very
caring daughter-in-law.

In the 1960s, Hanae's big worry was Yoshiko's conversion to the Christian sect. When they learned that the church would not allow their members to attend Buddhist or Shinto services, Hanae and Masami tried talking to Yoshiko to persuade her to give it up. They especially regretted her alienation from the family because she was not able to participate in family ceremonies, not even her father's funeral. In the end, however, they realized they could not force the issue. Yoshiko stuck to her decision just as she had earlier insisted on going to a music college and on choosing her own husband. Gradually the family accepted Yoshiko's chosen life. Nowadays Hanae sees Yoshiko as a genuinely good person, and recognizes that she is often the one who is most considerate and most helpful. For example, she is usually the most supportive when anyone is sick, and she comes to her mother's house every Friday to help out and care for her. Hanae also expressed concern, to me and to Yoshiko directly, about her children pursuing religious studies rather than going to college, fearing future financial insecurity for them. But she accepted their firm decision and did not keep on fussing about it.

Hanae had a distinctive style of relating to people and problems. She tried to teach her own children by explaining so they would understand and scolding them when necessary, and generally the children followed her leadership. She was not punitive or overly critical. Even when Masami hid on the roof to avoid his tutor, she was more relieved when he was all right than angry at his misbehavior. She laughs as she talks about his being a difficult child and a grumpy adult. These days, she deals with his moodiness by not interfering with what he wants to do. She has raised concerns about her grandchildren at times, but essentially defers to their parents' decisions on handling discipline. One time Hanae was worried about Michiko's youngest boy being too interested in playing and not studying enough. She gently chided him, saying that if he wanted to be a doctor as he had said, he would need to take his studies more seriously. And in her relationships with other family or close friends, she tries to understand the other's reasons. She may raise questions or give her own opinions, but even then will not draw a line or demand acquiescence or cut off a relationship. She focuses on the good qualities of people, and respects their right to make their own decisions. She enjoys seeing people reconciling and getting along (*nakayoku suru*).

In earlier years, my American suspiciousness of excessive politeness made me wonder whether Hanae's polite words were covering up something. The more I observed, however, the more I could feel the genuineness of her love of people and of people enjoying each other. Although she could recognize a problem, her always recognizing the good qualities of others was her very effective way of dealing with the complications of life.

I am impressed that Hanae's family members are all rather happy, successful individuals, and they have remained close and cooperative through the years. This is surely a tribute to Hanae and Takao as parents. The physician theme in the family has continued. With the exception of Yoshiko's children, all grandchildren, male and female, are physicians. Several have also married physicians. This is impressive, even in a society where the eldest son is expected to follow his father.

The oldest son Masami and daughters Masako and Michiko largely continued in the pattern reported in 1976. Masami and Masako each have close marital relationships, professionally and personally, while Michiko and her husband continue rather separate, although not incompatible, work and social lives. Masami's wife Kazuko continues working alongside her husband in the clinic, while enlarging on her own hobbies since childcare is no longer needed. Masako carries numerous responsibilities: clinic receptionist, bookkeeper, and even baby-sitter for her grandchild. Note that Hanae is now a great-grandmother.

The younger son and youngest child, Mamoru, seemed slightly more distant. Perhaps that was because he lived a distance away and his wife was not tied into the three-daughter-plus-daughter-in-law network around Grandmother. This was his second marriage. After a son was born to him and his first wife, his wife seemed sickly and her mother came to Mamoru and Hanae, requesting that the wife be allowed to divorce Mamoru since she was physically weak and unable to maintain the marriage and childcare. Hanae was annoyed that they had not been told of the bride's physical weakness before the marriage, even when Hanae had asked about it. There seemed no use in getting angry overtly, however, so they allowed the divorce. I noted the continuing influence of families in making decisions about a marriage problem rather than the pair working it out themselves Western style. Mamoru remarried and had a daughter with the second wife. He kept in touch with his son. Hanae has even visited the divorced wife's family. Now the son is also becoming a doctor, and has been friendly with Michiko's youngest son, as they were in medical school at the same time. Hanae was pleased with the friendship between the cousins. Now Masami's daughter is also on her way toward medical school. As Hanae's mobility has become increasingly limited by her knee pain, she has spent some time living at Mamoru's house; everything there is on one floor and it is easier to get around.

The middle daughter, Yoshiko, stands out as the exception in this family of closeness and professional compatibility. Not only did she not become a physician or marry one, but she converted to a Christian sect and raised her two children in it. She and her children have a different lifestyle and different value system from the rest of the family. Hanae describes their activities in an accepting, uncritical way. Yet she still seems astonished and dismayed to report that Yoshiko's son and his wife are volunteer missionaries in northern Japan, supporting their work by whatever they make delivering milk, and that Yasuko at age thirty is still tied to her mother, doing little besides teaching English at Bible school and reading the Bible at home. Yasuko, supported by her mother, says she would like to find a husband, but he has to be a member of their church although it does not matter if he is Japanese or not. Both Yoshiko and Yasuko expressed their pleasure that their husband/ father was now closer to the family and spent more time with them since he had retired from the main company and was working for a subsidiary. They were more accepting of his not joining their church, and he seemed more accepting of their belonging.

Despite her difference, Yoshiko has made a point of maintaining a helpful, supportive relationship with her mother and her siblings. She does not share their love of colorful clothes, nor does she participate in her sisters' loud talk and laughter. She continues in her quiet, modest, self-confident manner. I would speculate that her religion has helped her deal with her sense of being different from her siblings while maintaining warmth and closeness to her family. That is, it has helped her to reconcile this dichotomy in her own self. It has given her a way to feel all right being different and to feel correct in following her own judgment while saying no to pressures from her family and from her husband. And as she seems comfortable with herself and her family of origin, she and her husband seem more accepting of each other. I find that whenever I am talking directly with Yoshiko or Yasuko, they are both easy to talk with and quite straightforward in discussing their beliefs and activities, rather more serious and thoughtful than their more exuberant relatives. Yoshiko's religion is unusual in the larger society and distinctly different from the other Tanakas, but Yoshiko is as much a professional housewife as her sisters or the others of her generation. She has done her best in caring for her children and her husband, and has tried to improve herself through her religion. Perhaps as the middle child she needed some way to declare her individuality within this rather happily conforming family.

In looking at the Tanaka second generation (Hanae's children), they seem representative of those born during or soon after the war. They have enjoyed improved technology at home and elsewhere, with a steadily improving standard of living. They have found that upward mobility brought great pressures for academic achievement for themselves and their children. They have had fewer children than their parents did, and have taken on some Western ways in terms of housing, heating, beds, and baby carriages. The marital relationship began to take on more importance and to become more companionable, and child rearing became more indulgent. The women put less emphasis on the professional housewife and her particular skills. The third generation, the grandchildren, take modern, Westernized living for granted. They have more leisure time and somewhat shorter working hours. They are all professionals, men and women, though they still stress the importance of childcare. When I mentioned the term *sengyou shufu* to Hanae in 2000, she looked surprised and said that she seldom heard that term anymore.

REVIEWING A GOOD LIFE

As Hanae reviewed her life in 2006, she stressed that she was blessed with good fortune, had experienced no tragedies or very difficult struggles. She was *maemuki*: she looked forward to good times and did not dwell on problems. To some extent she thanked the *mukyoukai* (the no-church church) of her youth for this emphasis on love and positive thinking. She felt that she had a happy childhood, a good marriage, enough money, healthy children, many friends, and a hobby she still enjoys. She does not attribute this to any skills of her own. She says the only thing she could really brag about is that the students she taught during her three years as a kindergarten teacher still remember her with visits and cards, and even made a book of pictures thanking her for teaching them. Of course, they all are about seventy years old by now and several hold important positions in the community.

Hanae emphasized that marrying her husband was fortunate for her (and for him, I am sure). He was a learned man who earned a good living with his medical practice. He planned and thought ahead. Although generous with his family and friends, he was frugal and scrupulous. In one year he saved enough to buy a piece of property; indeed he bought five such properties so that he could give one to each of his five children. He was fond of an old saying that a man who spends money on mistresses and vacation homes will not go far. He was a leader in the community, both among his fellow professionals and his fishing friends. Since Hanae respected him, she felt it was natural to follow his leadership. He was the typical good father of those days in that he did no housework, but he played with the children and took the family on weekend outings. In fact, he was much easier to get along with than Masami. And it was only after he died that she learned that he had given money not only to his father, but also to her mother.

Hanae achieved one of her major goals for her later years: She got along well with her daughter-in-law and she was able to live with her eldest son and his family. She is always pleased to report that there are no disagreeable feelings between them. They lead separate lives, but they also cooperate. Hanae can sometimes call Kazuko to pick her up if she is not too far away, and she always leaves notes to let the younger couple know when she will be home.

My own impression is that Hanae was (and is) as healthy, happy, and successful a professional housewife as any I have met. She was a "good wife and wise mother." Her family thrived under her care, as she lovingly raised her children and supported her husband. Her skills in the domestic arts of flowers and tea contributed to the family's cultural accomplishments. She not only accepted her role as housewife but enjoyed it, and never felt demeaned by it. The value of her role was recognized by the family, by the community, and by herself.

She may have been unusual in the flexibility and creativity she demon-strated in forging a new life for herself after she was widowed. Although I was surprised by her unconventionally bright colors, I could see that she was not rebelling against her feminine role but enhancing it. Just as she had gained confidence from her popularity as a kindergarten teacher, she seemed to gain confidence during her widowhood as she took up the necessity of making her own life with real vigor. Perhaps by then she felt secure as a woman and a mother, so she had the courage to assert herself as someone looking to bring color and happiness into her life and that of her family. Her bashfulness gone, she enjoyed standing out. This was perhaps made easier by the many changes other Japanese women were making. Certainly she heard only praise, and no criticism, from the people around her.

I have occasionally pondered what the last half of her life would have been like had her husband not died so early. I am sure that she would have enjoyed doing things with him, but would she also have had the particular joy and the artistic accomplishments she had as a widow? Hanae, as a natural fit for the professional housewife role, excelled and found fulfillment in the role. As Japan modernized, she went on to more individual and perhaps more professional accomplishments with her flower designs, all socially sanc-tioned as consistent with her feminine wife/mother role.

NOTES

1. I have changed the personal names and some place names in this book to protect the privacy of these women and their families. Although I usually called Mrs. Tanaka "Tanaka-san" in the Japanese manner, I will use her first name and the first names of her family members to differentiate between different members of the family.

2. Uchimura was a Christian evangelist in Japan during the Meiji and Taishou eras.

3. Takarazuka is an all-female musical troupe based in Takarazuka, Hyougo prefecture.

4. Merry I. White, *Perfectly Japanese: Making Families in an Era of Upheaval* (Berkeley: University of California Press, 2002).

Chapter Three

Mrs. Itou

Resisting the Role

Mrs. Yaeko Itou immediately challenged my stereotype of Japanese women as quietly modest and deferential. She was the only wife who wore Western clothes among the main research group of six families in 1958–1960. The others wore kimonos, both at home and in public. She introduced herself as the youngest in the group (at age thirty-one), the most modern and progressive, and the most Westernized. Was she just trying to appeal to us as Americans? Or was she really different? I soon discovered that she really was unique among these housewives, less constrained by either the prescribed feminine manners or by the mandates of the professional housewife role. She was nonconformist just for putting herself forward as distinctive in a society in which women were respected for blending in, for being *otonashii* (gentle, docile). Ordinary (*futsuu*) was positively valued, while different (*kawatteiru*) was negatively valued. Deference and modesty, not self-assertive individuality, were the esteemed traits for Japanese women of that day.

So how did such a nonconformist survive and even thrive in a society as structured as Japan? Like many Americans, I had the image of Japanese women as self-effacing and self-sacrificing, but Yaeko was living proof that there were other varieties. I wondered how such a woman coped with the social pressures of the "good wife/wise mother" ideal that most women found so immutable. And as our friendship has deepened and we have passed through various stages of life, I have been intrigued, often astonished, to hear how she has managed her life and her relationships in the midst of such pressures. She has been characteristically open and enthusiastic in telling me about herself and her family, and I have been an eager listener, always enjoying her lively conversation and broadening my knowledge of Japanese women through her experiences. Her lifestyle would probably elicit admiration from many modern Americans. Perhaps she was just ahead of her time, struggling to adjust herself to a historical role that did not fit her. In twenty-first-century Tokyo, assertive women like her have become more accepted.

Despite her affinity for Western ways, American postwar influence in Japan was only the most superficial explanation for her personality style. Her basic orientation was set long before the American Occupation and even before the war. Yaeko explains her personality as due to being an *obaasanko*, an only child spoiled by her grandparents. That is undoubtedly correct, but I would quickly add that she grew up and lived in an adopted son-in-law (*mukoyoushi*) family, both as daughter and as wife. That meant fewer limits on her individual assertiveness, and she learned to fight those restrictions she did encounter. As noted in chapter 1, the *mukoyoushi* family was a variant within the system of inheritance in traditional Japan whereby families with no son in the family would adopt a son-in-law. The *mukoyoushi* wives tended to be more assertive than other wives because the elder parents were their own parents, not their in-laws. Correspondingly, the husbands were weaker because they were adoptees, even though they had officially taken over the mantle of the head of the family.

In Yaeko's family, the *mukoyoushi* pattern appears in her mother's line. Yaeko's mother, whom we shall call *Obaasan* or Grandmother since that is how Yaeko referred to her, had two sets of parents. One set was her biological parents, the Tsunodas, who ran a thriving printing business in Nihombashi in central Tokyo, surrounded by their large extended family of children and grandchildren. The second set was the Itous, Tsunoda relatives in the countryside who had adopted Obaasan and two of her siblings when Obaasan was in elementary school. Since the elder Itous had no children, they had been given for adoption the youngest three of the Tsunodas' twelve children, including Obaasan. Obaasan had then grown up and gone to school in the countryside with the Itou parents and her brother and sister. This brother was supposed to be the Itou family heir, but he rebelled, deserting the family and joining the Imperial Army in Manchuria. Her sister then died in the 1923 Tokyo earthquake. This left Obaasan as the only heir of the Itou line, making it necessary for her to marry a man, perhaps a third or fourth son of his birth family, who could become an adopted son-in-law. Maintaining the family line, along with obedience to parents, took precedence over the biological bond of mother-child or the emotional bond of husband-wife.

Obaasan lived many years with the Itous in Inatori, a fishing village on the Izu Peninsula south of Tokyo. After her marriage, however, she and her husband Yoshimatsu, a carpenter, lived with the Tsunodas in Tokyo, and their first and only child was born there in 1927. They named her Yaeko using the same *kanji* (Chinese character) from the name of Obaasan's sister who was killed in the earthquake. Nevertheless, Obaasan's and Yoshimatsu's primary allegiance was to the Itous. Since they had both taken the Itou name and were listed as Itou heirs, their obligation was to those parents above all.

Yaeko was greatly indulged as an only child and the only grandchild at that time living in the Tokyo household of her Tsunoda grandparents. She spent more time with, and had a stronger attachment to, these grandparents, the Tsunodas, than to her parents, who were frequently away in those earliest years visiting the Itou grandparents in Inatori. And according to a common saying, the first three years determine a person's personality for life (*mitsu go no tamashi hyaku made*). Yaeko has many happy memories of living in this rather large and well-to-do Tokyo house, even when her mother was away in the country. Even though boys at that time were more valued than girls, both boys and girls were often indulged and subjected to little discipline during the preschool years. Yaeko recalls being the center of attention, allowed to play at whatever she wanted in a relatively large and luxurious house, with chocolates as treats. She became accustomed to getting her way, playing as she wished, with others catering to her.

Not only was Yaeko more emotionally bonded to her Tokyo grandparents than to her mother, but she also considered herself a child of the city rather than the country. Obaasan related an amusing story to her when she was older. She had once taken three-year-old Yaeko with her to Inatori. The train conductor did not think that Obaasan looked like Yaeko's mother since the child was neatly dressed as a city child while the mother was dressed like a countrywoman. He thought Obaasan was a maid who was kidnapping the child, and he started to take them to the police box until he heard Yaeko say "*okaasan, oshikko!*" (weewee). That convinced the conductor that they were mother and child.

When Yaeko was six, all this changed. Her parents had to move full-time to the countryside to take care of their adoptive parents, who were getting old and whose house had burned down. There Yaeko first confronted a less indulgent and more demanding world, one that expected her to behave more like a girl. Even Obaasan thought Yaeko had been spoiled by the Tokyo grandparents and sought to teach her discipline. Yaeko defied discipline, however, and her tantrums frequently bested her mother. Yaeko explained that her independent spirit, born of being spoiled as a young child, was further nurtured in rebellion, most often successful rebellion. Yaeko has never liked to lose a fight.

Mother-in-law/son-in-law conflict arose in the family, much like the fabled mother-in-law/daughter-in-law conflict, except more intense. An adopted son-in-law was in a tough situation. Wanting to assert his male leadership, he was likely to resist being as passively obedient as a daughter-in-law was expected to be. The Itou grandmother was quite strict and demanding toward him, insisting on good manners and criticizing his drinking. Yoshimatsu, who was proud of his hard work as a carpenter, resented being criticized and ordered around. He drank more, argued with his mother-in-law, and sometimes took out his anger on his wife. Yaeko was horrified to see him hit her mother. Yoshimatsu wanted to take his wife and child and move away from the Itous, promising to pay them compensation in return. Obaasan, however, refused to leave. Although divorce was disgraceful, she felt that deserting elderly parents was even worse. Loyalty to and care of parents (*oyakoukou*) was more important than loyalty to a spouse. Finally, after many arguments, Yoshimatsu left the house, was divorced (erased from the family register), and never sent money back. From this traumatic experience, Yaeko came to hate men who drank or became violent. She swore never to depend on such a man—better to depend on herself.

Her mother also had to depend on her own strength, and so she did. She worked day and night at any available job, even gathering and selling seaweed in the nearby fishing village to support herself, her child, and her Itou parents. She also had to nurse the parents when they became bedridden for several years before their deaths when Yaeko was in sixth grade. Yaeko helped with their care and other household duties, even coming home from school at lunchtime in order to feed them, since they could not cook for themselves.

Yaeko's resentment of her father's desertion (as she defined it) grew during those years of hardship. She knew it was shameful not to have a father, but she thought it more shameful to have a drunken or a violent father. In talks with her mother, she would rail against her father, declaring him an enemy for throwing away his family, even his child, promising she would never have anything to do with him. "*Kankei nai!*" (no connection, no relation), she declared, both then and now. In fact, she has used this phrase several times in recalling conflictual events in her life. She kept that promise never to have anything to do with him. When she married, he offered to build a house for her, but she refused him, even though her mother told her she should accept this offer. Her mother pointed out that it was not all his fault, that grandmother Itou had treated him badly, and that he was now a well-respected, prosperous businessman with a new family in a nearby town. Years later in his old age, he asked her to meet him once before he died. She refused. She did, however, allow her daughter Katsuko to go meet him, as he had pleaded for someone from Yaeko's family to come. And Yaeko relented and attended his funeral, where she was welcomed but made a speech saying that she should not be given the honor chair of the eldest daughter because she was from a different family.

Yaeko found strife at school too. Although she was quite smart and excelled at schoolwork, she was never quite accepted by her classmates. She was teased (*ijime*) or even excluded because she had no father, no money in her family, and a mother who had to work too hard. Yaeko took pride in her brains, as she felt that was all she had. She was beaten in the election for class representative because she was said to be arrogant. Determined not to be totally defeated, she succeeded in impressing her teachers who gave her a major role in the school kabuki play.

She yearned for life in Tokyo. She never liked life in the country village. Being a spunky kid, she ran away to Tokyo once while in the first grade, her first year in the country. This was a brave and difficult trip for a seven-year-old, over two hours on trains with transfers. She took a basket of food with her, and was able to tell the train conductor and a worried policeman exactly the names and addresses of her Tokyo relatives. Her mother's older sister Motoko was contacted; she agreed to receive Yaeko and arrange for her mother to come and get her. While there, Yaeko learned that her grandparents had died, a fact that her mother had wanted to spare her. That sad news meant there was no longer any purpose in running away, so life in Inatori was all she had for several years. When she finished the sixth grade, she again determined to go to Tokyo to live with relatives and attend the better city schools. Although most of the country girls were intimidated by the big city, Yaeko was not. She felt she knew Tokyo, and that if she studied she could do well. Her mother opposed her plan, saying that she belonged in the village and she should stay there as her mother had done. Tokyo would not be a good influence on her and she would probably be teased for her country ways.

Meanwhile, after the Inatori grandparents had died and mother was left alone, Obaasan wanted to marry a fisherman, Takematsu, with whom she had become friends. Yaeko strongly opposed her mother's remarriage, saying she would only be asking for a repeat of her past suffering. Yaeko suggested that they move together to Tokyo where she would work in future years and take care of her mother. The arguments between them were quite severe for some time, with Yaeko accusing her mother of selfishness for choosing her lover and marriage over her child (Yaeko). She quoted the moral thinking of that time: that a good mother was never selfish, always putting care of the family, especially the children, above her own welfare. When the fiancé came to visit, Yaeko had a temper tantrum, declaring he was not a family member and should be given nothing to eat in their house. Yaeko never quite forgave her mother, and declared from that time on that she was under no obligation to look after her mother. Indeed, as an adult she did not live near her mother and stepfather or extend herself to care for them, although she did keep in touch. Correspondingly, her mother continually criticized Yaeko for being selfish, neither taking care of her mother nor, after marriage, of her own husband. When Obaasan died years later, she left what money she had not to Yaeko but to Yaeko's oldest daughter Mari, who had been quite devoted to her grandmother.

Looking back, Yaeko sees that both she and her mother were strong-minded and determined. These two strong women finally, although somewhat grudgingly, made a deal, each agreeing to accept the other's decision. Obaasan, who had previously stuck to her decision to care for her parents, now stuck to her decision to remarry. After that, she remarried and she did live an easier life. Yaeko never quite accepted her stepfather, referring to him for years simply as "that man." Now she realizes that he was a good man who supported her in many ways. When we first met Yaeko in 1959, however, she referred to him as her father, hiding the embarrassment of a divorce in the family, as most Japanese would.

Yaeko went to Tokyo and took the entrance exam to a good *jogakkou* (a four-year women's high school, which was a good education for a woman at that time), with her mother's tacit acceptance. She then attended school there from age thirteen, living with her mother's eldest sister Motoko. Her mother's brother, returning from Manchuria apologetic for not taking care of the adoptive parents, promised to pay for Yaeko's tuition. Obaasan regularly brought presents to the aunt for letting Yaeko live there. By the time she left for school in Tokyo, Yaeko had established a pattern of actively pursuing her own interests and of battling any obstacles with a determination to come out on top.

HONING SKILLS

In Tokyo as a teenager, Yaeko continued to follow her own interests and ambitions, and again found herself in conflict with another woman, this one even stronger, stricter, and more domineering than her own mother. This proud woman, the aunt with whom she lived, was a graduate of an elite woman's high school at a time when few women went past the six years of compulsory education. She was also a smart businesswoman, the manager of a photography shop. From today's perspective, Yaeko realizes that she learned a lot from this aunt about the rules of society, about the use of polite language (*keigo*), and about competent business management. At the time, however, Yaeko thoroughly hated this aunt because she was so critical, rigid, and authoritarian, making Yaeko work like a maid and insisting that Yaeko learn to be quiet and obedient or else no one would want to marry her. Her uncle, this aunt's husband, was more sympathetic with Yaeko. When her aunt railed against Yaeko, for example, the uncle would ask her to run an errand for him, just to let her escape the aunt.

While going to school, Yaeko also helped in the photography shop. There Yaeko, who was never timid, eagerly conversed with many male college students. She got them to help her with her homework and asked them many questions to satisfy her curiosity about the world. She was not at all interested in them romantically. She disliked romantic love marriage from what she had seen of it. She knew little or nothing about sex, and had no interest in exploring it. However, she preferred the companionship of men to women, especially educated men, as she considered men smarter, stronger, and more confident than women (*shikkari shite iru*).

Yaeko confronted a family crisis at the beginning of her fourth year in school in Tokyo. Aunt Motoko, who off and on had had arguments with her husband, calling him stupid (*baka*) for drinking and slacking off, had been having an affair with a young photography assistant. Yaeko had been shocked to see them going into the darkroom together. Aunt had given her candy, asking her to tell no one what she saw. Once when the assistant developed acute appendicitis, Yaeko helped her aunt by taking clothes to him in the hospital. The crisis hit when Aunt Motoko gave birth to a baby boy, and no one thought he resembled Uncle. Uncle pressed Yaeko to tell if she had seen anything, while Aunt Motoko forbade her to say a word. In the midst of this pressure, aggravated by her own total disillusionment with her aunt and uncle, Yaeko again ran away—even giving up on school—this time to her mother in the country. Since she had no money and did not want to borrow, she had to sleep on a park bench along the way. Mother and step-father, who did not know why Yaeko had left school, firmly returned her to Tokyo. Since Yaeko insisted that she did not want to stay with that aunt anymore, her mother arranged for her to stay one month at a time at the homes of each of the mother's elder siblings, including the aunt of concern, who were still living in the area. Although she obediently returned, she was disheartened and unmotivated for her studies for a time. One teacher inquired why she was not studying as well as usual when she had been a good student. She finally confided in that teacher, the only person she ever told what she knew. The teacher scolded her for not studying, advised her to stay in school at least through graduation, and not to let her aunt's misbehavior concern her so much. It was her aunt's problem, not Yaeko's, and Yaeko should look after herself. Yaeko could not help but agree with that. She immediately ceased her rebellion and recovered her interest in her studies. She even helped her aunt to care for the new baby.

Yet Yaeko clashed with Aunt Motoko once again. She badly wanted to go on to teacher's college after graduation. On her own initiative, she applied and took the entrance test, even though her mother urged her to return to the village where she belonged, and her aunt told her she could not be a good teacher since she was too outspoken, disobedient, and unfeminine. When the announcement of her passing the test arrived, Aunt Motoko received it and tore it up. By the time Yaeko learned of her acceptance, it was too late for her to enroll. That was the final betrayal, in Yaeko's eyes. She considered Aunt Motoko an enemy after that. She did not see that aunt again until the uncle's funeral, after she had been married several years. It was only then that she learned that her aunt and uncle had divorced soon after the war.

Although Yaeko hated the aunt, she continued to keep the aunt's secret about the child. Telling on the aunt would have been too destructive, she explained later. Her aunt might have had to go to jail. She did not tell me the full truth until 2000, forty years after I first heard the story of this harsh aunt. Thinking about it now, I see that she and her aunt were a matched pair. Yaeko had honed her skills by living with and battling two strong women in her life: her mother and then her aunt. We will see more of the aunt's traits in Yaeko's continuing story: sharpness of mind; quick planning and action; outspokenness; little concern for others' criticisms; and marriage to a softer, rather passive, somewhat devalued man.

Yaeko wanted to stay in Tokyo rather than return to the country, in spite of her mother's and her aunt's insisting that she belonged in the country. Even her teachers pointed out that it was now wartime (1944), schools were hardly operating, and her parents surely needed her help. She reluctantly returned to Inatori, but she soon found a way to get out. She went to look for work at an army base nearby, one with an officers' training division. Although most of the villagers stayed away from the city, Yaeko was not afraid of air raids. She was more afraid of being stuck in the country. In Japanese society, then and now, one usually goes through connections and proper introductions to look for employment, but Yaeko struck out on her own. She evidently impressed the officers with her school background, her energy, and her ability. She was hired as a civilian assistant, helping with whatever was needed, including some secretarial tasks. She was sent to work at Kisarazu, a naval air station in Chiba prefecture, on the other side of Tokyo from her parents, and lived in the nearby dormitory for base employees. There she enjoyed working around the officers, who were mostly rather educated young men. She was not timid about talking with them, so she learned a lot. She read Soseki with them, and was treated very kindly, rather like a mascot.[1] She befriended a captain named Kataguchi, whose studies at Tokyo University had been interrupted by the war. She greatly admired Tokyo University men. Although there was no romantic or sexual aspect to their relationship, by the end of the war Yaeko knew that she would like to have him, or someone like him, for her husband. He seemed fond of her as of a younger pal, calling her *Itou-kun* (instead of *Itou-san*), the "*kun*" being a way to address a close, familiar, younger male friend. They talked about Yaeko's concerns about marriage. Kataguchi explained that he could not marry her since he was the eldest son of his family and he would have to look after his parents and marry someone they thought suitable. He could not be a *muko-youshi* and join the Itou family with Yaeko. He suggested, however, that perhaps he or his parents might find a suitable husband for Yaeko. Yaeko made clear that she wanted to marry a college-educated man.

As the war ended and everyone returned home, Captain Kataguchi sent her by way of his home in Tokyo and carefully explained to her the best way to proceed from there to Inatori, avoiding danger as much as possible. He instructed her to walk all the way, not taking buses or trains even if they were running, walking at night and sleeping during the day, thus avoiding people who might want to steal food from her. She took very little food or water with her, but she had rested and eaten while at the Kataguchi house. When she arrived home after three days and nights of walking, her stepfather cried for joy, saying that as long as they were all safe, nothing else mattered. Her mother was more matter-of-fact, simply assuring Yaeko that she and the stepfather were reasonably well.

Yaeko had no particularly traumatic experiences during the war. None of her close relations were killed, she had not directly suffered from air raids, and she had not gone hungry. She had gained work experience and enjoyed the company of officers. Her self-confidence and assertiveness had served her well.

THE SELF-ARRANGED MARRIAGE

The *omiai*, or arranged marriage, was a way of protecting and providing for young women (and young men). Marriage partners were selected by the parents, or at times by the man's employer, to provide young people with a socially appropriate and secure partner. Often the young people, especially young women, were not involved in the searching or the planning. They met their partners for the first time at the arranged meeting, after many of the negotiations had already been worked out. By mid-century, Japan had liberalized to the point that the young couple had a formal meeting or two before a final decision, and each person had the right of refusal. Most often, young women passively followed their parents' advice due to lack of experience with the outside world and the positive moral value given to allegiance to parents. Yaeko, however, was definitely not passive. She was, in fact, the controlling force behind her own *omiai* and marriage.

After a couple of years at home with her parents recovering from the war and attending sewing school, Yaeko went back to Tokyo, this time taking a job at a bookstore. Kataguchi had advised her to work around books because she liked learning. Meanwhile, her parents, fearing Yaeko would soon be beyond the most desirable age for marriage, tried to find a suitable husband, and arranged introductions to several local men of suitable age and station. Yaeko turned them all down because they were not college educated. Then Kataguchi, remembering Yaeko's wish to marry an educated man, suggested an *omiai* with Tokuzou Aoki, Kataguchi's cousin who had been repatriated after the war from his post in Korea. Tokuzou was the fourth son of a Kyushu family and a college graduate with a degree in accounting, who had come to Tokyo looking for a job. He refused the *omiai*, saying he was not ready to think of marriage, but then Kataguchi suggested that he just go to Inatori for a weekend of rest and get acquainted with Yaeko. Kataguchi's father traveled with Tokuzou to Inatori, assuming the role of go-between (*nakoudo*). Tokuzou seemed attracted by Yaeko's liveliness, and sympathized with her as an intelligent woman who had been prevented by the war from going to college. He had no objection to changing his name to become a *mukoyoushi*. Yaeko certainly did not play the demure flower that weekend, perfectly dressed and sitting quietly while she was looked over, as in the stereotypical *omiai* meeting. She wore her everyday work clothes, her country *mompe*, and engaged Tokuzou in long discussions. She asked him everything she wanted to know about him. She satisfied herself with his qualifications and recommendations, and decided he was the one she wanted to marry.

Tokuzou returned to Tokyo, however, still telling the Kataguchis that he had no interest in marrying for the next four years at least. Ten days later, Yaeko's mother went to Tokyo to talk to Tokuzou. Tokuzou refused to consider marriage, but took Obaasan to the kabuki theater because she had come all the way to Tokyo just to see him. Tokuzou liked Yaeko's mother, both then and afterward; he found her to be an honest, open, unpretentious countrywoman. After her mother's effort, Yaeko took up the campaign. She started writing Tokuzou letters, and he responded. She now tells me that she was trying to entice him. Meanwhile the Kataguchis frequently invited him to lunch, and brought marriage into the discussion. Tokuzou revealed that his main concern was money. He thought he had to save enough money to pay for a wedding and a new household before thinking of marriage, but so soon after the war (1949) neither he nor the country had stabilized enough to make that possible. His parents in Kyushu, who had just been repatriated from Korea, also had no money to pay for a wedding. Gradually the Kataguchis convinced him that a young couple could live cheaply for a while and forgo some of the extravagances of a traditional wedding.

Yaeko was not worried about money. She did not want an expensive wedding and had no wish to ask him to live with her parents. She readily agreed to live in Tokyo, and later Chiba prefecture, where he worked. She was happy with the *omiai* she had engineered and was not pushing for love marriage after the problems she had seen in her mother's and her aunt's marriages. Yaeko, her usual outspoken self, even told him of her wish to have a boy child who would be given the best education so that he could get into Tokyo University. She asked Tokuzou to cooperate toward that goal, and he agreed. This "campaign" was so successful that Yaeko and Tokuzou were engaged within two months and married a few more months later. Yaeko was twenty-two and Tokuzou was twenty-six when they married in 1949 in the Itous' fishing village, Inatori.

FROM *SENGYOU SHUFU* TO *KYOUIKU MAMA*

To her delight, Yaeko gave birth to a baby boy within a year, and named him Ken. She was pregnant again within a few months, but she decided it was too soon to have a second child. She and Tokuzou opted for an abortion, a rather accepted method of birth control in Japan. As was the custom, the fetus, another male, was commemorated as a *jizou* at a local temple. Yaeko became pregnant again two years later, this time delivering a baby girl she named Mari. She was disappointed that the baby was not a boy, and somewhat regretted her previous abortion. She spent these early years of marriage taking care of house and children, like any professional housewife. She was a genuine housewife/mother, but at the same time she was eager to do more and developed a home business of dressmaking, utilizing the skills she had developed while in the village after the war.

By the time Ken entered first grade, Yaeko took on the more serious and all-consuming task of the education mother (*kyouiku mama*) with the goal of getting her son into Tokyo University. First she wanted him in the best possible nearby school. While they lived very conveniently almost next door to the hospital where Tokuzou worked, their local school district was not considered quite as good as the one next to it, Honchou Elementary School. To enroll Ken and later Mari in the Honchou School, she had to find a resident of that district who was willing to allow Ken and his mother to claim their address. Then Ken, as a supposed resident of the Honchou district, could be accepted. Since such finagling was common for ambitious parents, it was accepted rather uncritically. Later on, Yaeko explained that she had to make more strenuous efforts to get him into an elite junior high school. Since many believed that the first applications would be given the most desirable early hour for taking the exam, parents lined up early to submit their applications on the day when they were being accepted. Yaeko arrived at the school the evening before and stayed up all night to be the first to hand in her child's application.

Like many Americans, I thought that such drive to get a child into the best schools to get into an elite university was extreme. I have since learned from more authoritative sources that turning in the earliest application does not help get the earliest exam time. Yaeko was only one in an army of middle-class mothers, all with the same goal for their children. After the war, Japan's drive for success surged from the 1960s and 1970s through the bubble economy of the 1980s, greatly supported by these *kyouiku mama* and their hardworking, successful children.

Most parents at that time were permissive and indulgent with babies and small children, introducing strict discipline at school age. Yaeko was different: She encouraged responsibility and grown-up behavior as early as possible. I observed the parent-child interaction most intimately in 1959–1960.

Ken was eight years old, in third grade, and Mari was five, not yet in kindergarten. Yaeko readily explained her philosophy and methodology. She did not want to spoil her children or baby them. She encouraged them to do things on their own as much as possible, to speak their thoughts and wishes clearly, to take responsibility for their actions and choices, and to be obedient to parents and teachers. She acknowledged that many people thought she was too strict, and she wondered about this herself. She clearly enjoyed the children, however, and delighted in telling us of their rather grown-up and amusing behavior and comments. She did not like whining or clinging, and she insisted that the children use words to say what they wanted. She kept "skinship" to a minimum, in contrast to most Japanese mothers of the day who slept with their babies at night and carried them on their backs all day: She did not enjoy physical closeness with the children. She was even reluctant to let Mari sit on her father's lap. The more they grew up and she could talk with them like friends, the more she enjoyed them. She really wanted to hear what they had to say, found their way of thinking interesting and smart. She would discuss some issue with them at length, and did not scold them for their opinions. If Ken asked questions of us foreigners, questions that some mothers might worry about giving offense, Yaeko did not scold him but rather enjoyed his active curiosity. Even when Mari would say "*iyada*" or "*urusai*" (words of refusal or complaint) when told to do something, her mother would not get angry, but would laugh and stick to her request.

My impression was that both children were extraordinarily grown-up and responsible for their ages. Both had been breast-fed and weaned at ten months and toilet trained by a year and half. They learned to dress themselves early, and to put away clothes and toys. At times they helped their mother clean the house. Skilled with words and self-expression, they easily learned to read and write. They did not sleep on the same futon with either parent, but separately on bunk beds placed close to the room where the parents sat in the evenings, since Mari had complained of feeling lonely when their beds were on the far side. Ken did his homework without help, and practiced violin. Yaeko oversaw the homework, even though she expected him to do it on his own. If he slacked off, she reminded him that he needed to study hard or else he might lose his rank as the best student in his class. Or she might promise him a family ski weekend if he persevered. For the first two years, Yaeko also monitored his violin lessons, going with him to the lesson and supervising his practice. In the third year, however, she stopped. She thought he made faster progress when she was watching him, but she also found that she could not stand it if he was not the very best in the class. Since she had no ambition for him to become a famous violinist, she decided it was better not to pressure him so much, so she restrained herself. She took great pride in his school achievements.

Several incidents impressed us with how strong, confident, and responsible (*shikkari shiteiru*) these two children were. Once when Ken was going fishing with his father and his father's friend, Yaeko reminded him to take care of his bus pass and not lose it. When he came home, he looked a bit sheepish but did not get up the courage to tell his mother until later that evening. He could not find his bus pass. Mother sternly announced that he would have to walk to school, which for him would be a one-hour walk since they lived outside the district. The next morning after breakfast, he started walking, with his mother wondering if he would break his good record of no tardiness. After he left, she worried about him and asked Tokuzou to get on his bike, see how far Ken had gotten, and make sure he was all right. Tokuzou came back, saying that he rode his bike all the way, but saw no sign of Ken. Yaeko then was really worried and went to the school herself. When she peeked into Ken's classroom, she saw him sitting quietly and peacefully at his desk doing his work. Consultation with the teachers told her that he had been early for school. Armed with that knowledge and a promise from the teacher not to tell Ken that she had come to school, she awaited Ken's return, expecting him to complain of tiredness, to apologize for losing the pass, and to ask if he could get another one. To her surprise, Ken made no complaints and no apologies. He continued to walk, or run, to school for a full week. That weekend, his father returned to the fishing site and found the pass where it had fallen. The following week, Ken resumed riding the bus, without any words. Yaeko seemed disappointed that he would not say "sorry," but she also admired his guts and responsibility for his actions. This was one time that Yaeko thought she might have been a bit too strict.

Another time Yaeko went to the school for a meeting, taking Mari with her. Since the meeting lasted until suppertime, she asked Ken to take Mari home with him after school, and then either to stay in the house with her, or to let her go to her friend's house if he wanted to play with his friends. When she arrived home in the late afternoon, she was surprised that no child was there, and Mari was not even at her friend's house. When the children arrived home a bit later, Mari was crying. After Mari calmed down, both children told the story. Ken had brought Mari home, but then wanted to return to the school playground to play ball with his friends. Mari refused to go to her friend's house, insisting she wanted to go with Ken. Finally, Ken agreed to take her with him, but reminded her that she would have to walk home. Mari agreed. As one might expect, Mari became quite tired during the long walk. Ken had ridden his bike much of the way, but would not let Mari ride on the bike since she had said she would walk. Yaeko noted that Mari was crying from exhaustion, but was not angry with Ken, since she accepted that it was her responsibility to keep her promise. Yaeko mildly scolded Ken that he should have been a bit more sympathetic with his little sister.

Yaeko even let Mari stay home by herself for as long as five hours when she was too sick to go out, and let Ken go to the dentist by himself, or even to Inatori (several hours away, with train and bus changes) by himself. One time, however, when Mari wanted to go with him, he refused to take her, saying he could be responsible for himself but not for her too. In contrast to most of the mothers we knew who were true *okusans* (housewives) and almost never out of the house, Yaeko was often involved in outside activities and not at home when the children arrived home from school. Although Tokuzou spoke of the importance of mothers' being home for the children, he only asked Yaeko to *try* to be home. When his mother was not home, Ken would leave his books at the house, then go to the hospital where his father was working, and play or study there until suppertime.

While Tokuzou also expected good behavior from the children, he seldom scolded them or got angry. He did not criticize Yaeko's strictness; he usually backed it up or found a way around it, like going to find Ken's bus pass for him. Correspondingly, the children openly stated their preference for their father. He was the one who was always there, affectionate and reassuring. He was unusually stern with Ken on one occasion, however. When Ken was about six, Tokuzou caught him lying. When Ken did not immediately apologize, Tokuzou took him to the cemetery and threatened to leave him there unless he apologized. The apology was forthcoming.

Yaeko's approach to child rearing was consistent and dependable, and in many ways similar for both children. She encouraged straightforward, responsible, adult-like behavior, and did not cater to babyishness. But she showered Ken with the most attention: the highest expectations, the strictest demands in terms of responsibilities and achievement, and the greatest praise. She acknowledged that she liked men and boys best, and she had wished for Mari to be a boy.

Yaeko knew that Mari did not receive equal attention. Yaeko was usually at home before Mari entered school, however, and she would take Mari with her when she went out unless there was a reason she could not do so. Yaeko talked with Mari in her relatively grown-up way, and Mari at age five was unusually articulate and grown-up. Mari herself did not like to play with younger children, looking down on them as too babyish, and much preferred older children. One observer once commented that Mari was so grown-up acting that she was not very *kawaii* (meaning cute and childishly appealing). Mari could criticize her mother as *urusai* (bothersome) and Yaeko would laugh it off, or Mari could be stubbornly silent when told to apologize for some misbehavior. Yaeko told me that Mari was jealous of Ken, and indeed I saw many signs of that. Mari tried to do everything Ken did, even though she was three years younger; she was often miserable when she could not. Mari's mood turned sour when Ken was praised so much and she was not noticed. Mari was also unhappy when her mother was involved in a conversation with someone else. She would interrupt my conversations with her mother, clearly feeling left out, bored, and in need of attention. Her mother would tell her not to interrupt, with good humor or with sternness, depending on how often it happened. I noticed that several times after such an incident, Mari would go off and find something to eat. Later I started hearing that Mari was getting fat.

Yaeko became an active participant in the Honchou School PTA, an appropriate activity for a housewife, second in importance only to seeing that Ken did all his homework perfectly. Through the PTA she got to know the teachers, the principal, and the other mothers. She learned from them how to help her child study, what was necessary for success, various mothers' methods, and the teachers' advice. It was via the PTA and the school principal that we were introduced to her. Since the principal had been asked by the nearby National Institute of Mental Health to introduce us to six "healthy" families, Yaeko was one of the first mothers with whom he consulted about the selection of families in the school, as she was always eagerly available and knew the school population well enough to have suggestions.

Yaeko was quite successful as a *kyouiku mama* during these years, as she educated herself on the ways of the school world and saw to it that Ken did his best work. Ken excelled all along the way, even graduating from the most elite high school in all of Japan, Hibiya High School. Ken was studious and responsible, obedient to parents and teachers—at least until his senior year of high school, as we shall see later. Mari was also a good student, even though she did not do quite as well as Ken. Yaeko paid less attention to Mari's studies. Mari was a girl, so it was not so necessary for her to be the best. Yaeko was too busy concentrating on Ken, or involved in the PTA or other outside activities. Tokuzou offered much love and attention to the children, so they could always go to him if their mother was not available. They could find him at the hospital if they needed him after school, and Tokuzou fed the children when Yaeko did not come home early enough to cook dinner. Everyone found Tokuzou to be "*yasashii*," that is, easygoing, warmhearted, and a bit passive. He loved playing with the children, particularly sports on the weekend.

Yaeko gave birth to a girl named Katsuko in 1963, when Ken was thirteen and Mari ten. Yaeko, of course, had hoped for a boy. Katsuko was well cared for, but Yaeko gave little attention to her studies, much less than even Mari had received. Katsuko was allowed to go to the neighborhood school, rather than the more highly reputed Honchou School. Her early years seem to have been rather free and natural, without much pressure, playing with the neighborhood kids. Yaeko reports that while Ken and Mari were essentially obedient children, however, Katsuko was more inclined to talk back, argue, or resist her mother on a day-to-day basis, much as Yaeko had been toward her own mother.

A HOUSEWIFE NOT ALWAYS AT HOME

Wives were usually addressed as *okusan* or *kanai*, both of which referred to the inside of the house. The traditional housewife was expected to be always in the house, available to care for all family needs. When visiting in 1958–1960, I did not need to phone ahead to see if the housewife was home. Yaeko was usually there, except for a daily shopping trip in the neighborhood. She adhered to most aspects of the full-time housewife/mother role during the first ten years of her marriage, particularly while the children were babies. But she was probably out of the house more than most of the mothers. She frequently went out for PTA meetings, as well as for shopping. She also went out for her own pleasure, to a movie or other recreational activities, despite the pervasive disapproval of selfish endeavors. She liked to be busy and to make money, so she ran a dressmaking business from home. Although she would have liked to move up in social status, the role of the housewife with cultural activities at home did not appeal to her.

Yaeko enjoyed having visitors come to the house, whether it was Tokuzou's fellow workers at the hospital, neighbors from Inatori, other mothers, or even service people. Having lived in the country and the city, she knew how to talk to all kinds of people. She was quite egalitarian in her attitudes, and did not consider it a burden to serve guests. She did not limit herself to kitchen and serving duties, as the most socially approved wives did. Rather, she usually dominated the conversation. I remember well New Year's Day of 1960 when as hostess, wearing a beautiful kimono, she skillfully served and conversed with all of us.

She was restless, however, and wanted to work. There was no economic need for her to work, as Tokuzou's salary was quite adequate. She clearly preferred being active, always learning something new, meeting new people, busying herself with new projects or new challenges. As soon as she was able, she became active in outside activities: after the PTA, then a health food cooperative (*seikatsu kumiai*); then an after-school tutoring school (*juku*) which she organized and directed for several years; and still later, in a department store in specialty sales. She met people easily and thrived on being the leader, organizing and directing others. She was not deterred by the fact that her mother, her in-laws, and many neighbors disapproved of her working outside the home and being so outspoken. Others admired her competence, and were jealous of her independence and self-confidence.

Her own children criticized her severely. I was present during one family discussion in 1975. The children all agreed that Father was *otonashii* (good-tempered), *gamanzuyoi* (patient), and *kawaisoo* (deserving sympathy), while Mother was *warui* (bad). Ken especially expressed sympathy for Father and criticized Mother, because Father worked all day and had to come home and work more: cooking, cleaning, and feeding the kids. He mentioned coming home in the evening to find Father and Katsuko alone, with Father complaining softly about Mother's late return. When Mother did come home and thanked Father for looking after things, however, Father only said *kamaimasen* (it's okay). Katsuko took to Mother's defense, saying that Mother was also busy and also did housework. By 1975 Mari often took the role of the peacemaker, seldom complaining, often filling in for Mother's limitations, doing housework, supporting Father, and even serving guests. Tokuzou highly praised Mari, saying she was the greatest help, and he especially wanted to see her have a happy life.

Interestingly, Yaeko herself seemed undismayed by her children's criticism and let them speak freely, much as she had not scolded Mari as a five-year-old for openly wishing her grandmother to go home, or telling guests to go home if they interfered with her fun. Yaeko emphasized the positive aspects of their family life: They had much fun and sociability together and learned about the larger world from the many people that came to visit their house, mostly her friends and acquaintances. She also mentioned that she occasionally cooked something very special that Tokuzou liked. The children laughed, saying it was very occasional indeed, and that Mari was a better housekeeper and wife than Mother. Tokuzou invariably defended Yaeko, seeing her as a capable woman who had been deprived by the war of the opportunity to go to college. "*Dekiru hito*" (a capable person), he emphasized with admiration. He recognized that she was more pleasant to live with when she was enjoying her life.

I could see, both from their conversations and from my observations during visits, that Tokuzou did much of the parenting and was the consistent, steady presence at home, who had to look after many of the household responsibilities. He valued a clean house and longed for a proper *zashiki* (living room or drawing room), whereas these were not important to Yaeko. He often had to do the cleaning. From an American male point of view, he was exceptionally passive and tolerant, even as he was supportive of his wife. At the same time, she was the lively, sociable, and fun-loving one, who brought different people and new ideas into their home. She was entertaining in the way she told stories of what others, especially the children, did and said, speaking their words in a very realistic and expressive way, much as skilled actors on the stage might act out a story. While she tended to dominate the scene, she also enjoyed others' expressiveness and valued their individuality.

They had a partial reversal of roles. He was the more nurturing, she the more instrumental. She took the lead; he backed her up. He was quite masculine and athletic in appearance, with broad strong shoulders. She was quite small, no more than five feet tall, slim, rather attractive, and certainly not masculine in appearance. He had an established career; she was always seeking one. Yaeko expressed pleasure in her life: a stable home, a son on his way toward success in life, and a husband who allowed her to be active outside the home.

Tales of problems in the traditional family were typically of mother-in-law/daughter-in-law conflict. The older generation maintained power and authority over the younger couple in the extended hierarchical family. The mother-in-law trained her elder son's wife in the ways of the family and often the daughter-in-law (*oyomesan*) was treated like a twenty-four-hour-per-day servant, taking care of the family from early morning until late at night, under the strict supervision of her mother-in-law. The young wife would be the first to rise, and the last to bed.

In this *mukoyoushi* family, however, the power relations were different. As mentioned earlier, Tokuzou had taken the Itou name and was the official heir to the family headship, but he had negotiated to live separately as his job as an accountant required. Similarly, Yaeko did not live with her in-laws and did not have to be instructed by her mother-in-law. She also did not live with her own parents or take care of them. Her parents did not expect care from Yaeko since she had never been caretaking toward them. (Later the Itou parents took in a young man who helped with the fishing and cared for the older couple, but his name was not written into the family register as a legal descendant.)

Yaeko lived in the city, independent of her parents in the country. She visited them occasionally. Her children spent more time with these grandparents, enjoying the countryside, the ocean, and the attention of the grandparents on school vacations. Mari took over the role that her mother had left vacant, being attentive and caring toward these grandparents. Obaasan criticized Yaeko for not practicing filial piety (*oyakoukou*) and for being selfish and uncaring, yet she seemed to accept her that way. She showered her love and appreciation on Mari, and when she died she left her money to Mari, not Yaeko. Notably, Takematsu, the stepfather, whom Yaeko had initially rejected, was the one who was kind and sympathetic toward Yaeko.

Yaeko did not have the stereotypical problems with her mother-in-law either. Even though the first son, Tokuzou's eldest brother, had died, the second son had assumed the primary responsibility for his parents, who were based in Kyushu at his house after returning from Korea. In 1959, however, these paternal grandparents came to stay with the Itous, planning to stay for a year perhaps, as they slowly traveled around, living for a while with each of their several children.[2] When they arrived, Yaeko expressed a genuine wish to make them feel welcome and comfortable, knowing that they would not be there forever. When she introduced them to us, she did so in very polite and complimentary language. Nevertheless, conflict soon arose between the grandmother and Yaeko. Again, Yaeko had no trouble getting along with the man, the grandfather. But the grandmother criticized Yaeko's manners, calling her selfish because she was out of the house so much with outside activities and gave insufficient attention and respect to the elders. Yaeko thought that this grandmother was unhappy with the attention she and Toku-zou lavished on the children rather than giving the elders priority. Grand-mother even criticized Ken and Mari for being too selfish and outspoken, rather than quiet and deferential (*otonashii*), not as lovable (*kawaii*) as the Kyushu grandchildren. The children for their part were not pleased with the grandparents. Mari openly stated her wish that the grandparents return to their home in Kyushu, and the grandparents were shocked that she would be allowed to say such a thing. Ken wondered why the grandparents were given two futons when the rest of the family had only one. When Yaeko explained the care, respect, and deference given to elders who had worked so hard all their lives, Ken expressed his rejection of that way of thinking, since his father also worked hard and should have equal consideration. Clearly these children belonged to a new generation with different values from the grand-parents.

After a few months of increasing tension between the generations, the paternal grandparents decided to return to Kyushu, with Grandmother saying that her fragile health could not take the Tokyo winters. This seemed to be a metaphor for how she felt about the emotional climate. Grandmother pro-nounced Yaeko the worst of their daughters-in-law; and the daughter-in-law in Kyushu, wife of the second son who was now heir of the family, was the best. Tokuzou criticized neither side in the midst of this, understood Yaeko's feelings, and yet was considerate and patient (*gamanzuyoi*) with his parents. Yaeko was reassured that he would not side with his parents against her. After the grandparents left, Yaeko, Tokuzou, and the children could relax.

SELF-QUESTIONING

From the time we noticed that Yaeko was the only wife in our group who wore Western clothes and announced her distinction as the most "modern," we wondered how she dealt with the social expectations surrounding her. While we noted her self-confident behavior and her clearly spoken words, we also became aware of her underlying concerns for what others thought of her and even her questioning of herself, wondering how to evaluate or judge herself. In any society, it is often the person who is a bit different, who does not quite fit the norm, who is the most self-aware. Those who fit in easily have less need for self-reflection.

She soon began to compare herself to the other women in our group, commenting that they had larger houses and higher incomes and social stand-ing; they were probably more gracious in entertaining and careful in their speech. In contrast, she was open and frank, and casual and informal in entertaining. The others were modest and rather restrained within a group, whereas she quickly stepped forward, spoke her opinions, and often took over leadership. Yaeko readily acknowledged enjoying the leadership role; she liked to organize things and to direct others' activities. As she declared that she was more modern, she also indirectly and directly asked us for our opinion of her. We usually tried to avoid comparison, saying something empathic or appreciative of her endeavors without criticizing the other women. She recognized that she was often criticized for being too aggressive, even brash, but that did not change her behavior.

The other women did comment about Itou-san's talkativeness and assertiveness, with implied criticism, but we noticed that they also let her be the leader, perhaps needing someone willing to take responsibility for group decisions, since they themselves shunned leadership. She had been elected a PTA officer, although women of higher social standing, or sometimes their husbands, more often held the top positions.

The post-Meiji "good wife/wise mother" ideal demanded 100 percent devotion to the care of the family—children, husband, and parents. Selfishness was criticized; pleasure for oneself was not condoned. The wife had all home responsibilities, while husbands were expected to devote time and energy to their work. Yaeko knew she could not and did not live up to that ideal, and recognized that many were critical of her for that.

After Yaeko and I had grown comfortable with each other, she had a minor crisis in her marriage that caused her to question herself: whether she was being unfair to Tokuzou, and whether he was more displeased with her than he showed. For a brief time she even suspected him of having an affair with a woman employee of the hospital. She approached this topic gradually and indirectly at first. While talking about a friend who was starting to have an affair and whose husband had a mistress, Yaeko wondered if she had coerced Tokuzou into marrying her against his will and speculated that she really was not a good wife to him. Since Tokuzou had criticized her friend as being selfish, she wondered if underneath he harbored critical feelings toward her for being selfish. She sometimes thought that she was too selfish and not quite fair to Tokuzou. Perhaps once a day, or maybe just once a month, she pondered, she criticized herself and told herself that she really should be a good traditional wife to Tokuzou. She realized that she ate what she wanted and went to bed and got up when she pleased, and Tokuzou often had to fill in for her, even changing diapers. She sometimes played mahjong in the house with her friends till 3:00 a.m. Tokuzou said this was okay if she was enjoying herself, yet she would get furious if he was drinking with his friends in the house. He was very generous with her, but she could not be so generous with him. Yaeko realized that when she tolerated his drinking or when she occasionally made an effort to do something he liked, she did it out of reason or logic, not for love. She knew that she needed to make him happy sometimes in order for the two of them to be able to live together happily.

She could see that Tokuzou was generous, reliable, and consistent, whereas she occasionally blew her top. She went along with sex for his sake, even though she had become rather bored with it, since she appreciated that he did not complain about her outside activities. She confided to me that she and Tokuzou were both totally inexperienced with sex before marriage. The *nakoudo* had told Yaeko to follow Tokuzou's lead. But Tokuzou was quite shy, even about undressing, and did not immediately initiate sexual relations. She was the one who was curious and found books that taught her about sex, suggested that they get a double-size futon, and learned about using condoms.

As this discussion continued over a few weeks, Yaeko started to mention that her marriage was in a slump and that she was bored with housewife life, and she asked me for advice about getting a job or further education for herself. This "slump," it soon came out, was really anger at Tokuzou for having dinner with a woman at work one evening after a staff meeting while Yaeko was away from home. Her anger increased when she heard that this woman was the only woman going on a ski trip with several male employees of the hospital, including Tokuzou. She was so angry that she did not go to see Tokuzou off at the train station. Tokuzou refused to defend himself, saying that if Yaeko did not trust him, he could say nothing to make her trust him. Yaeko felt a bit guilty as she acknowledged that he would trust her even though she went to dinner with a man, but she could not stand to think that he might be unfaithful. Yaeko, unable to downplay her suspicions for long, soon told Tokuzou that she had been hearing from her friend with the marital problems that Tokuzou was in love with the woman he went to dinner with and was probably having an affair. After spending all night talking with Tokuzou, she was impressed with the depth of Tokuzou's trust and his love, and realized hers would never be that total. Spurred on to further investigation, Yaeko talked with a different hospital staff member and learned that another young woman there had started the rumor about Tokuzou out of spite. Evidently this young woman had expected Tokuzou to strongly recommend her in marriage negotiations with an attractive man of her choice. Tokuzou did not want to intervene, however, or take responsibility for the match since he did not think that the young woman was a very good worker. He never said anything critical, but she was angry that he did not give her strong support, hence her spiteful behavior. Tokuzou had simply been true to himself; he never took sides in any of the hospital political struggles or personal disputes.

Yaeko's suspicions were then washed away. Yaeko reported that she understood Tokuzou and herself much better. She could see that if she had any doubts about Tokuzou, she seemed to need to provoke a confrontation so she could know the truth without any doubt, and to test how angry he would get at her. She was impressed that through all this Tokuzou did not express any anger or criticism toward her, although he did once say that if she really could not trust him, he would commit suicide. She recognized her own self-ishness, and saw Tokuzou as a more loving, generous, steady, and trust-worthy person.

During these weeks when Yaeko was doubting her marriage, I noticed that she sometimes complained of not feeling well, of having mouth sores, or of being dissatisfied with the PTA, and that she was less reliable with me about our meeting times. I interpreted this as a sign of stress, and noticed that she returned to her lively self after the resolution of the problem.

ENTREPRENEURSHIP

I had appreciated Yaeko's open and honest discussions with me and admired her energy, abundant skills, and remarkable awareness of herself and of the world around her. I wondered how the contradictions in her life and her family relationships would evolve. As I continued my relationship with Yae-ko and her family, I came to realize how thoroughly Yaeko by nature was not comfortable with the professional housewife role, and that her talents lay elsewhere. Although she did necessary housework and cared for the children, she never liked household chores, she was too active to tolerate staying at home, and she had only moderate interest in child-raising except for oversee-ing Ken's academic success. She also did not care for the finer cultural arts that characterized the professional housewife role. Her greatest interest and enjoyment was in the world outside the house. She was strongly motivated to meet people, to organize, to be a leader and entrepreneur. She sewed at home to have a business going even while staying home with small children.

While this reflects her personality, it also connects to her origins as the daughter of a farmer-fisherman family (Obaasan and her husband) and of a small business family (Aunt Motoko and the Tsunoda grandparents). These women worked hard in their respective businesses and did not have the time or inclination to aspire to the niceties of a proper housewife. While Yaeko was upwardly mobile and moved into the middle class with her professional husband, she never tried to emulate the domestic or cultural skills of the professional housewife. She gravitated toward roles more often occupied by men, particularly at that time, in community or political organizations, or in business.

Yaeko learned much about the community from her active involvement with the PTA for many years. She also gradually developed her work as a seamstress. In 1963, after Katsuko was born, the Itous built a second floor onto their house, and Yaeko used one room as her sewing room. She could look after baby Katsuko while working at home. Then she gradually went out more, giving Katsuko a bottle more often than she had the other babies. She hired three or four helpers and farmed out some of the sewing to them, as the number of her customers for dresses, *yukata*, or other clothing increased.

Next she gradually expanded into community activities, often taking on an entrepreneurial role, organizing and steering various groups. She and other mothers organized a group to help women teachers feel at home in the community and develop relationships with mothers, so that the mothers could be more helpful to their children in dealing with the school's expectations—clearly a useful group for all the dedicated *kyouiku mama* (education mothers) of that day.

Yaeko also helped organize a community group interested in using recreational facilities available at a nearby medical/dental college. The purpose was to promote good relationships between the college and the community, enabling the community to make use of the facilities while also raising money for the college via luncheons or other social events. Yaeko and some of her friends played tennis on the college's courts early Sunday mornings.

By 1975 she launched into two other major activities. She helped to organize a consumers' cooperative (*seikatsu kyoudou kumiai*). About 1,800 households contributed money toward hiring trucks to bring fresh produce from selected rural areas of Chiba, enabling members to buy organic produce without going through middlemen. As a member of this group, she actively campaigned for a Socialist candidate who was seeking a seat in the Diet. She commented to us that many people were shocked to see her in front of the local station campaigning with a loudspeaker, because they had never before seen a woman do that.

Then she founded her own *juku* (after-school tutoring classes) for students in grades four through nine preparing for exams to get into junior high or high school. She did not aim for the best students, who could easily find a more prestigious *juku*, but for mediocre or underprivileged students whose parents were looking for an inexpensive way to improve their performance. She enlisted the help of a recently retired school principal, hired several teachers, and for several years used both Ken to teach English and Japanese classes and Mari to teach math. Our son Steven also helped teach English conversation on Saturdays while he attended high school in Tokyo. Katsuko was a student at her mother's *juku* during junior high.

While running this *juku*, Yaeko held frequent meetings of teachers and mothers for mutual support and education. She invited me to a couple of these meetings, both so I could learn about the group and so the group members could meet an American woman. At one meeting, the principal talked for about an hour about how to teach math and then the group discussed raising and educating children. As the group turned to gender differences, various women, including some of the teachers, addressed the women's liberation issues newly in the air at that time. Some wanted husbands to help with children or the house, or objected to husbands calling wives *omae* (a term applied to those in inferior status), but they also noted that wives were gaining the right to work outside the home or to go out of the house for various activities—no longer having to always be the *okusan* inside the house. Yaeko talked quite a bit in this group, offering her observations and advice. I could see from these groups how Yaeko often took on a counselor's role with both the teachers and the mothers, as many women came to her to discuss personal problems. She has followed this pattern throughout her life.

During these years Yaeko developed considerable competence and confidence in organizing community groups. She expressed pleasure with her activities, enjoyed her leadership roles, and felt that she was less criticized than she had been in earlier years, both because opportunities for women were opening somewhat and because many people respected what she did. Many of her activities, like those above, were directed toward helping people less privileged or more troubled than her own family.

I certainly noticed that many people respected Yaeko's initiative and organizing abilities, and benefited from her initiatives. But she was still caught in a bind: While the society needed female leadership, those who took on such roles were frequently criticized for being too outspoken—for not being good enough housewives and mothers.

The *juku* operated for about eight years, closing in 1980, after the co-founder, the school principal, felt that he could not teach anymore. Also, there was less need for that *juku*; many others were coming on the scene. Earlier she had faced the inevitable conflicts within any organization, including a slight rebellion after she fired one teacher. But Tokuzou came to her defense, and this quieted the complaints since everyone respected his calm judgment.

Her involvement with the co-op ended after several years, however, when she confronted a conflict she could not handle, as some co-op members rejected her ideas and then her leadership. That time Tokuzou advised that she should resign because there was getting to be so much negative talk even around his hospital that it was not worth the trouble to try to work things out with that group.

In later years, Yaeko thought perhaps she had been too stubborn in dealing with the co-op, but she was not deterred by such a setback. She always had several projects going at the same time, and was able to find new ones if one did not work out. She began to spend her time in business. She worked in a cake shop until a conflict arose with the owner. Meanwhile, she developed her own consulting station within Isetan Department Store, where she worked for twelve years. She sold clothes that she bought from a Yokohama fabricant and acted as a fashion consultant for customers. She enjoyed this work the most and felt most successful at it. She was her own boss, and she proved to herself that she could earn money just as well as a man. She reluctantly quit this job in 1989 due to Tokuzou's illness.

THE OBEDIENT SON REBELS

Everything went fairly smoothly until 1968–1969, when the most treasured member of the family suddenly became the biggest problem, the greatest trauma. Ken, as we have seen, had always been an excellent student, conscientious, responsible, and observant of all rules at home and at school. He had successfully entered the junior high that led to Hibiya Koukou, the high school reputed to give the best preparation for passing the Tokyo University entrance exam. He seemed to be well on his way to fulfilling his mother's dreams, doing well in his junior year at Hibiya. During that year, however, as the student rebellion of the 1960s was gathering steam, Ken began to slack off in his studies and was caught drinking coffee, eating cake, and smoking (although Ken denied the smoking) with friends at a coffeehouse near school. The school suspended Ken and his friends, confiscated their school ID cards, and summoned their parents to school. Yaeko rushed to the school and apologized deeply, and the ID card was returned. While she was there, Yaeko conferred with the parents of the other students who were suspended, among the top students in the class. Yaeko was shocked to hear that these elite parents did not see anything wrong with drinking coffee or smoking, and were not worried about the suspension because they felt certain their sons could get into Tokyo University anyway. While Yaeko and Tokuzou took for granted that school rules had to be obeyed totally, these parents seemed to have been influenced by the greater freedoms and liberal attitudes since the war. Tokuzou in particular could not respect such irresolute parents.

Ken's final year at Hibiya High was the year of the most violent student demonstrations. The storming of Yasuda Gate at the entrance to Tokyo University, the occupation of the main building, and the ensuing injuries and arrests not only shocked Japan but generated headlines in newspapers around the world. The Hibiya High School students also demonstrated, marching around Shimbashi station (a central Tokyo station). Ken was arrested there, along with other students. He staunchly refused to give his father's name to the police. A Shimada Hospital (where Tokuzou worked) employee happened to be there, however, and brought Ken home to his parents. Tokuzou, who was usually so gentle, was furious and indignant this time, much more so than Yaeko. He had grown up during the imperial days and had been in the Japanese army, and he felt that disobedience to school, parents, or country was unacceptable. He declared that no son of his would do such a thing, and threatened to kill Ken. Yaeko, fearing that he might indeed strike with the sword he had in his possession, quickly handed Ken some money and a bag of belongings, and escorted him out of the house, telling him to stay away for a while.

Ken did not return home at all, and sent no word. Yaeko phoned her mother in Izu, expecting Ken would have gone there, but her mother reported that she had not seen him. After several days of phoning and searching around Tokyo, one of Ken's friends approached Shimada Hospital saying that four student friends needed money to get out of jail, but this friend reported that Ken was all right. Yaeko then found him in an apartment rented by Fujita-kun, the close friend with whom he had drunk coffee, but Yaeko had not called them sooner because Tokuzou did not approve of them. Unknown to Yaeko and Tokuzou, several classmates had been meeting there frequently after school. Ken refused to return home, declaring that his name should be removed from the Itou family registry.

Yaeko and Tokuzou attended the Hibiya High School graduation, but Ken did not appear, even though he was listed as graduating. Tokyo University cancelled its entrance exams. Ken stayed with Fujita-kun, and started to work in the factory owned and operated by Mr. Fujita, while living in the company dormitory.

Almost five years passed before Ken came home again. Meanwhile, Yaeko and Tokuzou recognized that society was changing around them. Tokuzou's anger softened. He recalled that he was taught that America was the enemy when he was in the army, but he had come to see that some Americans were not so evil. During those years, Ken had continued working at the factory. But after a year, he started thinking about going to college. Even though Fujita-kun took the exam for Tokyo University and entered after one year of *rounin*, Ken declared that he did not want to go there.[3] He had been living out his mother's ambitions all his life, but now he was going to do what he wanted. He surprised his parents with talk of entering a fine arts college. While his mother had been aiming for him to be a lawyer or politician, he now declared he was no good at debate. Yaeko said she would debate for him. He replied that was precisely what he feared, that she would use his achievements for her own aggrandizement.

Ken applied to the fine arts college and passed the written exam, but he was turned down because he had little experience with painting. Yaeko laughed as she told the story of his taking the drawing exam. When he was told to draw a picture that included a Coke bottle in it, he tried to get himself a break by asking to go to the men's room. Being told that he should wait, he just turned in a blank sheet of paper—and ever since he does not like to see advertisements for Coca-Cola. He then applied where he knew he could pass: the law faculty of Chuo University, a rather good private college. He wanted a college degree, and he graduated four years later with excellent grades. His parents had refused to finance any college other than Tokyo University, so Ken paid his tuition and living expenses from his own earnings at the factory where he continued to work part-time even while in college. His parents were impressed and proud of him when he brought his diploma home to show them. They had to recognize that even though he had been living as a hippie, he had done nothing really bad. He had taken responsibility for himself in a mature way. Of course, Yaeko continued to be disappointed that he did not fulfill her dream of Tokyo University, and that he had no interest in attending Harvard while living with the Vogels.

As he was graduating, he talked of his wish to marry his "first love," a young woman he had known since his high school days. Since she was an only child, she wanted Ken to join her family as a *mukoyoushi*. Her mother was especially opposed to her joining the Itou family, as she felt Yaeko would make a difficult mother-in-law. Once during all the demonstration turmoil, this girl and her mother had watched on TV a group discussion of mothers of high school and college students talking with three Tokyo University professors. When the professors asked the mothers how they felt about the university's response to the demonstrations, Yaeko had talked at length about how the university should have stood firm (*shikkari shite*), whereas the other mothers simply replied with a word of sympathy (*komarimashita*) for the university. The girl's mother had said "*sugoi*," indicating that Yaeko was an unusual mother—unusually tough. Yaeko and Tokuzou also refused to give permission for the marriage. They could not allow Ken to marry as a *mukoyoushi* since that would leave the Itous without an heir. Ken did not argue with that decision, and before long the girl was married to someone else.

Ken came back home to live around this time, making a small second-floor room into his room. He tried his hand at being an entrepreneur, forming a small business with a few friends working with him. He reminded me of his mother as he talked of enjoying using his own head to figure out how to make things work and as he tried a variety of approaches to making money. For instance, his company made and marketed records, served as middlemen in distributing certain food orders, and creatively designed and constructed specific items. I was impressed by his inventiveness when he showed us a special little machine that squeezed water from eggs and shaped them into a firm tetrahedron, making it possible to decorate them with various designs. Ken was like his father, low-key and modest, less like his mother in personal manner.

Evidently this business did not go too well, but Ken continued to work at different things for some time, including making TV and movie commercials, and helping with his mother's *juku*. He had a creative, artistic bent. He continued to live at home for almost ten years, supporting himself financially although not paying for room or food at home. He drank more and more, perhaps because he did not feel successful at business. Twice he was brought home by the police, once for sleeping in the park and once because he had been hit by a car while riding his bicycle. Yaeko had always hated drunken behavior. Finally, she kicked him out of the house when he started to fall down stairs and to throw things, seeming out of control and upsetting the household. This then ushered in another period of alienation from the family.

For a while his address was unknown, although he would occasionally communicate with Katsuko or Mari but not his parents. He was working during that time, Yaeko learned later, making commercials for TV or movies.

Incidentally, Tokuzou also drank beer nightly, but Yaeko never made an issue of this. She was annoyed at times, at least when he stayed up late drinking with hospital colleagues. His behavior was never a problem, however, so Yaeko felt she should allow him this pleasure.

INDEPENDENT DAUGHTERS

Yaeko's daughters also refused to follow in the path Yaeko would have preferred, but she never pressured them as much as she had pressured Ken. They were like Yaeko in having their own minds. Yaeko's relative lack of pressure on Mari and Katsuko could be seen as a neglect of girls, or as trusting them with freedom and independence. Yaeko's relationship with Mari, for example, was never as intense as that with Ken, or as tumultuous. Mari was probably jealous of the attention showered on Ken, and turned to her father, and to food, for support and nurturance. Her father took good care of her when Yaeko was not home, and she took good care of him when he later needed it. He wanted to make sure she had a good life. She enjoyed food and she was a good cook. By the time she was in fifth grade, she had become noticeably fat and she has remained that way ever since. She tried to lose weight once at age twenty-seven or twenty-eight, but she did not succeed and tried no more. She always did well in school, but not as well as Ken. And since he also excelled at sports, Mari had little recognition in her own right. She was always known as Ken's little sister. Yaeko did not push her to study, and Mari herself avoided competition. She went to the local public junior high. She passed the paper exam for Hibiya High School but failed the physical exam, perhaps because of her weight. She attended a nearby private high school, where she did well, but not the very best except in math where she made 100 percent. She played the violin, as Ken had, until junior high; and after that she studied the *shamisen*.

She attended a four-year fine arts college in Shinjuku, an area of central Tokyo. Yaeko had encouraged her to be a teacher, as she thought Mari did a good job with the children in the *juku*. Yaeko offered to help her get into a prestigious private university. Yet Mari preferred making pottery to teaching. She wanted to handle her schooling in her own way. She developed a love for old Japanese arts and crafts, particularly craft (*mingei*) pottery, instead of learning English, going to the United States, or studying violin or modern Western arts as her mother would have liked. She had asked her father if he had enough money to send her to college, and if he did not, she would go to work. Since he said he had the money, she chose the college she wanted, while continuing her study of the traditional crafts. She was happy with her studies at that college, and had many friends there.

Tokuzou and Yaeko both worried about finding a good marriage for Mari, fearing her weight was a serious handicap. However, Yaeko did not expend much time or energy in searching out a husband for Mari, both because Mari seemed to want to handle her life in her own way, and because Yaeko was occupied with her own activities. At age twenty-four, Mari received a proposal from a nursery school teacher asking Mari to marry her son. Family friends of the Itous, they stated that her weight did not matter to them; they wanted Mari as the son's bride, just as she was. The woman knew Mari to be smart, able, caring, considerate, and dependable. Her son said he liked fat women. Mari turned down this proposal because the young man planned to go to the United States to work for some years, and Mari felt that she would be too shy to fit into a foreign country, especially since American young women (she thought) were all so slim. Mari seemed to not want to be pressured on academic performance or feminine beauty or a prestigious marriage. She was not following Yaeko's model of looking for success or fame, but perhaps it was not easy to find another female role model. I wondered: Could it be that Mari's weight was an unconscious way of staving off sexual or marital pressures? Was it a way of insisting that the world accept her as herself? In any case, she remained unmarried and lived at home for several years after college, taking care of the house and her father while Yaeko worked at the department store. She continued playing the *shamisen*, making pottery, and gradually working more for a jewelry-making company, at first specializing in coral. Although she was shy about going to America, at her own house I always found her friendly, outgoing, and helpful—not at all a shrinking violet, really quite jolly and full of laughter with everyone.

Yaeko told a story about another young man that Mari liked, but mostly Mari liked to take care of him. Yaeko was the first one to take care of him. Kimura-kun was a rather insecure, nervous fellow whom she hired to work in the co-op. He resigned in support of Yaeko when she left the co-op, even though she told him not to do that. Not long after that, he called Yaeko, saying that he had run away to Kyushu, and he was going to commit suicide because there was no use for him in this world. But first he wanted to thank Yaeko for all her help and encouragement, for his three years at the co-op were the happiest of his life. Yaeko quickly asked where he was, how much money he had, and she told him how he could borrow enough money from Shimada Hospital for a train ticket back to Tokyo. She told him sternly that he must come back to Honchou to die, that thanking her over the phone would not do, that he must do it in person, and that running away was not manly. He complied. Tokuzou met him at the train station, then he and Yaeko talked with him, and they put him to work helping out at the hospital. I noted Yaeko's skill in saving a suicidal person. In my opinion, her sternness without a tint of feeling sorry for him saved him. Later he became a nurse's helper, then went to nursing school, and became a nurse—in fact, one of the best. Mari became his constant source of encouragement during these years at the hospital.

Katsuko is described as "just like Yaeko": independent, rebellious, frequently arguing with her mother since she has always freely talked back. Katsuko grew up casual and relaxed. She did not study very hard but she had a good time with many friends. Katsuko grew up more attached to her father and her siblings, not feeling obliged to obey her mother. Yaeko seems to have accepted this rebellious independence; she compares Katsuko's relationship with her to her own relationship with her mother. I should note, however, that while Yaeko and Katsuko have fought, Katsuko has never had a lengthy period of estrangement from her mother, unlike her brother and sister. In fact, Yaeko and Katsuko have been rather close, despite the quibbling.

Katsuko attended a nearby prefectural high school. There she became interested in math and science and graduated second in her class. She also developed a close relationship with a classmate, Masaki Matsunami, who ranked in the middle of the class. Since Katsuko had done well and expressed an interest in becoming a medical technician or pharmacist, Yaeko encouraged her to think about attending the Chiba Medical University. As a national university Chiba was hard to get into but not expensive. Katsuko preferred a nearby private university with a less strenuous entrance exam. Yaeko said they would pay tuition for Chiba, but not the more expensive private university. She wanted to encourage Katsuko to work harder to realize her ambitions: She should not get something for nothing. Furthermore, she thought most parents would not spend as much on a daughter's education as on a son's, and the national universities were more respected anyway. Katsuko did not follow her mother's advice, as usual, and decided to get a job rather than go to college. She commuted into Tokyo and worked as a secretary for the Ministry of Education for four years. Yaeko told me that Yoshirou Mori, who later became Prime Minister, was the Minister of Education at that time. Katsuko's children are impressed that she worked for such a famous man.

Masaki, the high school boyfriend, went to a national agricultural college, majoring in economics. As Masaki was graduating, Katsuko's future with him was uncertain. He had found another girlfriend at college. Mari then took matters into her hands. She asked Katsuko if she still loved Masaki, and with that confirmed, she used her connections with a local newspaper to have an article written about a local boy and girl who had remained good friends after high school, stating nothing more than that. That succeeded in bringing Katsuko and Masaki together again, and soon there was discussion of marriage. Masaki declared his preference for Katsuko over his college girlfriend, and his parents agreed.

As was the custom, the Matsunami parents visited the Itous to formally ask for Katsuko to join their family as the bride of the eldest son (*oyome ni iku*). Yaeko asked them why they wanted Katsuko, since she was headstrong, selfish, and no good at farmwork. (The Matsunamis lived on a farm in Chiba prefecture.) Tokuzou scolded Yaeko, saying she need not have disclosed Katsuko's faults. The Matsunamis replied that they liked Katsuko's self-discipline and her good manners. Yaeko explained that she had meant that Katsuko should not be expected to do farmwork, and the Matsunamis agreed to that condition. Masaki at that time expected to live on the family land and to inherit and serve as the eldest son. He talked of wanting to build a sports club on the land. The newly married couple went to live in Funabashi, near the Matsunami farm, while Masaki continued working as a salaryman in Yokohama.

In 1980, Yaeko came to the wedding in Cambridge of our oldest son David, whom she had known when he was two to three years old. She came by herself via airplane, transferring in New York, despite knowing only a few words of English she remembered from our lessons in 1959–1960. She got lost in the New York airport and missed her connection, but found a rescuer, an African American airport attendant, who got her on the next plane to Boston. She arrived a few hours later than planned, but she was in good spirits, undaunted by her first trip abroad. I could not help but think of the many Japanese who would have been terrified at the thought of making such a trip alone. At the wedding and the reception, she was her usual sociable self, circulating among the whole party, noticing everything and everyone. What especially impressed me later was the number of guests who voluntarily reported that they enjoyed talking to Yaeko. I still do not know just how she communicated, since she could speak almost no English. Somehow she managed, and she was her usual jovial, interested, extroverted self.

THREE FAMILY CRISES

Yaeko was more serious when she welcomed me to the house on my first visit in September 1988, soon after I had arrived for a Fulbright year of research and consultation at St. Luke's Hospital in Tokyo. Tokuzou's appearance shocked me: he looked old, tired, bent, and rather shaky. Yaeko explained to me that Tokuzou had a stroke at work the previous June. He did not collapse or lose consciousness, but suddenly felt weak and shaky and had some slight paralysis. He was hospitalized for two weeks. He seemed better when he came home, but when he returned to work, he promptly got sick again and was rehospitalized. He got better again, his doctor declared him cured, and he was eager to return to work. But when he returned to work, his boss told him he was too sick to work and sent him home. He immediately lost all his energy and motivation, and declared that he was no longer any use. Since then, she reported, he had stayed home, doing very little except trying to take a walk at times. He reported that he could not think, that his mind went blank. He was supposed to decide by December if he would retire. (He was sixty-six at the time.)

Yaeko confided that for several years Tokuzou had been worrying about things at the hospital. Since the original Dr. Shimada had retired and died about eight years earlier, his son and a nephew had struggled over who would take over the hospital. Tokuzou had been very loyal to the respected doctor who had hired him, so he was inclined to support the son, whom he saw as a good man and a good doctor. However, the nephew seemed to have been a better businessman, or just more shrewd, and had taken over the administration of the hospital. As the head of the business office, Tokuzou had been aware that this nephew was using hospital funds for personal purposes: to take trips, or buy cars. The nephew had instructed Tokuzou to keep this a secret. At first it was only small things, so Tokuzou felt obliged to obey his boss, but he became more troubled and conflicted as time went on. His discomfort became more acute after Dr. Shimada, the son, caught on to what his cousin was doing and came to Tokuzou with questions. Dr. Shimada was shocked to hear of the misuse of funds, as he always used his own money for trips or such. He told Tokuzou of his worries about the financial condition of the hospital, concerned that the hospital might go bankrupt or have to be sold. Just the previous week, Dr. Shimada had come to the Itou house, wanting Tokuzou to vouch for him and give an accounting of the money. At this request, Tokuzou's whole body shook; he stood wringing his hands, and could not do or say anything. Yaeko told the doctor that she would go to the hospital and vouch for him if need be. Tokuzou would just get nervous, claim his head was no good, and say nothing.

Tokuzou had discussed this saga with Yaeko, but not with anyone else. He was terribly conflicted and could not decide what to do. He feared the nephew was destroying the hospital. He worried that he would get sick and die if he openly battled the nephew. He feared someone would come and search the Itou house. He viewed Dr. Shimada as a gentle man who cared for the patients but had no courage to battle his cousin.

Yaeko saw her husband as conscientious and idealistic. He stuck to morals as perfectly as any man, and thought others should do the same. Yet he was also a softhearted, gentle man who wanted everyone to get along. The hospital conflict presented him with an unresolvable moral dilemma: loyalty to his master (the hospital, his boss) versus integrity and concern for Dr. Shimada. Mari felt that her father had lost his backbone (*ikuji ga nai*). Yaeko defended Tokuzou, saying he used to be stronger, that twenty years ago he had testified about the financial affairs of a Korean man doing business with Shimada Hospital. He had declared that he would tell the truth even if he died, but he worried about the effect on Yaeko and the children. Yaeko now saw him become so worried that he really could not think, could not decide what was best. Mari commented that her father was fleeing into illness.

I proposed to arrange a consultation for Tokuzou at St. Luke's Hospital with Dr. Takeo Doi, the eminent psychoanalyst and our family friend. I thought Tokuzou was depressed and that antidepressant medication might help him. Yaeko liked this idea, particularly because she thought she could tell Tokuzou that they were going to the hospital to see me rather than labeling it a psychiatric visit. We agreed that I would arrange an appointment at St. Luke's in two weeks.

Yet this was not the end of the trauma for the Itou family. She recounted Ken's drinking and her kicking him out of the house four years previously. He had not been home since. Katsuko had invited him to her place, however, and the whole family had gathered there. Ken was living by himself in an apartment near Tsukiji in Tokyo, working in design and advertising.

The most recent crisis had been a separation and a threat of divorce for Katsuko. Living so close to Masaki's parents, it was not long before Katsuko and her mother-in-law got into conflict. Yaeko went to help and became embroiled in the struggle with Mrs. Matsunami—a battle of the mothers-in-law, I joked. But when Tokuzou went to try to work things out and was insulted by being given only leftovers to eat, Katsuko could tolerate it no longer. She left the Matsunami house and returned to Honchou with her firstborn baby. She moved into a small apartment that Yaeko had bought thinking that Ken might marry and want to live there someday, and where Mari stayed sometimes.

Meanwhile, the Matsunami family confronted a crisis of inheritance. The Matsunami grandfather and father had agreed that the eldest son would inherit the family farm. After the grandfather died, however, the grandmother and her sisters wanted the four Matsunami children to inherit equally according to the new laws on inheritance, and they succeeded in convincing the father. One aunt even accused Katsuko of pushing Masaki to keep all the land, and complained that Katsuko's mother—whom she called a pushy woman—was pressing Katsuko. Yaeko proclaimed that there was no truth to such accusations, that the aunt was delusional. Masaki was angry with his father for giving in. When the land was divided four ways, he found that his portion was not large enough to make a golf course, as he had intended. So he gave all his rights and obligations as the oldest son to his brother, the second son, who liked farmwork, and Masaki left his father's place to join Katsuko in Honchou.

Yaeko certainly did not want them to divorce. Since Katsuko was the only child who married, Yaeko wanted to support that marriage. She was afraid people might blame her, saying that her children could not get along with anyone since she was such an outspoken person. And Yaeko liked Masaki.

Katsuko was critical of him for not being aggressive enough, but Yaeko figured that Katsuko, like Yaeko, needed an easygoing husband. A consultation with a fortune-teller confirmed her own recommendation that the couple should work it out. (Yes, middle-class Japanese frequently consulted fortune-tellers.)

Since Masaki did not really like farmwork and did not have space for his desired golf course, he was not upset at giving up his rights to the farm. Yaeko helped Masaki and Katsuko find jobs in a resort area on the Izu Peninsula where both could work—work that Masaki enjoyed. Yaeko also bought them an expensive car.

When I phoned Yaeko two weeks later to confirm the appointment, Yaeko told me that Tokuzou refused to go to the hospital to see Dr. Doi. He did not want to bother such a famous doctor and did not think he needed a psychiatrist. He had been going for massage and felt a bit better, but Yaeko doubted that massage would be sufficient. She agreed to call me if and when Tokuzou was willing to go to St. Luke's.

I did not hear from Yaeko after that. I knew she was busy working at the department store about thirty hours per week, plus the commute was over an hour one way, although that was not excessive for Tokyo. When I sent them a Christmas present, I received a phone call inviting me to come during New Year's (*oshougatsu*) and to spend the night with them on January 3. Just as I was leaving for Honchou, however, I received a call from Yaeko, telling me not to come. She curtly noted that they were in Izu at Katsuko's house, that she had been busy working, that Tokuzou was still sick, and she added something about trouble with Mari. I was puzzled by this, as this was not usual Yaeko behavior, but I was all the more concerned when I heard nothing more from her for almost two months. I finally wrote her a letter asking how they all were and whether I had offended them in some way. Yaeko called immediately in response to the letter. She assured me I had done nothing offensive: "After all," she declared, "we have known each other so long, and I even went to David's wedding. I would have told you if there were a problem between us." She mentioned, however, that she wanted to discuss a family problem with me.

Mari was indeed the problem this time. On January 1 and 2, they had all been at Katsuko's house in Izu. Yaeko had baby Jun'ichi on her knee and was feeding him some of her food with a spoon. This was against Katsuko's rules of child rearing, as she believed in having everything individual, even separate dishes and spoons for the baby. When Mari saw how her mother was feeding the baby, she said something about "interfering" and pushed her mother, causing her to fall backward, as there was nothing behind her to support her. Although she was not physically hurt, Yaeko was so insulted at being pushed that she left the house, walked (quite a distance) to the bus station, and took the bus and train back to Honchou. Ken went after her, trying to talk her into returning, but she just kept on walking. She declared she had never in her life been treated that way. Yaeko could tolerate disagreements but not an insult to her pride.

Now two months later, Mari and her mother had exchanged no words. Mari was living in the house, in what had been Ken's upstairs room, because there was no other place for her. But since she and Yaeko went to work at different times, their paths seldom crossed. On a rare occasion when Mari cooked supper for her father and Yaeko was home, Yaeko refused to eat it and cooked her own.

Katsuko had tried to talk with her mother about this, asking her if she could understand the cause of Mari's behavior. Yaeko had just brushed her aside, refusing to discuss it. Yaeko was actually thinking about it a lot, more than she was willing to let on to Katsuko, and she could understand Mari's feelings rather well. She made it clear to me that she wanted to reconnect with Mari *if* she could do so without losing face. Even though she had given a cold shoulder to Katsuko, she had silently admired Katsuko's understanding and her straight, honest presentation.

Yaeko figured that Mari, who was usually patient and understanding, had been accumulating resentment over some time, and then suddenly arrived at a breaking point and exploded. Probably Mari's feeling at the moment she lashed out was a defense of Katsuko's autonomy in her child rearing, partly coming from Mari's identification with Katsuko and the baby because Mari had helped care for them since Katsuko moved back to Honchou. But the underlying issue, Yaeko judged, was that Yaeko had sold the apartment after Katsuko and her family had moved out and went to Izu. Mari had been staying in the apartment much of the time for several years. Her friends looked for her there. Back at the house, she did not even have a room of her own. She stayed in Ken's room, which was still full of many of his things, even though he had not been there for four years. Furthermore, Yaeko had completed the sale quite suddenly and allowed the new owners to move in right away, all without consulting Mari ahead of time. When Yaeko announced this, Mari had merely said "*shikata ga nai*" (it can't be helped), but that word of resignation probably covered up resentment that her mother so little considered Mari's feelings, even though Mari had been taking care of her sick father for so long. In fact, Mari probably felt even deeper resentment that Yaeko always treated Ken as someone important and Mari as unimportant, even though Mari did so much to help and Ken did nothing. Despite Yaeko's remarkable understanding for Mari's feelings, she never actively sought reconciliation. She believed that parents should not "bow their heads." Her pride would not allow her to recognize that she had been unfair to Mari. It was two more years before she and Mari resumed normal relations, letting Katsuko gradually bring them together.

While Yaeko was recounting all these family conflicts, she began complaining that the house was full of stuff, much of it belonging to Ken. I asked whether Ken should be responsible for his own things: sorting out, throwing away, or whatever. Yaeko was surprised by this question. She seemed to assume that she was responsible for her son, despite his very grown-up age. I wondered if the greater freedom and indulgence given by mothers to children after the war meant that their caretaking responsibilities never ended. But then, I thought, maybe she wanted his things to maintain a tie between them. Before the sale of the apartment, she had asked Ken how he felt about it. When Ken said he did not want it, Yaeko had decided to sell, all without consulting Mari, who was actually using the apartment and who was the mainstay at home.

Tokuzou's response to the conflicts with Mari was to try to pacify everyone, rather equally allocating some blame to both sides. He once said that he might as well die if mother and daughter were no longer speaking to each other, but Yaeko had countered that his dying would not repair the mother-daughter relationship.

As Yaeko described his behavior, I was all the more convinced that he was clinically depressed, even though Yaeko said he was not like the depressed psychiatric patients at Shimada Hospital who simply sat, head down, wringing their hands and vegetating. She reported that he was less shaky since he had officially retired from his job in December, but that he did nothing all day, did not go out, did not want to see anyone. In fact, he shut the doors and windows, and would not respond if someone came to the door. He had trouble sleeping and woke up early in the morning, but stayed in bed much of the day. He seemed not quite there sometimes, though not disoriented. He worried unnecessarily about money since he was not earning a salary, although he was getting a pension, and he even let Mari pay for the rice delivery.

Yaeko had quit her job at Isetan in the middle of February so she could look after Tokuzou. She had enjoyed that job and was proud that she made good money, almost as much as Tokuzou's salary. She planned to take up a new more flexible career as a fortune-teller, and was already reading books and consulting with people about it. As usual, she was quick at finding new things and thought she would enjoy talking with different people.

By the end of March, Yaeko succeeded in getting Tokuzou to keep an appointment with Dr. Doi at St. Luke's Hospital. Dr. Doi agreed that Tokuzou was depressed, and recommended that they should move away from Shimada Hospital since being next door, the hospital continued to occupy Tokuzou's mind. He stressed that it was now Yaeko's turn to take care of her husband, since he had cared for her all those years. To my amazement, far from being offended, Yaeko laughed as she told me how she admired Dr. Doi's wisdom and his straightforward manner. She knew he was right. She even told me that Dr. Doi had said it was no wonder that Tokuzou was depressed, having had to live all these years with such an outspoken wife, and having had to suppress his annoyance. Yaeko could accept these truths because she respected Dr. Doi and did not feel insulted by him.

TO THE SEASIDE

Yaeko and Tokuzou promptly followed Dr. Doi's advice. When I was in Tokyo the next summer, I found Yaeko and Tokuzou comfortably ensconced in their new home, a third-floor condominium with a view of the Pacific Ocean and the beach just across the street. Yaeko had given up any idea of continuing work, had sold their house in Honchou, and had moved to Choushi, a small town on the Chiba coast. There they not only had the comforts of the ocean, but they were not far from Asahi-city and a general hospital where a good doctor recommended by Dr. Doi could be accessed if needed. Yaeko reported that the move was good for Tokuzou. He was no longer restless or agitated. He ate and slept better, and took long walks by the ocean. He still complained of a lack of energy, however, and he never wanted to go anywhere. Yaeko got restless at times, so she would go into Honchou, or Tokyo (two hours by bus), or even Izu. She would have preferred to keep working in Tokyo, but contented herself with these occasional excursions. Tokuzou reassured her that he could take care of himself while she was gone for a day or two. Mari had her own apartment and place of business in Honchou, but she visited Choushi frequently. Ken was still in Tokyo but he also came out fairly often; he was gradually getting on better with both his mother and his father. Katsuko and family were still in Izu, but came to visit at times. And on rare occasions, Tokuzou would agree to go with Yaeko to see the grandchildren.

A year or two later, Yaeko thought Tokuzou was sufficiently stable that she decided to take a job at a department store in Asahi-city, only a bus ride away. She enjoyed working there, but one evening she discovered that Tokuzou, who always went to bed early, had not turned the gas off completely, and gas was seeping into the apartment. With this clear alarm, Yaeko gave up working.

Within another year or so, Yaeko was telling me Tokuzou was a bit perkier, more interested in family affairs. He was able to talk to her more about the troubles at the hospital. He was sad that his long years of work there ended in discord and animosity rather than in the appreciation he had always expected, and he regretted not being able to save the younger Dr. Shimada.

Yaeko deeply empathized with those feelings. Certainly his long years of service deserved celebration. I wondered why the hospital dilemma had undone him. Could it be, as is often the case, that his greatest strength was also his greatest weakness? Could it be that his idealism, remarkable in its purity and strength, was not sufficiently flexible to deal with a conflict between ideals? He seemed unable to prioritize his values, choosing one while risking losing another, at least not in his later years. Being honest and maintaining his loyalty to his benefactor and friend (Dr. Shimada) would have meant being disobedient to authority (his boss) and risking the loss of his job, his reputation, and the welfare of his family. Could his quiet stoicism during much of his life also be seen as passivity and a wish to avoid conflict? While he undoubtedly had confidence in his steadfastness and his ability to get along with everyone, did he also have an underlying anxiety that he was weaker (less of a man?) than Yaeko, and inadequate in dealing with conflict? Perhaps Tokuzou's psyche also reflected the conflicts in the *mukoyoushi* role. He was flexible and compliant enough to fit into that role; he was not authoritarian in posture or nature. Maybe that meant accepting a slightly lowered status. And perhaps that is why Yaeko valued his support of her dominance, but devalued him somewhat at the same time.

After my yearlong stay in 1988–1989, I began coming to Tokyo every year in summer or fall. Of course, I had a lengthy visit with the Itous each time. By 1991, Yaeko reported with obvious pleasure that Ken visited quite regularly, about twice a month, and that she and Ken seemed to understand and accept each other better than ever before. She realized that she had always been saying "*Toudai, Toudai*" (Tokyo University) to Ken, and that just drove him to rebellion. At the same time Ken had drunk too much. Ken regained confidence as his film editing and TV commercial business went better. Yaeko respected him for his independence and his success. Ken explained that he did not want to go to Toudai and work in the Finance Ministry as his mother wished, because he was not that kind of person. He also volunteered that he was not married, that he liked beautiful women but beautiful women were usually dumb, and he did not want dumb children. Furthermore, he worried about anyone he would marry, because he expected that she would be tormented by his mother. Yaeko laughed, and agreed.

Ken's success was more evident a year or two later when he was written up in a magazine for having produced the preview for the film *Princess Mononoke*, which played widely both in Japan and in the United States. He asked his mother if she now accepted (*mitomeru*) him. Yaeko quickly responded: "*mitomezaru o enai*" (I have to accept you). After we had discussed how Ken was just like her, a "my way" person, she commented that next time she talked with Ken she would be more positive about accepting him, her son after all.

During these years, we had relaxed times together, talking, eating, drinking beer—Yaeko, Tokuzou, the three children, and even the son-in-law and grandchildren. Tokuzou was a fairly silent but warm presence while the others all talked. Mari was a jovial participant. She continued living and working in Honchou for a maker of coral jewelry, and became friendly with a coworker named Miwada, a man of about fifty, divorced with two grown children who lived with their mother. As Mari and Miwada became closer, they split off from the original company and started their own business, at first making various kinds of jewelry and later also selling supplies for doctors' and dentists' offices. Miwada would sell on the road while Mari kept the books, cared for the office, communicated with customers, and also made various pieces to sell. She seemed to have a real head for business. While Yaeko had been troubled by Mari's apparent lack of marriageability, she gradually recognized that Mari and Miwada were partners, business and personal, even though not married and not living together. Tokuzou wanted to help Mari somehow, and Yaeko did too once she and Mari were reconciled. So they gave money to support Miwada's business, with the understanding that it was really Mari's money that she was putting into the joint enterprise. Miwada also became like a member of the family, coming to visit Mari and helping occasionally—once transporting me from Tokyo to Choushi in his car.

After the move to Choushi, Katsuko and her growing family, a husband and three boys, born two years apart, took over a larger space in Yaeko's life. Masaki continued to work at recreational sports activities, particularly golf courses, although he changed companies a couple of times. Katsuko's relations with her in-laws mended, and she took the children to visit them regularly. Masaki and Katsuko seemed to me to represent the new generation of cooperative working parents. They worked hard and cooperated on childcare. Katsuko worked at various jobs whenever she could, sometimes part-time, sometimes full-time, but she resigned and stayed home with the children when pregnancy was disabling or when Yaeko was unable to care for the children. Yaeko did care for one or two children while both parents worked for a time, but mostly either Katsuko or Masaki would care for house and children while the other was at work. Masaki had to commute one or two hours each way to work for a while, and also had to work seven days a week for a long stretch. At those times, Katsuko was mostly at home.

Katsuko and Masaki garnered a lot of attention and love, perhaps because they were the only real family in this generation of Itous. Just as Mari had mothered Katsuko and Jun'ichi while they were in Honchou and continued to visit them often, Ken also maintained a close relationship with them. He considered them the perfect young couple, and loved Jun'ichi as his own child.

Katsuko taught me about young mothers of her generation. Since *renai* was gradually replacing *omiai*, couples married because they wanted to be together, she reported. After children were born, however, children took precedence over the marital relationship. While husbands were more helpful within the household than they were fifteen to twenty years before, Masaki was better than most in sharing responsibility. Katsuko noted that most of the Izu mothers never used baby-sitters, only occasionally left children with grandmothers, and complained continually about their husbands. Katsuko found that she did not fit into such a group very well, because she never complained about her husband, but rather thought he was terrific. She and Masaki had very little time together anymore, however, because usually one was at work and the other looking after the children.

Yaeko and Tokuzou thought Katsuko was too strict with Jun'ichi, but Katsuko replied that Yaeko had been that strict with her. Yaeko had to agree with that, yet continued to complain of Katsuko's strictness. Katsuko explained to me that she did not like the way many young mothers were raising their children. Since they were having fewer children, usually just one or two, they were overprotecting the children and keeping them dependent. The children did not have a chance to play freely with other children unsupervised. They were pressured to study in any spare time and expected to fit into the group. If there was fighting, the mothers would blame the other child and defend their own. Katsuko's philosophy, in contrast, was to raise her children to be independent, to do as much as possible for themselves, and not to need excessive care. She emphasized being considerate and not causing others trouble (*meiwaku o kakenai*). When a child did something wrong, Katsuko would make the child apologize, looking the other person straight in the eye and speaking with an honest heart. She also stressed saying "thank you." I could not help but think that Katsuko as a mother was very much like Yaeko: strict, stressing independence and responsibility, while also enjoying the children and talking with them animatedly on their level.

Meanwhile, Yaeko had transformed from the strict mother to the doting grandmother. Yaeko had her worst fight with Katsuko toward the end of Katsuko's pregnancy with the second baby, Junji. Yaeko and Tokuzou went to Izu to help Katsuko at the time of delivery. Katsuko, being quite large and near delivery, was tense and anxious. One afternoon, Katsuko locked Jun'ichi out of the house for four hours as punishment for misbehavior, leaving him crying at the doorway all that time.[4] Yaeko was so angry at Katsuko that she went home to Choushi, leaving money for Katsuko to pay for child and household help at the time of delivery. Tokuzou, of course, had tried to intervene, pleading with them to stop fighting. About two weeks after Junji was born, Katsuko came to Choushi to introduce the baby and to apologize for being ill-tempered before the delivery.

Yaeko's resistance to Katsuko's rules had also been the issue in Yaeko's feud with Mari a couple of years earlier. Was this a new form of the eternal mother-daughter struggles? Katsuko considered her mother selfish, for instance, when she made her own plans without thinking that she might be inconveniencing the Matsunamis. While relaxing at a hot spring together, Yaeko would suddenly decide to go to the bath at 10:00 p.m. and ask for company, even though the Matsunamis had already decided on an early bedtime. And Katsuko thought her mother quite presumptuous to be quite so free in telling others how to live their lives.

I spent a few days with the Matsunamis and Yaeko in Izu in 1992 at a time of another crisis when the oldest boy, Jun'ichi, was in first grade. Jun'ichi had been happy in kindergarten. He was well liked and played well with others. His first-grade teacher was surprisingly strict, however, not interested in children's play, and very soon complained that Jun'ichi was slow, forgot to bring things to school, did not do his homework, and could not read a book.

One day Jun'ichi came home from school, saying the teacher had called him a fool (*baka*), had hit him with a pencil and a small flag, and had told him to copy the teacher's sentence since he could not write his own. Katsuko wrote the teacher a note asking about this incident. The teacher responded with anger and accusations that Jun'ichi had lied. She demanded that Jun'ichi write her a letter of apology. Katsuko's investigations convinced her that Jun'ichi was not lying. He surely had been called *baka* and had been at least tapped with the flag, although he may have felt more threatened than the teacher intended. Then she and Masaki went to talk with the teacher and the principal, expressing understanding of the teacher's trying to do her best, and looking for some warmth and understanding toward Jun'ichi in the school's attitude. Masaki had tried to explain that they thought the most important thing about first grade was to get the children used to school, that perfect academic performance was not the main thing. They were met, however, not only with an ironclad defense of the teacher's methods, but also an attack on the Matsunami family child rearing. The teacher labeled Katsuko a neglectful mother because she worked as a waitress at night, even though Masaki was always there to care for the children at night. This teacher seemed to adhere to prewar child-rearing standards.

Masaki and Katsuko decided to move as soon as possible to put Jun'ichi in a different school. Meanwhile, Yaeko went to the school board with the matter via a friend of Ken's. The teacher never acknowledged that she knew that they had lodged a complaint, but Katsuko noted that the teacher was red-faced one day and absent due to illness the next day. Then the teacher made a speech in front of the PTA, a meeting of parents, teachers, and children, in which she emphasized that school was not a place for fun and that lying could not be tolerated. Jun'ichi came home saying that the speech was aimed at him. Katsuko could see that Jun'ichi knew very well what was going on, and she felt bad about his beginning school in such a humiliating way. She also knew that they had to move as soon as possible: Their relationship with the school had been irreparably damaged.

The Matsunami family members thoroughly supported each other through this ordeal. Katsuko and Masaki held similar values. Masaki expressed no regrets about moving away from his parents and giving up the farm, saying neither of them would have been happy living there with his parents. They firmly supported Jun'ichi, as he had always been honest and they had heard complaints from other mothers about the same teacher. They had faith in Jun'ichi's athletic ability and his ability to get along with other kids. They did not think it necessary for him to excel at scholarship. Each recounted how they had not excelled at school. Katsuko had felt bad in grade school for not doing better. Her mother had neither pushed nor helped, but Ken had helped her with homework at times. Her mother had never been home, but father had welcomed her home after school, cooked supper, and told her that being healthy and happy was most important. She had not liked school until high school, when she had discovered several interesting topics, especially animal studies, and came in second in rank, a fact that Katsuko never mentioned but Yaeko pointed out. Masaki said he had never had a problem with school, but had always been a mediocre student. He had excelled in sports and been prominent in various activities. He was content if Jun'ichi followed this pattern.

Katsuko implied in this discussion that she had been disappointed that her mother had been absent and not too interested in her studies. Katsuko strongly identified with Jun'ichi, feeling bad for his being targeted, and wanting to save him from further humiliation. Yaeko later talked about feeling bad that she had not rewarded Katsuko's success in high school by agreeing to fund the college of her choice, since the older two had both gone to college. She was glad that Katsuko was married, however, and was trying to make it up to them with financial help.

Katsuko had no ambivalence about moving. She did not feel accepted in that Izu community. She complained that the mothers there were more conventional and narrow-minded, like country folk, than she was used to in Tokyo or Honchou. The young couples were still living with the husbands' parents, even while the mothers-in-law and daughters-in-law complained about each other continually. Katsuko worried that they were all pointing fingers at her, criticizing her for working and commenting on her conference with the teacher, implying that something must be wrong with her family. She and Masaki had worked hard to be accepted, but still they heard the gossip: one housewife was jealous of them for having two cars, wondering how they could afford it, another defended them as conscientious parents, and another criticized Katsuko for being "hysterically strict." Katsuko felt she had no close friends there. I was the first person outside the family she had confided in about the school problem. I reflected later that Katsuko was like her mother: she disliked living in the countryside, she refused to live with parents, she resisted pressure to conform, and she found an agreeable and cooperative husband.

Within a few months the Matsunamis moved to a larger town on the coast, and Jun'ichi started a new school. Then they moved on to Choushi, to the first-floor apartment of the building where Yaeko and Tokuzou lived. Masaki had a new job managing a golf course in the middle of Chiba prefecture, between Choushi and Tokyo, and Katsuko worked full-time at an Asahi-city department store. Yaeko enjoyed baby-sitting three afternoons a week, while having greater freedom to go to Tokyo or elsewhere, since the Matsunamis were there to look after Tokuzou.

This living situation seemed to work rather well for several years. Yaeko clearly enjoyed having the Matsunamis around. They provided companionship and stimulation. She became especially fond of the second boy, Junji, as he loyally followed her around, even when she was not baby-sitting. Katsuko liked being near her mother too, especially for baby-sitting help, and their occasional arguing did not seem to upset either of them too much. Jun'ichi did his homework acceptably, got along with his teachers, and spent most of his time at sports. Masaki, however, was burdened by having to commute for so many hours, and he worried about money. Due to the recession, the golf course did not do well and did not pay him well enough. Then Katsuko had to quit working when the third baby boy, Junzou, was born. Yaeko could no longer do much baby-sitting because she could not manage all three children for very long.

During these years, the Matsunamis taught me much about the younger generation in Japan. They criticized their own generation for wanting everything stable, no changes. People wanted everyone to be the same, to fit into the group. Actually they were themselves looking for some stability, as their situation had changed a bit too often. So when Masaki got a job with a more prosperous golf course a few years later, they moved to be closer to his work.

Meanwhile, Jun'ichi developed characteristically, only passable in schoolwork, excelling in sports, rather grown-up and responsible in personal style and relationships. No one in the family, not even Yaeko, demeaned his school performance. When Yaeko visited me in Cambridge in 2000, she made a point of bringing junior-high-age Jun'ichi with her, to introduce him to the world and to my teenage grandsons. He seemed to enjoy the trip, and the family said he had matured in awareness and in confidence. We enjoyed hearing him tell how he persevered and often prevailed in his judo matches by simply keeping his mind on a successful outcome. And when he returned to Japan, he won his biggest match and was awarded black belt status, becoming the only black belt in his school. His parents worried about his being able to pass a high school entrance exam. (Mandatory public education ends after junior high in Japan.) The next year he was accepted without an exam, however, into a reasonably good prefectural high school based on his athletic ability.

In high school, he focused on further judo training. His judo teacher, however, was punishing him cruelly. The teacher hit him, knocked him down, even banged his head against the floor so many times that his ear was damaged, bleeding so badly that he required a doctor's visit. Everyone, including the doctor, labeled this treatment *ijime* (teasing or tormenting, a notorious problem in Japanese schools, mostly between students). When I saw Jun'ichi, he had a small facial scar, and his ear was thick with scar tissue. Katsuko had collected evidence, and wanted to go to the school authorities. Jun'ichi, pleaded with her not to, as he said her complaining would only make it harder on him. Masaki supported Jun'ichi, saying that it was the boy's decision, and advised against complaining. Evidently, the males considered that this *ijime* was really a kind of hazing, the teacher's method of toughening up the students and giving them discipline. The Matsunamis heard that other students who had gone to the principal with similar complaints were dismissed with the simple response "*shikata ga nai*" (it can't be helped). Two of these students had quit judo. By the next year Jun'ichi was doing quite well in judo again, winning his matches, and the teacher no longer mistreated him.

LOSS OF THE BEST SUPPORT

To go back a few years in our story, however, the most important event during the 1990s was the death of Tokuzou in April 1995. He died quietly and painlessly in his sleep, evidently of a stroke. Yaeko planned for a modest funeral at the family temple in Inatori, and accompanied the body there for the funeral and cremation. Shimada Hospital was not notified of the death and no condolences came from there. On arrival, however, she was thoroughly shocked to find the temple full of flowers and guests, with a lengthy list of financial condolences. Tokuzou had an impressive funeral after all. Ken's boss, his sponsors from TV and movie companies, and his coworkers had all pitched in with their support. Yaeko was overwhelmed, and impressed with Ken's success as she had never been before.

The family shed many tears at the loss of Tokuzou. Ken at first blamed his mother for his father's death, because she had not always taken care of him. Mari insisted there was no point in blaming Mother, that Ken also had caused Father unhappiness, and that Mother had been caring for Father since the move. Yaeko blamed the stress at work for Tokuzou's illness.

Yaeko found the apartment lonely without Tokuzou. She mentioned even some years later that whenever she came home from Tokyo or Honchou, she always looked up at the window where Tokuzou used to watch for her and wave, wishing to see his welcoming face again. She realized how lucky she had been to have him for her husband. He was an exceptional man, really a strong man who stuck to principles and lived according to his ideals as few people do. He had been a constant support for her, not only helping with the house and the children, but also defending her. When she was criticized for her outside activities, Tokuzou showed his sympathy by explaining that she had been prevented by war and then marriage from going to college. He viewed her as a very capable person who could have done many more things under different circumstances. When the children felt sorry for him because she took little care of him or the children, he would say that he enjoyed being home, staying with the children, caring for plants around the house. He was never sorry he had married Yaeko: She made his life interesting and enjoyable. That reassurance meant a lot to Yaeko. Yaeko was glad she had quit work, moved with him to the ocean, and took care of him for the six years there. Those had been good years for them. Tokuzou was relaxed and at peace, and she was too.

When she thought about it, however, she realized that sometimes in her heart she had belittled him. She had liked his agreeableness, but wished he were more aggressive and more ambitious. She felt sad for him now because he had clearly sensed that in her. She recalled the time when Ken was about three years old, when a phone call from Kataguchi had prompted Tokuzou to ask if Kataguchi was the man she really loved, and if she was perhaps not a virgin at marriage. Yaeko was so insulted by his question that she lost her temper and did not speak to him or cook for him for three days. Finally, Tokuzou apologized, saying that he now understood that she and Kataguchi had just been friends, and he had misjudged the closeness he sensed between them. Yaeko recalled that Tokuzou, once while drinking, had said that she was more *erai* (accomplished, esteemed) than he. She also recalled that he had asked her if she really respected and loved him. At the time she reassured him she did, but she felt sad later to realize that he probably was wondering that all during their years together. Of course, she and Tokuzou were on the horns of a dilemma. She might have respected him more, and he might have respected himself more, if he had been more assertive. But if he had been, she would have been fighting him every time he disagreed with her, and frequent conflict would have endangered the marriage. His pride in loyalty and silence would not have allowed such aggression in himself. Even if not assertive, one had to respect that he was *gamanzuyoi*, a virtue highly valued even today, connoting patience and endurance.

Ken had been particularly grief-stricken right after his father's funeral and angry at Yaeko for not having been a better wife. But he soon mellowed, came to Choushi more often than ever before, and was more accepting of his mother. Yaeko felt deeply gratified to have a son who acted like a son. They enjoyed occasional long talks into the night. He spoke of how he had been critical of her as a wife and mother, but that he liked and admired her as a person. She told him she could understand his anger, especially for pushing him so hard toward Tokyo University. When she said she could understand his anger, he replied that all he ever wanted was her acceptance. When she wondered about his wanting to marry, he had said honestly that he did not think he should marry while she was alive, because she would be a frightful (*kowai*) mother-in-law. Besides, he did not think he would be a good father, never as good as his father. He was too selfish.

Ken was quite solicitous when the Matsunamis moved away and asked Yaeko to go with them so she would not be alone and could baby-sit while Katsuko worked. He advised against moving, saying that she would have no place to go when she and Katsuko argued. She should keep the apartment in Choushi. Besides, he wanted to keep the Itou family line going, and he wanted Choushi to be the Itou family homestead (*jikka*), since the Honchou house was not available. Ken would even be willing to pay for it. The plan was to have the Matsunamis' second son Junji take the Itou name when he grew up, since Ken had no children. Katsuko was furious at Ken for interfering, and at her mother for listening to Ken. Both Katsuko and Mari were angry that Yaeko respected Ken more than her daughters, even though the daughters did more for her. Yaeko recognized that Ken had always been most important to her. Of course she always respected men more.

It really seemed as though she and Ken had put their conflicts aside: They had come to a mutual understanding and they were positively reinforcing what had always been a strong bond underneath. Ken had even told her that while he used to think that she talked as though she were an expert when she really was not, he had come to realize that she had collected a lot of knowledge from reading and from experience over the years. He was awed by her strength and fortitude, noting that she never seemed to be really troubled or to suffer a serious setback (*zasetsu*), whereas he had had many setbacks.

A year later, Mari reported to me that her mother was again not speaking to Ken, and Ken was no longer coming to Choushi. Mari's story, later confirmed by Yaeko, was that Ken had come to talk with Yaeko about the woman he was planning to live with. They were not going to have an official wedding and probably would not have children, but her parents wanted to invite Ken's mother and sisters to a dinner in celebration of the union. Ken then explained that this woman was someone they had known previously. She was Katsuko's age. She had lived in the neighborhood, and attended the Itou *juku*. But she and her mother had felt offended by something Yaeko had said when they had gone to the *juku* with greetings. In the course of relating this to his mother, Ken suggested that she should adjust her personality. He was probably concerned about his mother as a mother-in-law. Yaeko was offended by this, and henceforth refused to meet the woman or to go to the dinner. Mari and Katsuko also declined to attend the dinner, partly to support Yaeko but also because Katsuko thought the woman was impolite when Ken had brought her to Katsuko's house to introduce her. Mari commented to me that Ken had shown poor judgment in telling his mother what the woman and her mother had said, as Yaeko would surely be upset. Mari felt Ken should have known his mother better and kept quiet about his partner's criticisms. Yaeko explained that she had no objection to Ken's marrying, but she could not tolerate the insults. Within a few months the dinner was held, Ken lived as a married man, and three years later his mother had still neither seen him nor spoken with him.

When Yaeko reported this, she did not appear sad, angry, or upset. She stated the facts, with a bit of a nervous laugh, and moved on to more pleasant topics. In fact, Yaeko did not tell me this big news about Ken right away, but first told me that she had met with her old friend Kataguchi. Was she reluctant to admit to a wound? Was the pain of yet another alienation from her son hard to acknowledge? In any case, she continued to accentuate the positive.

Yaeko was alone in the apartment after Tokuzou died, and felt let down and unmotivated for a while. But she was not so lonely that she wanted to move in with the Matsunamis. She was more isolated in Choushi after they moved. But she was not one to complain or admit weakness. She talked of enjoying her freedom. She met people easily and involved herself in various activities. Now well into her seventies, she enjoyed good health and still had energy. For a while she went to the nearby large public bath every day, talking with various women. Baths in Japan have long been gathering places where people relax and talk freely and rather openly. Yaeko quickly became a sort of counselor, with women telling her their life stories or their current family problems. Yaeko took an interest in all, and always had good sensible advice for them. I had heard over the years about various women who were coming to her for advice, and I had been introduced to a few. For a while she wondered whether she could become a real counselor. I told her she already was, and that she had lots of business! However, she was dissatisfied that she did not have a license. She wanted to be a recognized professional.

Then the bath closed down, and Yaeko showed signs of getting bored with Choushi. She talked of how the people were uneducated country folk. She went to Tokyo or Honchou for activities, business, or visiting. She helped Mari with her business, including one time when she thoroughly enjoyed a couple of months with Mari and Miwada in Yamagata, selling for them in a large shopping complex. She later took care of Mari when she was hospitalized for a mild stroke, which revealed that she was suffering from high blood pressure. She visited Katsuko and family or baby-sat for them, especially if a child was sick at home, even though they lived an hour away. She traveled around Japan, something she had never had the chance to do before. She read books, even doing some professional reading and research for me. She brought Jun'ichi with her to Cambridge where she helped me prepare to write this book. That inspired her to do her own writing, and she began keeping a journal. I was impressed all over again with how physically healthy and mentally alert she was, how full of curiosity and interest in all around her. She was just naturally doing research on all aspects of the world of Boston: people, housing, plants, even the birds and squirrels in the trees.

Kataguchi had called a reunion of those who had worked together during the war in Kisarazu. Yaeko enjoyed seeing everyone that day, and was pleased that he suggested they meet in Tokyo, just the two of them. They met at St. Luke's Hospital, walked and talked about both their lives. He wanted to know if she was glad she had married Tokuzou, or had felt pushed into it. She assured him that Tokuzou had been the best husband for her. Kataguchi told her that he had graduated from Tokyo University, married, had children, had a successful career in one of the government ministries, and was now retired.

I wondered if Yaeko would not be happier if she moved closer to Tokyo—perhaps Honchou near Mari or Narita near Katsuko, or even Funabashi in between. To think of this active, sociable, city-loving woman living by herself in the country, often with little to do, seems to me like a letdown. Yaeko has not wanted to be dependent, and she has busied herself with various interests, such as journal writing or counseling. She needs to be in control of her own life, and she even wants to manage her death. She hated the situation of a dying friend who was prevented by the doctor from eating the steak and beer he wanted. Yaeko maintains her independence and her initiative, still able to go to Honchou or Tokyo, good at finding new friends, new activities. She never reveals unhappiness, anxiety, or depression.

LIFETIME PATTERNS

Yaeko reflected on her life, as most of us do as we get older. In contrast to many Japanese women of her generation who are hardly aware of their feelings, she is quite articulate and objective in explaining herself. When not being attacked, she is not defensive and quite honest. She evaluates her accomplishments, her motivations, her relationships, even her personality, and ponders the meaning of it all. Particularly since we have been discussing her history, she often stops to think about her life and her world, and our discussions have clarified her own view of herself. Essentially, she enjoys life, past and present. She was never knocked down, remaining energetic, perky, and buoyant. She recognizes, however, that she has many critics, including her own family members, and she understands their criticisms. She also knows that she has friends and admirers, and acknowledges her own accomplishments. Her happiness, her liveliness, and her accomplishments come from her essential motivation to pursue her own interests and her own joy, and her ability to do so. In this, she was ahead of her time, and she brought on more criticism than such behavior would today. I think we both view her life in the changing context of the professional housewife ideal. Her criticisms, including her self-criticisms, come from inadequately fulfilling the demands of that housewife/mother role in Japanese society, exhibiting confidence (often seen as arrogance) in place of the preferred deference.

Yaeko feels lucky to have been healthy and most often able to do what she wanted to do. She admits, nevertheless, to some unfulfilled wish to have been more accomplished or famous (*erai*). If she had gone to college and if she had not married, she ponders, she might have become someone like Fusae Ichikawa, the great feminist leader after the war. But as it is, she is proud that she was able to be active in society in the PTA, in the co-op, with her *juku*, and in the business world, sewing and selling at various stores. She proved to herself that she could earn money like a man, especially when she had her fashion consulting business at Isetan. She learned a great deal from all those activities, and she has always enjoyed learning.

Her skill was again demonstrated when she helped organize a retirement party for me and gave a speech to the group, full of amusing stories about how the original six families were chosen in 1958 by the school principal with her help. When asked to be interviewed for almost two years by American scholars, she had been eager to participate but the other mothers initially refused, unwilling to involve their families and open up to foreigners. She told of their excuses, such as a fear of mothers-in-law finding fault, and recounted how she and the principal had persuaded the five others. Afterward, I heard many of the guests praise her talk, even one university professor who said she would make a great radio announcer, with her eloquence and well-spoken humor.

Yaeko describes herself as an active, decisive, practical-minded person, with many interests. If one project did not work out, became boring, or caused problems, she would declare "*kankei nai*" (no matter), and go on to the next. She has never been one to be paralyzed by worry or anxiety or to fall into a state of pessimism. Her strategy, now made conscious by our discussion, has been to confront each problem as quickly and directly as she can, assess the situation as realistically as possible, and take action. If she makes a mistake, she confronts it, reverses her decision, or seeks another path, at least if she can do so without succumbing to a direct attack. She claims flexibility as her general style, although her children sometimes thought she was rigid, and she could be completely stubborn when she felt insulted. She suggests that she is not an ideologue, standing by an ideal no matter what. She is proud that she has never done anything really wrong, has drawn back from going too far or doing anything too dangerous. She knows limits. Note her not telling on Aunt Motoko, or having an affair with Kataguchi, or lying or cheating to get her way. It was her honesty, not dishonesty, that got her into trouble at times.

Since it was probably inevitable that she marry, she feels fortunate that she married Tokuzou. He was a solid support for her and the children, which made it possible for her to do the outside things she enjoyed so much. She is glad she had children, although there remains a hint of her regret for not having had two boys. Yes, she acknowledges she may have made a mistake in preventing Ken from marrying his first love, and she knows she pressed him too hard to fulfill her academic ambitions for him. She burdened him and caused him unhappiness, yet she still thinks sometimes that he would have been more successful and therefore happier with himself if he had graduated from Tokyo University. When asked when in her life she has felt the most troubled (*komatta*), she readily replies "the troubles with Ken." She recognizes that she neglected Mari, especially in not helping her get married, and that perhaps she should have let Katsuko study at the private university she wanted, but these thoughts do not linger as much as the regrets about Ken. Yaeko was not unusual in stressing and overstressing academic success for her only son. She was perhaps a rather stereotypical *kyouiku mama*. She mentions one other small regret: the conflicts when she was cochairman of the co-op, which made it necessary for her to resign. She feels she did not do a good enough job of pulling everyone together. She was too outspoken and made too many enemies.

Until the latest alienation from Ken, Yaeko had been rather pleased with her relationships with her children and grandchildren. Although she knew the three children had all criticized her as being selfish and had preferred their father, she felt that they were doing alright in their lives, that she accepted them, and that they accepted her. She was enjoying rather frequent contact with each, with all being independent, but with each helping her and each other at times, and her helping them. The Itou family would continue, because Katsuko's son Junji, Yaeko's favorite and the studious one of the three grandchildren, was to take the Itou name when he grew up.

With her birth father, Yaeko's "*kankei nai*" (not related) was permanent; she staunchly refused to meet with him again. With her children, including Ken, however, she always had a realistic understanding of them hidden underneath her stern demeanor. Probably she can understand Ken's fear of her as a mother-in-law. (In fact, Yaeko and Ken eventually resumed contact once again, mediated by Katsuko and Jun'ichi.)

Yaeko was surprised when I told her I thought all the children were very much like her. Each was smart, able, independent, realistic, sociable, strong, and determined in pursuing his or her own interests and own path in life. Although that meant that each had rebelled against her at some time, that very rebellion was just like her. They had learned from her to know themselves and the real world around them, to pursue what made sense to them, and to resist outside pressures. I had noticed as children that all three surpassed the average, usually more shy, Japanese child, in ability to express feelings verbally.

And what about any negative effect on the children? One could connect both Ken's and Mari's difficulties in getting married to their mother's conflicts. Ken feared marriage and put it off for a long time for fear of his mother as a mother-in-law, and perhaps because of his own uncertainty about what kind of man he would be. His occasional alcoholic depression perhaps indicates a struggle with self-confidence, but he seems to have rebounded into comfortable success.

Mari's disinclination to fit herself into a housewife role is probably related to her conflicted feelings toward her mother as a housewife and therefore toward herself as a woman. My observations of Mari as a child lead me to connect her overeating to her jealousy of Ken and her lack of maternal affirmation. And her weight is probably connected to low self-confidence and avoidance of marriage. Her recent high blood pressure also seems to reflect stress. Katsuko, on the other hand, seems comfortable as a woman and satisfied with her marriage; her marriage is a modern, egalitarian, cooperative relationship. Katsuko was probably freer as a child to fight with her mother and to develop naturally with regard to her individual identity.

Despite Yaeko's ability to make friends easily, she realizes that she has had no long-term friends, except Tokuzou and me. Usually her friendships ended because of some competitive conflict or because she gets bored and lets the relationship dwindle. Then she readily goes on to others. Most of the people who seek her out are those who want her advice or support. She enjoys "counseling" them for a while, but then gets tired of them. She does not like passive, unthinking, or fuzzy-minded individuals (*ii kagen na hito*). Since many women are like that, she prefers men, who are generally more straightforward and clear in their thinking (*shikkari shiteiru*). She likes people from whom she can learn something. She has enjoyed friendships with men when that was possible, as in the photo shop or at the navy base. But male friendships are probably hard to come by, because of the tendency of Japanese to socialize by sex, wives with other wives and men with their male colleagues. She wondered aloud why she has had longer relationships with Tokuzou and with me. Her answer: She could trust Tokuzou, and she could learn from me. She views me as a foreign professional, and she does not see me too often.

In the last fifteen years, I have noted one friendship more significant than most. An insurance saleswoman came to the Itou door in Choushi and persisted in her friendliness until Tokuzou made a small purchase. Meanwhile Yaeko had learned that this woman, who was cultured and educated, had gone through a difficult divorce and had three teenage children to support, one a boy who was an excellent student and wanted to go to Tokyo University. After a couple of years of friendship with the mother and several long talks with the boy, Yaeko and he decided that upon high school graduation he should come to Boston, study English, and apply to Harvard or some other U.S. university. With his mother's support he did just that: He lived in my house for one year; and five years later, he graduated with an excellent record from Boston University. This young man's ambitions fit with Yaeko's dreams. On his coming-of-age day (adult day, at age twenty in Japan), he thanked his *three* mothers: the mother who raised him, Yaeko, and me. Finally, Yaeko had found a son, albeit a surrogate one, to fulfill her dreams of academic accomplishment.

As I reflect on my friend Yaeko, I ponder what price she paid for her rebelliousness against the strictures of the housewife/mother role of her day, and her insistence on doing things her way. Even with somewhat more openness since the war, she has been confronted with criticism, conflict, broken relationships, and painful alienation from her son for long periods. Her family members also paid a price. She knows herself well enough to recognize that she is better off living alone to avoid conflicts, even though she is lonely at times. Her energy, intelligence, and assertiveness have brought her a rich life, full of activities and interesting people as well as the satisfaction of following her own path. As an American woman, I have to say that her marriage relationship in today's United States would be applauded for its cooperation and equality, and her individual assertiveness would fit right in.

NOTES

1. Soseki Natsume was a prominent novelist in the Meiji era, often referred to by his first name.

2. Yaeko's experience parallels the storyline of the movie *Tokyo Story* by Yasujirou Ozu in 1953.

3. Students who fail unversity entrance exams and spend an extra year or more preparing to retake the test are referred to as *rounin*, a term for samurai without masters.

4. Japanese mothers tend to lock children *out* for punishment whereas American mothers keep them *in*.

Chapter Four

Mrs. Suzuki

Power and Submission

When I first met her in 1958, Mrs. Mieko Suzuki revealed no signs of internal conflict. She was charming, intelligent, and sociable, a successful and highly esteemed professional housewife. I admired her as a woman who was a mother above all else, as nearly an ideal mother as I could imagine. She seemed happy and comfortable with her role as a housewife, fully in charge inside the house while her husband worked and played outside. As I came to know her, however, I gradually recognized the profound underlying conflict arising from her resentment at her subservient role. She eternally struggled to maintain control over the areas that were most important to her: her children's upbringing, her household, and her body. She starkly confronted the reality of her husband's authority on her wedding night, yet within a week she began to devise her own strategy for dealing with these conflicts over control. She determined with all the strength of her intelligence and her confident personality that she would maintain the real control over what she knew best: the children and the household. Meanwhile, she would give in to her husband readily where necessary, consenting to sex and deferring to his nominal family leadership. This conflict persisted for her lifetime, but the balance of power versus submission shifted in the later stages of life. She was most satisfied and most successful during her child-rearing years when she enjoyed and ably managed child rearing, the household, and daily life. After the children grew up and her husband retired, she lost some of her effective control and experienced less daily satisfaction, and her body began to show some distortion. In the last years of her life, she submitted completely to one man, her eldest son, just as prescribed by tradition, despite her earlier assertions of her independence and of equality among the children.

In 1958, Mieko was thirty-eight years old and at the height of her career as a mother. Married to a successful businessman, she had five children, ranging in age from seven to eighteen. As an *okusan*—a housewife in the true meaning of the Japanese word, someone who stays deep inside the house— she almost never left home. She could usually be found working in the kitchen or sitting at the *kotatsu* with her children around her.

During this period, the ideals of the "good wife, wise mother" and the professional housewife were still strong, although changes were coming. Mieko demonstrated to me what was still the middle-class norm. A Japanese woman of her generation was a mother almost to the exclusion of all else. Almost all women married, and they married to have a family. Motherhood was more important than wifehood, especially since wives tended to mother their husbands. Although some mothers were sex objects or companions to their husbands, hostesses to their colleagues, or workers in businesses, these roles were encouraged only insofar as they were necessary accompaniments to the primary mothering role. Japan, the country of *amae*, where meeting dependent needs was considered basic to group solidarity, gave special importance to the job of nurturing family members. [1]

The necessity of being a full-time specialist in creating a nurturing environment confined a Japanese woman to her home, where she could be in charge and always available to her family. It kept her out of the man's world of employment, politics, and entertainment. Japanese society, especially before 1945, taught that a woman should always be financially dependent upon and obedient to a man—first her father, then her husband, and finally her son. Men officially held the power, even while depending on the caretaking of women.

Mieko lived within the social constraints of the housewife role, fully recognizing that she could not challenge her parents' or her husband's authority, and that her job was to meet her husband's needs as well as care for her children. She accepted that her life would be restricted to home and family. However, this acceptance created within her an ever-stronger determination to exert control within her home, to preserve absolute power over the upbringing of her children. Her story is one of considerable success in the deployment of this covert power during her long child-rearing years. She was not unlike other wives of her generation in practicing this art, as this pattern of authority and division of labor was typical of middle-class families of the time. Mieko, however, with her intelligence and her strength of character, was truly a master.

Despite staying inside the house, Mieko was impressive in her ability to bring the outside world into the confines of her home. Her warm personality and natural beauty attracted people to her. Neighbors, relatives, teachers, and friends often joined the group around her *kotatsu* and talked of business, education, family relations, and personal problems. While staying home devoted to her children's upbringing, she came to understand with a scholar's thoroughness both the personalities of those around her and the functioning of the world outside. Appreciating her keen analysis of personalities and social customs, always rendered with humor, one American scholar commented that she gave him more insights into Japanese society than the professors at Tokyo University.

While Mieko recognized the explicit authority held by men, she believed in her heart in equality and she was thoroughly aware of a wife's considerable covert power, typically based on a strong alliance with her children and on autonomy within the home. Although her methods were often quiet and indirect, her goals were clear and her strategies deliberate. Her approach included minimizing her husband's influence on the children.

Although others saw her as the perfect housewife, Mieko saw herself as a maverick. She was not strict in teaching her children such things as the proper way to sit, the use of polite language, diligent study methods, or obedience to authority. She used her power to create an environment designed to encourage independence and self-expression rather than to train conformity to the precise rules of Japanese etiquette. The paradox of Mieko's child rearing was that she maintained a pervasive control over the family for the explicit purpose of allowing her children to develop naturally and freely.

For me, Mieko embodied Japanese motherhood. When her methods were different from other mothers, it was because she adhered more truly to her essential purpose, not giving undue weight to lesser goals, such as manners, or to means rather than ends. Mieko's purpose in life (her *ikigai*) was raising her children in the very best way she could. Everything she did had some connection with her broad-ranging mothering concerns, and everything else was subordinated.

Mieko never doubted that her job as a mother was as important as and probably more important than any other job in the world. "Men only shuffle papers on their desks all day," she asserted. "If they make a mistake in the design or manufacture of a product, they can start from the beginning and redesign and remake the product. But mothers are responsible for the creation and quality of the next generation. Their responsibility is heavier because they cannot undo their mistakes, so they must use greater care and skill in their work."

Mieko was a self-confident and strong-willed mother, with definite ideas about how to raise her children. She was like most urban middle-class mothers of her generation in that she was the central nurturing and controlling force in the family. She focused on her children's needs twenty-four hours a day. She managed all daily events in the way she felt would be most productive for their physical, social, emotional, and intellectual growth. Although she had a very high level of effective control, higher even than that of a rather dominant American mother, she never seemed bossy or punitive. Her style was low-key, happy, and fun-loving. Her methods were based on a constant unspoken awareness of each child's personality.

Her only worry about her child rearing was whether such an indulgent upbringing might produce adults insufficiently strengthened by the hardship that Mieko and her generation had endured. My Western mind at times wondered whether children so nurtured and manipulated could develop true independence. I found, however, that the Suzuki children were poised and self-confident, free in play and self-expression, and considerate of guests but not restricted by the overpoliteness or shyness of some Japanese.

THE SILENT "NO"

Certainly Mieko's liberal views were made more possible by the secure socioeconomic status of her family and by the fact that her father and her husband, both of whom were younger sons, were therefore less bound by tradition than eldest sons. Her father was a white-collar "salaryman," well educated for his day, who had risen within his company as a competent and respected employee. The family was well established in a western suburb of Tokyo long before World War II. Mrs. Suzuki later lived in this same neighborhood with her husband and children.

Despite the fact that she was born in 1921, and grew up and married before the war, Mieko's upbringing had been relatively liberal and conducive to the development of self-confidence and social ease. Her father, the authority of the family, was an intelligent and understanding man who inspired affection and admiration in his daughter. Mieko was a happy, pretty, good-natured girl, treated with kindness and warmth but firm discipline.

Mieko's position as the eldest child in a family of five children (three younger sisters and one younger brother) with a weak mother contributed to her sense of autonomy and responsibility. She described her mother as a narcissistic woman with frequent incapacitating illnesses, who was concerned mostly with preserving her own good looks and had little empathy for others. Early on Mieko found herself not only taking care of the younger children, but also disinclined to see her mother as a role model or to turn to her for support or affection.

Mieko prided herself, as did many women of that generation, on having developed a silent inner strength and fortitude from submitting to stern authority and transcending adversity. She was obedient and never talked back, as was expected of all children before the war. "I cannot remember ever rebelling or even talking back to my elders, not to parents, relatives, or teachers. I do remember thinking that my mother handled things badly, and that I would do better when I grew up. And many times I thought 'no' in my heart although I said 'yes' with my lips. In fact, that determined silent 'no' is probably the source of my inner strength."

Mieko's school days were happy ones that were conducive to the development of self-confidence. Allowed to continue her schooling up to the age of seventeen, she graduated from a girls' high school, where she received a good education for a girl before the war. She enjoyed her relationships with her teachers and schoolmates. Even forty years later, her old school friends and one teacher still came to visit her. After graduation she lived at home, preparing for marriage in the traditional way, by taking cooking, sewing, and flower-arranging lessons, called *hanayome shugyou*. There was no need for her to work since her family's income was sufficient. One year later, her father chose a husband for her.

Looking back, Mieko thought that her father saw in her future husband a man who had the characteristics he himself admired but felt he lacked, namely business or moneymaking success. Although Mieko's husband had received only a grade school education with some additional courses, he was energetic and aggressive, an up-and-coming business entrepreneur who had founded a growing electronic parts manufacturing company along with his older brother. His business success would mean that Mieko would never have to worry about money.

After she was formally introduced, Mieko was inclined to accept the man recommended by her father, whose judgment she respected. While in school, she had at times thought of wanting to be a nutritionist, but she never even mentioned this to her parents because she knew she was expected to marry soon after graduation. She did ask for the chance to get to know her fiancé better, however, rather than marrying right away, and her parents were sufficiently progressive to agree. Thus for six months she and Takashi Suzuki exchanged letters and visited each other's houses about once a month. She saw more of him thanks to a great flood that surrounded Mieko's house with water. Takashi brought men and boats from his company to rescue Mieko and her family. The couple married in 1939. The bride was eighteen and the groom twenty-four, ideal ages for marriage at that time. They moved into a new house in what was then a sparsely populated neighborhood in the same district as Mieko's parents. This was home to them ever after.

Looking back in 1960 at her wedding pictures, Mieko commented on how young, pretty, docile, and naïve she had been, in contrast to how hard (*kitsui*) and determined she had become after the passage of years. She laughed in her usual jolly way about how stubborn she had become. "I feel sorry for the young bride, so pretty and doll-like and trustingly unaware of the world. There is nothing left of the doll in me now. And I feel sorry for my husband for no longer having a sweet, docile wife!" At the time of her wedding, the silent "no" of her childhood was only a seed of the inner fortitude that adversity would later cause her to develop.

In fact, her first confrontation with the necessity of submitting to her husband came on her wedding night. Just before her wedding, it vaguely occurred to Mieko that there might be something about marriage she should know about. When she asked what married life was like, her mother simply told her to leave it all up to her husband, just follow his lead. She had been taught nothing whatever about sex at home or at school. At that time there were no movies with love scenes. Her school days had been so full of friends and sports that she had not thought about sex, and did not even know where babies came from. She had known nothing about menstruation and was terrified when her first period came, especially since she was away from home at school at the time. She had only one teacher to turn to, who gave her a minimum of information and reassurance.

Mieko found herself in a state of shock after her wedding night. She could not stand to have her husband touch her for a week. After the week had passed, however, Mieko reluctantly came to the conclusion that sex was the essence of married life, so she fought it no more. This experience left her with a feeling of fatalism, having to obey passively and to sacrifice herself, without being allowed any will of her own. She had learned in childhood that passivity and self-sacrifice represented a sort of feminine ideal, but she had infrequently experienced them in her rather liberal upbringing. The shock was so great that she never enjoyed sex at all, even though she thereafter acquiesced to her husband's sexual desires with apparent willingness. While she submitted her body for her husband's pleasure, she kept control of her own feelings. And since her mother's response to questions about marriage had conveyed her mother's inability to provide counsel, Mieko thereafter kept these feelings to herself.

Nevertheless, in other areas of life, marriage gave Mieko the opportunity to express herself in a way that she never had before. From the beginning, she and her husband would joke, tease, and have fun together, and she expressed her own opinion, at least if not on a controversial subject, with increased assurance. After her first child was born she gained additional confidence and a sense of inner strength. "For the first time since leaving my parents' home," she recalled, "I knew I had *something of my own*, a baby to love and care for." Many Japanese wives going to live in alien families turn all their affection to their children and find their fulfillment through them. Mieko was less oppressed than many because her husband was a second son and did not live with his parents. An elder son's wife would have been more compelled to obey her mother-in-law as well as her husband, and follow family traditions.

STRATEGIC CHILD REARING

The child-rearing years were the busiest and the most fulfilling of Mieko's life, when she had full and unquestioned management of home and family. Mieko's first child, a daughter named Akiko, was born sixteen months after the wedding. Like all the Suzuki children, she was born at home with the help of a midwife and a maid, but no doctor or anesthesia. Her husband, like most Japanese husbands, was entirely uninvolved in the birth process and was informed of the birth only afterward when it would not interfere with his work. Mieko did not go to her mother's house for childbirth, even though most Japanese women in those days returned to their parental home for several weeks or months. When she spoke of independence and the value of natural childbirth, I understood her to mean that she wanted control of the birthing process without interference from doctors, drugs, husband, or mother.

The eldest son Susumu was born two years later, in April of 1942, in a shelter in their garden on the day of the first American air raid over Tokyo. He was a weak and sickly child from birth, a worry to his mother. The next boy was born in 1943, about one year after Susumu, strong and healthy like Akiko. Commenting on her fertility, Mieko laughingly described herself as "like a sandwich, one child carried on my back and another growing in my stomach: Why, I should have gotten a motherhood award from the Emperor! During the war he encouraged a high birthrate."

As the air raids over Tokyo increased in intensity, many families fled to the countryside. In late 1944, Takashi, Mieko, and the three children joined Takashi's older brother in the country home of their father. Takashi himself was fortunate not to go to war as a soldier: perhaps, she thought, a monetary contribution helped to convince government officials that his business was essential to the war effort.

Once in the countryside, Mieko found herself living in an unfamiliar world, that of the traditional extended family, where as a younger *oyomesan* (bride or daughter-in-law), she was expected to submit to the family's ways. Because her mother-in-law was dead, her husband's older sister and his older brother's wife explained to her the family's traditional ways of doing things and they expected her to follow their teachings, even on matters of childcare. Frightened in the midst of wartime, alone in a strange environment, and intimidated by the demands for family conformity, Mieko reluctantly complied. When her youngest child, at eighteen months old, suddenly became ill with a digestive tract ailment similar to Susumu's frequent troubles, she suppressed her misgivings and accepted the advice of her sisters-in-law and the local doctor, only to see her child weaken and die within a few days. They buried the baby in the family graveyard, and immediately after the funeral Mieko packed up their belongings and took the children back to

Tokyo. The air raids seemed less frightening than living under the social pressures of her in-laws. The two older children, who had mild illnesses while in the country, regained their health upon returning home. Even Takashi came back to Tokyo, agreeing that they should follow their own convictions and not allow interference from relatives. Mieko felt she could have handled her child's illness if the others had not interfered. After all, she was the one who knew the child's needs best. Losing this child was perhaps the bitterest experience of her life. She felt as though the in-laws had killed the child. She would never again submit to others' pressure in any matter involving her children's welfare. Her silent determination to follow her own best judgment hardened into a stubborn iron will. This also was the beginning of her distrust of doctors, which becomes more significant later in her life.

Back in Tokyo in 1945, life was not easy, with air raids and food shortages. For long periods the family lived in the dugout air raid shelter in the garden. Their neighborhood was never hit but fires often lit up the skies around them. The Suzukis raised their own vegetables in a nearby field. They came to know their neighbors well through the *tonarigumi* (neighborhood association), as they helped each other survive each day. In 1958–1960 several of those neighbors still lived nearby and were among Mrs. Suzuki's closest friends.

Three more children followed: Eiko, a girl, in 1946; Tomoko, another girl, in 1949; and Mitsuo, a boy, in 1951. Takashi, feeling the burden of raising children during the economic uncertainties after the war, suggested that Mieko, when pregnant with Mitsuo, have an abortion, since abortions were allowed under the new legal code. Mieko staunchly refused to destroy a child once conceived and suggested it would be wiser to prevent conception in the future. As it turned out, Mitsuo's delivery was a difficult one: The baby arrived a month after the due date and was especially large. Her fatigue after delivery added to the mutual decision to have no more children. Subsequently, Takashi and Mieko relied on condoms to prevent further pregnancies.

In 1958–1960, Mieko frequently talked with me about the varied personalities of her children and about her own rather clear-cut ideas on child raising. "It's amazing how different my children are, despite growing up with the same parents and the same child-rearing methods. Sometimes I worry that my children will grow into weak and selfish adults, as they have been so indulged as children. Nevertheless, I proceed to raise my children as I think best, even though my methods are unconventional. Sometimes I'm astonished at my own audacity in being so headstrong."

Mieko had clearly thought out her child-rearing principles, so she was able to articulate them to me: "I want my children to be natural, to be themselves, and to be free to do as they wish as long as they do not hurt others. I do not follow the traditional method of molding children's personalities or behavior to fit one prescribed style. For example, I bother very little about manners, such as the correct way of sitting or walking." Instead, Mieko saw that each child had what he or she needed and was encouraged to express his or her own opinions and follow his or her natural inclinations. She treated boys and girls the same, allowing both to help in the kitchen and to play with dolls and guns. Susumu was accorded no special privilege for being the eldest son.

I found the Suzuki children to be free and easy, fun-loving, open-minded, and warmhearted. I noticed when one daughter, uninstructed, put a plastic cover on a visitor's bicycle when it started to rain, and this made me appreciate that the children learned kindness and consideration from the generous feelings all around them.

In observing the household, the encouragement Mieko gave to her children to be expressive and independent was immediately apparent to me. She was warm and understanding, never bossy or authoritarian in manner. After longer acquaintance, however, I realized that her low-key approach was more effectively controlling than an overtly authoritarian one. She seldom if ever gave commands, demanded obedience, or meted out punishments. Rather, she carefully created and maintained a milieu that would be conducive to the type of interaction she considered most beneficial for her children's development. By utilizing her well-guarded autonomy in her home and by nurturing her children's closeness to and dependence on her, she established a secure power base from which she exercised an all-pervasive influence. Mieko was not really unconventional or different from other Japanese mothers I met in her goals, but only in her skill. She was more subtle and more effective in developing close relationships with her children, in preventing encroachments into her sphere of power, and in managing family life.

Like most Japanese mothers, Mieko began building a strong mother-child bond by being physically close to her infants and meeting their needs as completely as possible. She breast-fed her babies and carried them on her back to put them to sleep or to soothe them, or simply to transport them or to keep them out of trouble. The *ombu* sash took the place of a Western crib, carriage, stroller, and playpen. She bathed with them when they were little, put them to bed at night by giving the infants her breast, or by reading to the older ones and lying down with them until all fell asleep. She slept with the youngest child on the same futon until the next child was large inside her and liable to be hurt by the kicks of the older one. At that time, the older one would move to sleep on the father's futon while the new baby would sleep with the mother. No child was ever made to sleep alone or allowed to cry himself or herself to sleep, except at weaning. The children played together around the house and yard and did not attend any kind of school until first grade, except for Mitsuo who went to kindergarten, since there were no younger siblings for him to play with at home. Mother was always home, and usually siblings or other relatives and even a maid were about.

The Suzuki house was of traditional style with sliding paper doors and the family sitting on floors of tatami mats and sleeping on futons. It was spacious by crowded Tokyo standards. By 1958 the downstairs sprawled to include the entranceway, a kitchen the size of an average American kitchen (large for Japan), laundry, bathing and toilet areas, a study-bedroom for Susumu, two medium-sized tatami rooms for entertaining and for parents' sleeping, a small tatami room next to the kitchen with the *kotatsu* in the middle, and a large playroom. Upstairs were small bedrooms for the four other children, each with a bed and desk. The garden outside contained a small vegetable patch and play space for children as well as a well-cared-for garden of rocks, trees, small ponds, shrubs, and flowers. A high black-painted wooden fence provided protection and separated the house and garden from the surrounding narrow streets, while heavy sliding wooden doors closed in the entire house at night for added security. Both the house and the yard were spacious enough for five children to be able to play inside or outside quite freely and safely. The children easily slipped in and out of their *geta* (traditional wooden clogs) from the long verandahs that opened from the *tatami* rooms directly out to the garden during the day.

Although Mieko talked of allowing her children to be independent, I was surprised to learn that there were times with each child when Mieko had to *force* him or her to be independent. Weaning, which was difficult with each baby, was the prototype of forced independence. Each baby was weaned at about twelve to fourteen months of age, as he or she became able to eat soft adult food such as rice porridge. Digestive problems around weaning were common, as some of the adult food was difficult for the baby's stomach to handle. Mieko weaned them quickly, with trauma for both mother and baby. She recalled that neither the baby nor she wanted the weaning. Her breasts would fill with milk, especially at bedtime or during the night. She milked her breasts to relieve the pain. She put plaster or red pepper on her nipples to show the baby that nursing was to stop. During the day the baby would play happily but at night it would cry for the breast. Such times were like an endurance contest between mother and baby. If she once gave in to the baby, she would have to give in every time afterwards. She made sure that she won the endurance contest, letting the baby cry for a night or two until it would go to sleep contentedly without the breast. Wean a baby gradually and painlessly? She could not imagine how. No baby would want to give up the breast at any time and therefore weaning had to be forced, the more quickly and totally the better. Her mother and her generation were different. They nursed their children for two or more years and saw little reason not to give a baby milk if the mother had milk. Mieko knew she could only carry out her plan because they lived apart from the grandparents. Takashi tended to be sympathetic to crying babies but he could see her point of view in wanting the children to be independent and in weaning quickly, not agonizing over it for a long time.

Mieko assumed that children want to remain dependent on their mother and will do so unless they are weaned forcefully at each stage and pushed onto the next developmental level. Most Americans, I thought, tend toward the opposite assumption, seeing children as pushing for independence and having to be held back or punished for being too aggressive. While Mieko's power was usually latent, she sometimes took control more actively, making sure she "won the contest," ironically using the child's dependence on her to insist that the child give up some bit of dependent gratification according to the mother's timetable. This struck me as different from many American mothers who find more gradual and less painful methods of weaning.

To cultivate a constructive environment for her children, Mieko carefully studied the growth and personalities of each child. Akiko was healthy, outgoing, and sociable. The only thing that concerned Mieko was whether Akiko at eighteen was still too dependent and might not be strong enough to cope with the problems of the adult world. Susumu, who had been a sickly child until the third grade, was more reserved and interested in science and technology. Eiko was the most introverted but also the most willful child. Mieko attributed this to the fact that she was the first child born after the baby's death and so Mieko greatly protected and catered to her when she was little. She seemed to want protection forever from her mother, and did not want to have to adjust to others' demands. Sometimes she even turned to her younger sister for protection and guidance. However, Eiko was also the most fastidious and the most studious of all the children, always getting her work done perfectly and on her own. Tomoko contrasted with Eiko and resembled Akiko, except she was stronger. When Tomoko was born, Mieko was busy with four children and still needing to protect Eiko. Therefore, Tomoko grew up the most free, independent, fun-loving, sociable, and self-confident of all.

Mitsuo, who continued to be physically large and strong for his age, nevertheless seemed to feel more dependent and to act babyish longer than the other children. The other children scolded him for his babyish ways and reproached Mieko for spoiling him. He clung all the more to his mother for protection and she spent much time explaining to the other children that if they were less harsh toward him, he might mature more rapidly. He had a sensitive personality, could not stand for even insects to be killed, and did not like rough play with other boys despite his size. He usually played with Tomoko, following her lead in many activities. He was perhaps a typical *suekko* (a spoiled baby of the family).

Mieko found that later "weanings" at crucial points in a child's development were also necessary. Each child had a "second weaning" somewhere around five or six, before entering school, and some of the children had still later ones at difficult times, depending on their particular situation. This second weaning occurred when the child was old enough to understand when he or she did something particularly selfish or inconsiderate and needed a push toward maturity. She would take the child aside for a severe talking to and scolding, which lasted until the child thoroughly understood. Once it was over, everything returned to normal. She did not scold the child anymore, did not remind him or her of the scolding, and did not let bad feelings drag on— but there was always a noticeable change in the child's behavior afterward.

Mieko particularly mentioned the second weanings for Akiko and Eiko. Akiko received the second weaning before first grade, then a third when she was in fifth grade. At that time, she was particularly demanding, expecting to be catered to all the time, and she did not listen well when Mieko had a talk with her. On this occasion, Mieko told her that if she wanted to be the center of attention and to be catered to all the time, then she should go live at Mieko's parents' house for a week and try it out. Surely there, her grandparents, who dearly loved her as their first grandchild, would give her anything she wanted and play with her all day long. Then she should not come home until Mieko said she could. Mieko then took Akiko and left her at the grandparents' house, knowing all the time that Akiko would not want to stay there but would want to return home, despite being catered to at Grandmother's. Akiko would have plenty of time to realize that she preferred life at home even if she had to share the limelight with her brothers and sisters and was expected to take care of herself according to her age. After four or five days, Mieko allowed her to come back home. Mieko felt she needed to employ these stringent methods occasionally, because she otherwise indulged the children. They had been allowed to develop freely and spontaneously. She felt they were liable to become selfish and willful unless she forced them to think of others.

Mieko had another strict talk with Akiko when she was nineteen and a junior college student. Akiko was nearing the age of adulthood (twenty in Japan) and would soon be graduating from junior college and then deciding about marriage. Mieko felt that Akiko needed to think more about her future and take responsibility for her decisions, rather than just playing around and expecting her parents to decide everything for her. Mieko scolded her for leaving her shopping and packing for trips for her mother to do, and for complaining that she was not free to marry whom she pleased. Mieko carefully explained to Akiko that if she were able to find herself a suitable mate, that would be agreeable to her parents. But since Akiko had few opportunities to meet young men, she might want her parents to help find suitable prospects: she might want to have an *omiai* (arranged introduction). Her school, which she had attended from middle school through junior college, was full of very strict rules about dress (a school uniform in middle and high school), about makeup (none before college), and all aspects of proper behavior for girls, including never being seen on the streets with a young man. Mieko further explained that although her parents could arrange the *omiai*, it would then be Akiko's ultimate responsibility to decide whether she wanted to marry.

Mieko's message here seemed to be, "Akiko, don't talk so big about wanting to pick your own husband. You do not have the means to do so. You need your parents' help. Appreciate our willingness to help, and shoulder your own share of the decision-making process as well as your responsibility for taking care of your things. If you complain too much, you risk losing your best resource for finding a husband." Akiko was agreeably married two years later to the first man she was formally introduced to by her parents. He carried the universally recognized sign of success: graduation from Tokyo University.

In talking of Eiko's later weanings, Mieko explained that she had always treated Eiko gently. When Eiko was small, she seemed to lack self-confidence and was outdone by her younger sister. Mieko encouraged her to have fun and to express herself. Mieko praised her when she developed individual pride in a hobby different from Tomoko's. However, there were two particular crises in Eiko's development when Mieko had to switch her approach. In fourth grade, Eiko was becoming perfectionistic to the point of being neurotic. She was taking many lessons—dance, piano, and calligraphy—and was compulsive about getting all her schoolwork done in perfect detail. She was staying up until midnight or later. Suddenly she started to complain that she could not swallow, that food would not go down her throat. She seemed able to eat her lunch at school, but she was unable to eat anything at home. Mieko took Eiko to the doctor both to make sure there was nothing physically wrong with her and to have the doctor explain to Eiko that she was all right, that her throat was wide open. Despite the doctor's explanation, however, Eiko continued to complain that she could not swallow, that her throat hurt, and she came to Mieko looking for consolation and care. When she did not receive the consideration she wanted, she began to complain that she could not breathe. At this point, Mieko concluded that Eiko was becoming too extreme in her self-centered neurosis. She immediately packed up Eiko's clothes and schoolbooks and took her to her grandparents' house, telling her that she would surely get well if she stayed there. She could think of it as being a hospital and she could go to school from there, but she could not come home until she got well. At her grandmother's Eiko ate all three meals with no trouble and had no more pain; she was allowed to come home after three days. Mieko was happy to have her well and home, but told her that she would have to go back to grandmother's if she had the same trouble again. Eiko never had such symptoms again. As a clinician, I was impressed with this cure of a neurotic symptom. However, I doubted that it cured Eiko's underlying insecurity and her obsessive studying.

When Eiko was in seventh grade, Mieko felt she needed a strong force to push her to grow up. Mieko commented that it would be good if Eiko could be less rigid, more relaxed in her study habits, and more sociable and adaptable to others, so she would have less stress and more satisfaction in her life. Eiko responded to this in a casual, offhand manner by saying that she was happy with herself as she was. Mieko would not allow Eiko to treat her suggestion lightly, so she had a serious talk with Eiko that lasted until Eiko could accept her mother's advice. At first Eiko said it was simply impossible for her to change, that she had no way left but to die. Her mother responded that if she had to kill herself, to go ahead because a person who could not keep on growing and improving might as well be dead. Mieko insisted that Eiko should strive to make more friends, to study less hard, to be more relaxed and less exact, and to be more open-minded to new ways of doing things. In this talk with Eiko, she pushed the child away from her emotionally, not giving her any sympathy, but rather insisting that she give up her babyish, self-centered ways. After this talk, many people noticed a change in Eiko. She made more effort to be sociable, pleasant, and relaxed.

Perhaps it was Mieko's experience with her own mother and her immediately younger sister, both of whom she described as weak, dependent, helpless, demanding, and narcissistic, that made her quick to prevent any child from manipulating the family from a position of sickness or weakness. She stepped in to prevent Eiko from becoming too dependently controlling, as she had prevented Akiko from becoming rebelliously independent with her talk of finding her own husband. Mieko's low-key indulgent enjoyment of her children did not keep her from acting decisively to curtail any threats she saw to the child's development or to her control over her nest.

Mieko's job as creator and manager of the home environment included cultivating relationships and activities to enhance the children's social, emotional, or intellectual growth. While Mieko was encouraging all those around her to be free and easy and open, she was the one who set the tone, created the atmosphere, and often pulled the strings that enabled those in her nurturing environment to thrive.

By cultivating good relationships with neighbors and teachers, Mieko made it easier for all her children to feel welcome and comfortable wherever they went. She herself was natural and unpretentious, not hiding her true character or her kitchen from the world. Most Japanese wives do not want outsiders to enter their kitchen, which is considered a private workspace, but allow them only in the living room.

To encourage her children's intellectual interests, Mieko read widely among the topics of current interest to each of the children. Even with Susumu and his friends, she added incisive comments to their discussion of politics and economics. Furthermore, her continuing contact with many different people—her relatives, her husband's relatives, schoolteachers, PTA members, neighborhood friends, and all her children's tutors and friends—brought the world into her house and added to the stimulating atmosphere.

Mieko also constructed situations to further the children's social and emotional development. When Akiko was approaching marriageable age but had little experience with boys except her brothers and cousins, Mieko invited some young men, sons of friends or acquaintances, to come to the house and socialize with the family so that Akiko could become friends and feel at ease with them without the seriousness of dating or possible marriage.

Mieko also brought in two young men to provide Susumu with companionship and older male role models as well as tutoring. One was a young college student majoring in humanities; the other was an older graduate student in science. Since Susumu had no older brother and no cousins of similar age, and since his father was seldom around the house and not someone after whom Mieko wanted Susumu to model himself, Mieko felt that Susumu needed exposure to different types of male role models. Mieko often brought tutors or others into the household when she felt that one or more of the children needed to learn more about the outside world.

Mieko anticipated problems before Tomoko's sixth-grade school trip. This trip with her classmates, with one overnight, was to be Tomoko's first night away from home. Mieko noted that Tomoko had been growing rapidly and was at the age that menstruation might occur at any time. Since she did not want Tomoko to have the traumatic experience Mieko had at menses, she volunteered to be one of the mothers accompanying the children on this trip. Even though she had previously taught Tomoko about menstruation, she thought it would be difficult for her to handle two new things at once—a first overnight and a first menstruation—should it happen that way.

Every Japanese mother during these years was especially concerned with her children's educational success, since college entrance exams largely determined the child's later socioeconomic status. The fervor of the Japanese mother in guiding her children through this examination hell (*shiken jigoku*) caused many middle-class mothers to be called education mamas (*kyouiku mama*). Mieko put as much thought and energy into ensuring her children's future success as did other mothers, but her approach was more liberal and less anxious. Although examination performance was important for her children, the family's community standing provided her children with more resources and more options than were available to less well-situated families.

Mieko's approach was one of promoting her children's intellectual interests, social skills, sense of responsibility, and self-confidence—the whole person, that is—rather than focusing narrowly on exam study. She resisted the extreme pressures that caused some junior high children to give up hobbies and friends for round-the-clock memorizing, or caused grade school children to stay at school for extra study until suppertime and to start homework right after supper. She encouraged the children to do their homework well, sat with them to keep them company, and brought them snacks and drinks during study time in the grade school years. By the time they were in junior high, however, she no longer catered to them while studying and no longer attended most school functions. She vigorously participated in the discussion with each child about which educational path to choose, and then did everything she could to ensure their success. She found what was necessary for each school, helped the children get the requisite preparation, and encouraged their self-confidence.

A mother in Japan is considered responsible for her child's success or failure. The success of Mieko's methods was demonstrated by her children's sociability and their success in the examination system. Susumu, who had been a weak and sickly child, was given a home tutor to help him prepare for entrance exams, and then astonished everyone by entering Tokyo's most elite high school and then a top public university. The other children did not receive that extra support or pressure. Akiko entered an excellent Tokyo girls' private school in sixth grade that would carry her without further examination through junior college. The parents of girls frequently opted for this strategy when they wanted their daughters to do well but to avoid the examination pressure the boys faced. Eiko, who needed to feel secure academically and wanted to stay close to home, chose a nearby, low-pressure girls' school from junior high through junior college. Tomoko, with a greater zeal for competition, succeeded in entering and graduating from one of Tokyo's best private universities. Mitsuo, who always loved to read and learned quickly, passed the exam for one of the best private boys' high schools in Tokyo, but disappointed everyone later by dropping out.

Understanding Mieko's need to control her world helped me to comprehend why she did not take advantage of the opportunities she had for life outside her home. She never complained of not being allowed to participate in her husband's social life or of being confined to her house. She preferred staying home because she felt more at ease and better able to construct the situation as she saw fit. Her house was more fun than any other place, more full of diverse personalities and interesting activities. She did not like to go to social occasions where she had to be quiet and polite and could not act freely. She found pleasure trips with the wives of her husband's business associates boring because the talk was so formal and polite. She went out socially only when absolutely required, for a relative's wedding, for example. Otherwise, she always had a polite excuse. I once met Mieko with her husband at a formal occasion, and was shocked to find her so totally unlike the Mieko I knew at home. She was quiet, retiring, deferential, and polite—the perfect demure housewife. One would never suspect the freewheeling manner displayed at home.

In the beginning I had found it puzzling that Mieko almost never left the house, and that the family never locked up and went for a vacation together.

Mieko had many explanations: She could not go out by herself or with her husband because the children might be lonely or cry. They could not all go on vacation because they would need a *rusuban*, someone to look after the house since empty locked houses were vulnerable to burglars. The *nukamiso* (paste used to make pickles from vegetables) needed its daily stirring or else it would mold, she laughed. People looked strangely at women who went out often. Gradually, it became clear that she did not *want* to go out to meet the world. She preferred bringing the world into her sphere, where she was the manager, and she made it enjoyable for all.

Her skillful handling of social relationships was impressive. She was kind, always charming and full of fun, never hurting anyone, not leaving bad feelings. Still, she never let herself be pushed around or talked into doing something she did not feel was in the best interests of her family. Her path was clear, her strategy successful.

THE MARITAL RELATIONSHIP

As Mieko often pointed out to me, the parent-child relationship in Japan, at that time though to a lesser extent today, was stronger and more important than the husband-wife relationship. She focused her love and attention on her children. Her relationship with her husband occupied a relatively minute portion of her time and energy. During the many years when she was involved in raising her children, her husband was totally involved in his work and recreation outside the home. He was seldom home, and they functioned in separate worlds. She did not try to intrude into his world, but she also prevented him from interfering with or even influencing life at home.

Takashi's overriding concern was the success of his business and providing financial security for his family. He was away all day six days a week, and did not come home until late at night, often midnight or later, always after the children were in bed. As was typical of successful businessmen, his evening activities were often a combination of business and pleasure, namely going to bars or to geisha houses with business associates. In later years, Akiko and Mitsuo explained to me that their father never had a mistress and only visited the geisha houses for entertainment or to play mahjong.

On Sundays when Takashi was home, he mostly slept or watched TV. He was a jolly man with a friendly, expressive face who liked to tell jokes and be the center of attention. He enjoyed being affectionate with his children and telling funny stories. His most memorable gesture was the frequent one of pointing his finger straight at his nose when he wished to dramatize the fact that he was talking about himself. But he was not very good at listening to the children's concerns, and he knew little of what went on in the home.

The Suzukis' division of labor was like most Japanese couples at that time. Takashi had full responsibility for his business and for providing money for the family. Though he might at times talk of some goings-on at work, and Mieko or the children might comment, it was clear that it was his responsibility to handle his business matters and Mieko did not try to interfere. Similarly, Mieko had responsibility for the home and children and she made all final decisions, though others might express opinions at times. In this way, arguments were rare, and Mieko was free to do what she most wanted to do—raise her children according to her own best thinking without interference, even from her husband.

Mieko relinquished power to her husband in his arena in order to retain power within hers. She allowed him complete freedom in recreation as well as in business, and even catered to his wishes when he was at home. He could stay out late, go to geisha houses or anywhere else he wanted, and she would provide him with quick and uncomplaining service when he was home, bringing his clean clothes and towel to the bath for him, picking up his dirty clothes, serving him food and drink, and meeting his sexual needs. She allowed him to rest and watch TV or whatever he wished while he was home, and made no demands on him. She did not object to his bragging (*ibaru*) or acting like an emperor around the house, even to the point of letting him call her a fool or order her around like a servant. She knew that women were intrinsically equal to men but that men liked to act superior. "You have to realize that his calling me a fool (*baka*) or commanding me to come (*koi*) is his way of being affectionate. If I object to his insulting manner, I will lose in the long run. It is wiser to go along with his ways. If I let him act bossy and cater to his whims, he is pleasant and agreeable and unlikely to challenge me on matters of importance. If I give in to him in those small ways, then I can win the larger battle of control of house and children." And indeed, Takashi did not challenge her power at home. On Sundays while the whole family was laughing and enjoying themselves, Mieko even seemed to enjoy catering to her husband, playfully calling him the biggest baby of all.

Mieko reported that in the early years of their marriage, they had occasional arguments, typically about how to spend money or concerning relationships with relatives. Mieko wanted to save money for the children's future or their own old age. And Mieko was unwilling to place the Suzuki family traditions high on her hierarchy of values. Takashi conflicted with Mieko's mother; each refused to bow to the other. After a few years, however, Takashi and Mieko came to accept each other as they were, to adjust accordingly, and subsequent arguments were almost nonexistent.

Mieko described her husband as being selfish and childish, yet she never criticized him or tried to change him, although there were occasional good-natured jokes about each family member. She accepted him as he was, and structured their family life so that he could have little impact. He was treated like a guest, honored and indulged like a playful child, but kept somewhat outside the strong central mother-child coalition.

Mieko never argued with her husband if she thought the conflict would in any way hurt the children. Mieko handled matters so that little conflict could arise. She never told him about problems with the children or about her scolding sessions with them until matters were settled. If he were home while she was disciplining the children, he would be likely to feel sorry for them and interfere, so she never started such an undertaking when he was likely to be there. Similarly, although she thought him less than ideal as a model for her sons, she said nothing critical of him, but simply brought into the household other men who would provide different male role models.

Japanese husbands generally are in charge of earning the money, but the wives are in charge of banking it, spending it, and even allocating the husband's spending money. Takashi typically did not know what his wife bought or how she spent money. If on occasion he objected to her buying something, she probably would not buy it, as she would not want to cross him. If she judged the item a necessity for the family, however, she would find a way to buy it anyway, perhaps telling him she paid a lower price for it and making up the difference from money she had accumulated over the years and kept separately from the general funds (called *hesokuri*, meaning hidden in the navel) to allow herself independent action.

Mieko never objected to her husband's going to geisha houses. In fact, she felt she maintained control through her knowledge. "Oh, he even brags to the children about the beautiful and trained women he meets," she reported. He always let her know where he was in case he was needed in an emergency. She knew all about which houses he frequented, and which geisha he saw. "Because my position as wife and mother is socially and legally secure, there is no reason for me to be threatened by my husband's outside activities," she explained. "The women that men have affairs with are more prone to feel jealous, because their social position is insecure." I noted that the wives' social position was clearly not based on sexual attractiveness. Nevertheless, there were signs that Mieko resented her husband's geisha evenings, even though she knew he never had a mistress. And there were indications that Takashi felt a bit guilty about some of his "playing around." Mieko reported that when he came home late because of working late, he would bang loudly on the door, demanding to be let in and fed his dinner. When he came home late from playing around, however, he would sneak in as quietly as possible, trying not to wake anyone. Mieko expressed concern for Akiko and Susumu. She hoped Akiko could marry a husband who would be faithful to her. But more importantly, she wanted Susumu to grow up understanding women's feelings and acting responsibly. I wondered whether Mieko was determined not to be hurt by her husband's behavior more than she was truly free of hurt.

In sum, Mieko developed a pattern of successfully handling her children, herself, her social contacts, and her husband with a minimum of conflict and a maximum of pleasure. Her life and her house were filled with enjoyment. Her relationship with her husband was not a source of pleasure; it was a part of her life she adjusted to and minimized. She resented that she had to succumb to his sexual desires and to depend on him financially. This sexual submission and financial dependence made her determined never to rely on him emotionally, and never to allow her children to be vulnerable to his childishness. Although he continually asked her to wait on him when he was home, she asked for nothing, never demanded that he buy her anything, never looked to him for love or emotional support, or even appreciation.

LIFE AFTER CHILD REARING

When I spoke with Mieko at length in 1978, I realized she had entered a new stage in life: She was now a grandmother. Her children were all grown, living separately, and all married except Mitsuo. Mieko and Takashi were living alone in their house. Takashi had retired a few years earlier at the age of sixty, partly due to some health problems on his part, but also partly at Mieko's urging to make way for Susumu, who had decided to go into the family business.

Mieko was still her delightful self, warm and hospitable and deriving obvious pleasure in discussing her children and grandchildren. She did not brag about her grandchildren, but rather took an avid interest in the individual differences among her children, their chosen lifestyles, and the personalities of each of the grandchildren. Akiko and Tomoko lived nearby with their families. Susumu and his wife and baby lived in Tokyo, near the business. Eiko and her new husband also lived in the city, as did Mitsuo. Akiko and Tomoko and their children visited the Suzuki house almost daily, and the others usually came on the weekends. Typically on Sundays the house would be full, with all five children, four spouses, and five grandchildren gathered together, laughing, talking, drinking, and eating. The house was still a center of lively activity that attracted everyone to it.

Mieko could give no final opinion as to the rightness or wrongness of her child-rearing methods, which she had often contemplated in earlier years. She was satisfied that each child was doing what he or she wanted, although at times she still wondered if they were too dependent on her and should have been forced to be more independent and more able to endure hardships. In any case, she said she felt relieved and more relaxed now that her child-rearing responsibilities were over and each child carried the responsibility for his or her own life.

The four older children were clearly successful, well educated, and well married. The eldest three had married via formal introductions (*omiai*) and their marital relationships resembled the older generation's in the sense that the parent-child tie was stronger than the marital bond. Tomoko, however, had a "postwar modern" marriage. She had met her husband at college and married him for love (*renai*), and their relationship was given precedence over childcare. They were like an American couple in that they went skiing or socializing together, and left their child with a baby-sitter, usually Mieko, but occasionally another relative (never an unrelated person).

Eiko had been a worry for a while as she continued to be shy, sensitive, perfectionistic, a flashy dresser with too much makeup, still dependent on her mother and unable to marry. Her mother had assured her that she did not have to get married. After passing up several formal proposals, she decided to marry at age thirty, rather late for a Japanese woman at that time. The man she married, according to Mieko, was no better or worse than the others she had passed up.

Although neither Takashi nor Mieko had intended for Susumu to go into the family business, Susumu decided to do so after several years at an engineering company. Susumu knew well that his father would be pleased, but that father-son conflict would be inevitable. Susumu often consulted with his wife and his mother about how to handle his father: that is, how to make his own business decisions without antagonizing his father too greatly. Wife and mother, far from competing, were allies in supporting Susumu. Mieko was even self-sacrificing in encouraging her husband to retire to keep him from interfering with Susumu, even though her husband's presence in the house was a strain on Mieko. (Later in our story, we will see just how much of a sacrifice this really was.) Thus the Suzukis, without intending to, continued the classic Japanese pattern of the son following in the father's business while maintaining his strongest attachment to his mother. Mieko was pleased that Susumu also had a good relationship with his wife.

Mitsuo was the biggest challenge. After entering one of the best boys' high schools in Tokyo, he became discontented with school and seemed unable or unwilling to adjust. For two years he discussed his unhappiness with his mother only. Mieko listened to him but argued that he should graduate from high school for the sake of his future. Nevertheless, he eventually dropped out, moved into an apartment of his own, and took up writing and singing. Since then he eked out a small income to add to his inheritance (given to him at age twenty, the same as the older children) by singing French chansons in nightclubs. Mieko and her husband resigned themselves to letting Mitsuo find his own way in life, though they could not help worrying at times whether he would ever be able to marry or support himself adequately. They considered him a product of the affluence of the 1970s and 1980s when a new youth culture was emerging in Tokyo. He came home often, but they never went to hear him sing. Akiko and the other children occasionally went to hear him.

Mieko enjoyed having her children and grandchildren around her and was pleased that they wanted to come so often. At times, however, she found the care of the grandchildren to be a burden. If her daughters complained that she or Grandfather spoiled the grandchildren, Mieko would tell them to take care of their own children and not bring them to her so often. She let her children know that she still had the upper hand because they needed her more than she needed them. I felt that she did not enjoy her grandchildren as totally as she had her children, perhaps because she was more tired and not as in control of them.

Mieko looked tired, even old and haggard. Her conversation was as charming and lively as ever, but her earlier beauty was only a memory. She was almost toothless and quite emaciated, except for a protruding abdomen. Her hair was gray, uncurled and pulled back into a neat but not very becoming knot. She wore a simple, Western-style housedress, less elegant and less flattering than her earlier graceful kimonos, partly because it revealed her skinny arms, her bowlegs, and her "potbelly." Although she was still in her fifties, she looked more like eighty, certainly much older than her husband.

After she told me about the children and grandchildren, she talked of life since her husband's retirement, and I began to get a clue as to why she had aged. Thirty years of raising five children was less exhausting than four years of everyday care of her husband. Mieko openly envied her widowed friends, with her lighthearted laugh, of course, and lamented her fatigue from nursing the "biggest baby of them all."

"Even in retirement," Mieko complained, "my husband cannot rest or sit still. He is forever in motion, fiddling with the pet bird, or with something in the garden." Even when he was watching television, he was continually talking about it. He could not stand to be alone and wanted someone's attention all the time. Now Mieko had to wait on him hand and foot every day, not only on Sundays. She had to respond to his continual questions and conversation. Only when he went to the office to play mahjong would she have some time to herself: to rest, read, think, or talk with friends. He had no interest in being anywhere except at the office or at home because those were the only places where he could be himself: brag and command attention at will. He never had any interest in going any place where he had to be restrained or quiet. He never wanted to bow his head to anyone. And when he retired from work, he also retired from his nighttime recreation. He said he was too old and sick to drink, dance, and play mahjong all night. He would eat dinner at home and go to bed early, only to get up in the morning by 5:00 a.m.

Since Takashi had given up most of his activities and his nighttime companions, he turned totally to his wife, children, and grandchildren for company and attention. He loved the grandchildren, the smaller the better, and enjoyed having the children visit, often asking them to come and stay. But when they were there, he talked loudly and at length, telling them of things that amused him, but he had never learned to listen to others. His relationships with his children and grandchildren remained shallow. They did not talk to him of anything of any consequence. In fact, if they really wanted to talk, they came to talk to Grandmother when Grandfather was not home.

Takashi occasionally wanted Mieko to go on a trip with him. She did so a couple of times, but after that refused as it was altogether too exhausting for her. She had to do all the trip preparations, carry the bags, and then keep up with his enormous level of activity and conversation. Not only was taking a trip with her husband all work and no fun, but it was more work than Mieko's body could bear. She encouraged him to go by himself or with friends, but he did not feel comfortable going anywhere without her to provide for all his needs.

Instead, the Suzukis built two vacation houses, one for winter and one for summer. They started spending many months in each of these homes where they could relax somewhat and enjoy the weather. But since they could not tolerate being alone together too long at one time, they encouraged their children, other relatives, and friends to visit them. Generally, there was a constant stream of people coming and going. If Takashi and Mieko were alone, they really had no interests in common and did not enjoy close companionship. Mieko felt Takashi to be a drain because he continually wanted her to listen to him and to bring him things.

When Takashi was hospitalized for an appendectomy for one month, he wanted Mieko to sleep in the hospital with him as had been customary in past times, even though the hospital had plenty of regular nurses as well as private duty nurses. Takashi could not be comfortable without her, as he felt that no one else would adequately understand his needs. Therefore, Mieko stayed with him in the hospital for the whole time, looking after him day and night. He felt much better when he came home and became as active and lively as ever ("unfortunately," she laughed), but then Mieko became sick and stayed in bed for two weeks because her strength was spent.

Mieko seemed to be expecting, or almost planning, to die before her husband. There were no clear medical indications that this should be so. As far as she knew, neither one of them had serious health problems, although both had occasional weeks of feeling sick and staying in bed. Both had some high blood pressure, controlled by medication. She had a uterine tumor, but it was benign. Perhaps it only *seemed* as though she were planning to die first because she was so worried about her husband's welfare if she were not there to care for him. Or perhaps, I could not help wondering, she wished to die first as the perfect revenge, leaving him bereft of the total care he took for granted.

In any case, she talked at length—and with relish—about the difficulties he would have if she died first. "My husband is incapable of caring for himself. He is unable to even make a cup of tea. He will never be content with a housekeeper or nurse, as only a family member's care is acceptable to him." Even though the traditional expectation was that the eldest son and his wife would care for an aging father, he would not feel accepted by them. He would probably prefer for one of his daughters to care for him in his own house, but this would be impossible. The three daughters could not leave their own homes and husbands. Their families would not want to move into the house. Takashi would not feel comfortable in anyone's house except his own; hence, he would not want to move in with any of his children. And even if he could tolerate feeling ill-at-ease in a daughter's home, the daughter and her family would not want to have him there because of his demanding and difficult ways. Takashi without Mieko would likely have to face feeling unwanted and uncared for. Her death would be a most painful "weaning" for him.

If Takashi should die first, however, Mieko felt confident that she would be all right. In fact, then and only then could she retire; only then would she be able to quit her job of caring for her family. She knew she could live alone and care for herself well enough, happy to see her children and grandchildren occasionally. Or if she were physically weak or sick, she would be content to go into a nursing home, not wanting to burden her children, and not needing to be catered to by anyone.

Although Mieko had always seen that her family, including her husband, received good medical care, she herself had refused to see a doctor or a dentist for over ten years. She laughed lightly and described herself as a believer in nature. She would let nature take its course without interference. She trusted herself to know her own body and her own needs more than she trusted doctors. The doctors had told her of the uterine tumor years ago and recommended its removal, even though it was benign and posed no immediate danger. She had consistently refused an operation, even though her abdomen had enlarged and the tumor was crowding her other organs. She also refused to see a doctor when she had a persistent cramp that prevented her from straightening her leg. She exercised it gently herself, and after six months the leg returned to normal.

Since she had not been to a dentist in years, she had lost many of her back teeth. When they became infected, she pulled them out herself. She could not chew because she had no molars. Her appetite had diminished and she ate very little. Instead, she drank beer from morning until night. She laughed and said that beer was her gasoline, that it kept her running. She did not drink so much during her earlier years, and ate more. She sat down with the children and ate scraps of their food with her rice. Now she served her husband, but she would not eat with him, partly because he constantly needed something brought to him. "Yes," she admitted, "the children worry that I am not taking care of my health. But they know how stubborn I am." Her husband's brother even scolded her for not taking better care of her appearance. He felt sorry for Takashi because he no longer had a pretty, young-looking wife. He tried to talk her into dyeing and curling her hair, getting false teeth, buying new clothes, and wearing makeup. Mieko chuckled as she reaffirmed her belief in nature. I surmised that she still might be subject to her husband's sexual desires, but she would not pretty herself for him.

Once a friend praised Mieko for her devoted care of her husband and commented on the Suzukis' great love for each other being demonstrated by their always being together. Mieko immediately responded that responsibility, not love, held them together. Takashi, she reasoned, felt responsible for Mieko financially and was with her all day and night now not because he loved her, but because he had no place else to go. Mieko claimed no love for him, but she felt responsible for his care.

Mieko continued, "I am not a real woman (*onna ja nai*). I have never really loved my husband and I have never enjoyed sex. My husband never seemed to notice, or to mind that I didn't enjoy sex, since I never refused him after that first week. He seems no more aware of my feelings or preferences than if I were a piece of furniture."

Mieko herself was never able to turn to anyone for support. There was no one she could depend on—not her mother, not her husband, not even doctors. "Maybe the problem is within myself," she reflected: "I don't like to lean on anyone or anything, not even on machines. I refuse to ride on planes and I am always the last person to buy a new appliance. I only depend on myself."

Some Japanese wives grow stronger and more confident as they get older. Wives who earlier were subjected to the domination of mothers-in-law enjoy gaining control of their households after the older women die. Some wives find closer companionship with their retired husbands than was possible earlier, or they enjoy the freedom to pursue their own friends or hobbies. Some who are burdened by retired husbands wanting to be serviced all day, like Mieko, get divorced. Mieko, however, seemed to have lost, rather than gained, power and satisfaction. After her nest emptied of children, her husband's retirement subjected her to his ever-present demands. Characteristically, she responded by strengthening her control in the area that remained. She became ever more determined to control her body, resisting doctors, dentists, surgery, beauty treatments, and family advice. While her children were growing up, she was not opposed to using doctors and dentists. But now her stubbornness, even to the point of emaciation and possible early death, was her refusal to submit, her silent "no." When I said goodbye to her that summer of 1978, I wondered whether the protruding abdomen reminded her of happier days with growing babies inside.

TUMOR AS METAPHOR

I noted the progressive deterioration of her physical condition during the 1980s and the early 1990s, and she spoke ever more lengthily about the strains of living with her husband twenty-four hours a day. She aged rapidly, looking more like an old and sick lady. She became thinner, gradually lost most of her teeth, and her cheeks were sunken. One year she explained that she had been sick. For a month or two her whole body was bloated. She did not see a doctor, but talked with one by phone and was given some medication. "When I feel sick, I rest but I do get up to cook breakfast and dinner," she reported. "On such days, my husband may eat lunch out. I am feeling a bit better today, mainly because I rested up so I would be *genki* (well) enough for our meeting today. I arranged for my husband to go to Tokyo for two days so we would be free to talk."

Although Mieko went on to talk about the children and grandchildren, she kept returning to the topic of her *guai* (condition of her health), and even of death. "My body has at times become swollen, with the top half thin but the bottom half so swollen that I look like I am in the last stages of pregnancy, almost ready to deliver. My stomach is so big I can't see my feet! My legs and feet are swollen too, so that I can't get my socks on. Sometimes my legs hurt so badly that I can't walk for a while." She believed the swelling was due to water accumulation from heart weakness and/or the tumor pressing against her internal organs. She took medicine to manage the high blood pressure and to get rid of the water.

When I expressed my puzzlement as to why she never had surgery, she talked of how she has had a big stomach for most of her life, either with pregnancies or with this tumor, and that she is a stubborn person who never wants to give up anything. Later she went on to explain that she had a lot of pain after Mitsuo was born, and she was told it was due to a tumor. Since the tumor was benign, however, there was no immediate need to remove it. She thought she would wait until Tomoko went to school before going to the hospital. After some time the pain stopped so she decided to wait until Mitsuo was in school. So she kept on putting it off, not wanting to risk an operation and not wanting to be away from the children.

Nowadays, she went on, there was no pain from the tumor directly. She began to feel less well after she entered her fifties. (She was now in her sixties.) She was again told that there was no urgency, that the tumor would not kill her, but that she ought to have it removed before it got too big. Last summer she was told that it had become too big, but was advised that surgery might be too much of a strain on her heart. Takashi advised her to go into a hospital for a thorough exam and consultation, assuring her he would pay for nurses to care for her. Again she found an excuse not to go.

"If I had had a life-threatening illness, I would have had an operation and I would have been cured," she explained. "But without such a clear and immediate threat, I kept putting it off until now, when surgery could be dangerous and would require a very long recuperation." She never liked being sick, being dependent, or needing care, and did not like doctors doing things to her. She did not fear dying from cancer or a heart attack or a car accident, but she would hate to have a stroke and be disabled.

She returned to speaking of her husband, much as she had during my last visit, relating how difficult it would be for him if she died, and for the children if they had to take care of him. She insisted that he was neither a tyrant nor a bad person, just rather childish. "He never gets things for himself unless I am sick in bed." She laughed as she told how particular he was. "He won't eat anything if it does not suit him just right." Recently Tomoko had made him some *norimaki* and left it for him wrapped in plastic, as he was coming home late, but he rejected it saying that it was too dry. He was always restless, needing something, wanting to do something, acting bored and lonely. He liked going out but now had no place to go. He would bike around the resort town at times, or even go to Tokyo to play mahjong with his friends, but he had few people to really talk to, either at the vacation house or in Tokyo. Because he had no one else, he turned to Mieko to be his conversationalist as well as his caretaker. Mieko would try to listen to him as well as to serve him, but their interests were different. He would talk of books, history, and economics, but she was really only interested in real life, in things that meant something to her. She would encourage him to do things on his own, or stay over at the children's houses, but he would not stay away long. He also seemed afraid of losing her.

"Sometimes I tell him to find himself a young woman who can take care of him better than I can. But he won't do it because he knows such a woman would only be interested in his money." She seemed to enjoy contemplating how everyone would miss her and have a hard time if she died. She probably liked feeling needed but never needing. She further explained to me that she wanted to take care of him as best she could, as she felt sorry for him, alone and helpless, and she could not discard him because he meant a lot to those she loved, namely the children.

"In contrast to my husband," Mieko said, "I am never lonely. Family and friends always come to see me, and I am always busy. I still have no time for myself. I enjoyed raising my children, even during the war when times were difficult, more than I enjoy caring for my husband. Now that I am older, I would like to be by myself more, and to rest."

Mieko's aging body led her to talk of death, but not morbidly, mostly with humor about others' difficulties if she died, and with a sentimental tone as she talked of the death of her mother and her mother-in-law, and with anger at the death of her baby. She remembered where she was when each of the mothers died, and reflected that she preferred her mother-in-law to her own mother. Her mother-in-law was much more accepting and helpful, whereas her mother only thought of herself, and especially her looks. Mieko and her siblings always turned to their father for advice and understanding. By being totally unconcerned for her looks, she seemed to be declaring her refusal to be like her mother.

I received another surprise in the 1980s when I told her of my divorce. She and Akiko both immediately replied, "*Omedetou gozaimasu!*" Congratulations! And then added that they felt "*urayamashii*," that is, envious. I was surprised by this spontaneous response, but I understood that it came from their disappointment with marriage and their wish for independence. My other Japanese friends had all expressed sadness, sympathy, and surprise to the point of disbelief.

Early in the 1990s, Mieko finally had the tumor surgically removed, but she was rather weak afterward, as it seemed her spindly legs barely supported her. I was nevertheless hopeful that she might gradually regain some strength.

Mieko always enjoyed talking about the children when I visited. In the mid-1980s, her report on the children was mostly one of satisfaction. Akiko had some of the same complaints about her husband's helplessness that Mieko had experienced, and some of the same longings to be on her own. She and her husband led rather separate lives within the same house. However, they were hoping to take some trips together in order to create common interests and a stronger relationship. Their children were both growing up well enough, but were perhaps overprotected. Susumu and his wife finally succeeded in having one child, a daughter. Mieko was proud that he was a considerate husband and that she and this daughter-in-law got along well, as they agreed on giving maximum support to Susumu. Eiko, finally married, was wishing for children and urging her husband to get a job, even though he had enough money to do without one. Mieko had been worried about her, this most sensitive child, because she was so shy and so concerned about her looks, wearing excessive makeup and ultra-stylish clothes. Tomoko, with her modern love marriage of sharing interests and social life, was now busy with two children, as well as with her activities with her husband. There were hints that even she occasionally felt burdened by the dependence of her husband as well as her small children. Mitsuo, still singing chansons in Tokyo, wanted to get married, but Mieko knew that would be difficult for him due to his very strange and unsettled lifestyle. He visited her often, but she still had never gone to hear him sing. I speculated to myself that he might be gay.

Later in the 1980s, I heard of a family tragedy a few years after the fact since I had not been in Japan for several years. Tomoko had been suddenly diagnosed with cancer and died quite rapidly. Her husband and children were living nearby with his parents. Eiko was now divorced as well as childless, and was working as a pharmacist in Tokyo. Mieko suggested that with her sensitivities, she had found marriage too difficult.

TAKASHI GOES FIRST

I had received news of Takashi's death before my arrival in Tokyo the summer of 1994. A mutual friend and I visited the Suzuki home, bringing flowers. Mieko took us into the inner room to show us the *butsudan* (Buddhist altar to the dead) with pictures of Takashi, Tomoko, and the baby who had died.

Takashi had died suddenly and peacefully in his sleep about two months previously. The *atoshimatsu* (things to be done after a death) were voluminous and difficult: paperwork, prayers, and ongoing negotiations. Takashi's death had generated divisive family issues. Of course, the major question was the inheritance, especially since he had left no will. The second question was where Mieko should live and with whom. The family members were beginning to agree on what had become customary after the war, namely that the widow would receive half the inheritance, and the five children would divide the other half equally among themselves.

By tradition, the widow should live with the eldest son. Susumu and his family did not want to move to the suburbs to live with her, however, and she did not want to move to their condominium in Tokyo, which she had never even visited. Besides, she would find it more difficult to live with her daughter-in-law than with her daughters, even though they had generally gotten along well. Meanwhile, Mieko remained in her own house with a live-in maid to take care of everything. Eiko and Mitsuo took turns coming to stay at the house, and visited daily. Mitsuo was there on this day, so he joined our conversation occasionally.

Mieko told me she was seeing me for a diagnosis. "Am I depressed (*utsujoutai*)?" she inquired. "I have trouble sleeping at night. I get up to go to the toilet and then I fret over everything. Eiko tells me not to think of worrisome things, but I can't help it." I reassured her that depression is normal for some months after a death, but that she should start to feel better soon.

I called to make a date to visit about a month later, since I heard from Akiko that the children were worried about their mother and I would be leaving Japan soon. Mieko said, laughingly, that I should come again for a diagnosis (*shindan*) and counseling. And this time I talked with Mieko alone, even though the maid and Mitsuo were in the house. Mieko readily told me that she still could not sleep. "Even the sleeping pills I was taking don't work anymore. I wake up during the night, and feel terribly anxious, unless one of the children is nearby. The maid is not enough. I need help with the *atoshi-matsu*. My legs are weak and it is hard to walk. I can't go out by myself. I am surprised at being so upset by my husband's death. I never expected him to die first."

Her biggest worry was about the children. They disagreed about how to take care of her, when the main thing she wanted for them was to get along with each other. Susumu proposed that she live with him and his wife and daughter in their central Tokyo condo, so they could look after her. Akiko, Eiko, and Mitsuo suggested that she stay in the house she has always lived in, with Eiko and Mitsuo taking caring of her, and Akiko nearby. Eiko and Mitsuo would not mind: They lived alone, they had flexible lifestyles, and they found their childhood home a comfortable place to be. These three argued that they were the ones who knew best how to do things around the house. Susumu came very seldom, particularly since the others, who saw him as wanting control of mother's money, frowned upon him. "In truth," Mieko noted, "Takashi and I never visited Susumu's house, and I do not know how I would feel away from this house and this familiar neighborhood. Of course, Takashi never went anywhere, not even to Akiko's nearby for lunch, as he was only comfortable in his own place where he was king." Occasionally she would interrupt her own narrative with a particular lament: "Why did I raise my children to be so individualistic and independent?" She seemed to blame her liberal child rearing and the children's independence for their persistence with their different points of view.

In the months prior to his death, Takashi's arguments with Susumu had escalated. Takashi was worried about the business, and tried to tell Susumu how to deal with the problems. Susumu insisted that the economic depression was the cause of the troubles, however, and resisted his father's suggestions. Takashi would fume and fuss around the house all day, angry with Susumu. Mieko tried to tell Takashi to leave the business to Susumu, and to quit storming around so much. Finally Mieko could not tolerate it any longer and escaped to the hospital for two weeks. (I have heard of several cases where going to the hospital is a conscious escape from a stressful situation one cannot change.) After leaving the hospital, however, she had to go to Akiko's son's wedding, a strenuous outside event for Mieko. Then after the wedding Takashi had died. So Mieko found herself arguing all day with the "*hotoke-sama*" (her husband's soul). "It was cruel of him to die and leave me with this mess," she bemoaned. Mieko's world had turned upside down.

Although Mieko talked in her usual reasonable and rather humorous way, I knew she was quite anxious and agitated. I agreed with her diagnosis of depression, but I figured that she would not consider seeing a psychiatrist. As I left her house and soon departed Japan, I expressed hope that this grief would heal naturally with time and that an amicable settlement could be worked out.

DEPRESSION, SUBMISSION, DEATH

Yet Mieko's condition deteriorated. She was not only depressed; she had submitted completely. I found her in the hospital, where she had been for six months. She had caught a bad cold during the winter, and she had stayed in the hospital even though the cold was long gone. She was lying peacefully. I could not talk with her much because she was weak and the nurse and several family members were there. Since I was told that the doctors found nothing wrong with her at this time, I knew that the true diagnosis was the one she had given herself two years earlier, depression, and that she had not been able to get herself out of it. The doctors and the family hardly understood a depression that was not a flagrant psychosis, and simply treated it with bed rest.

I was even more saddened with how I found her the next year. Akiko told me that her mother had stayed in the hospital for a total of eleven months, and finally left with Susumu for his condo in Tokyo. Although she was well cared for by Susumu's wife, the *oyomesan*, plus a full-time *tsukisoi* (traditional caretaker), she was not allowed to be visited by any of her other children or grandchildren. When Akiko and Mitsuo had gone to visit on New Year's Day, the *tsukisoi* told them visitors were not allowed and turned them away. And Akiko heard her mother's voice in the background saying "*okorareru*," meaning "they will get angry." Susumu and his wife had explained that if any of the family wanted to see *Obaasan* (Grandmother), they would have to make a prior arrangement to meet at the Okura Hotel. The other children were all so angry that they had not requested a meeting. Akiko had telephoned once or twice and had been allowed to talk with her mother, but her mother had never phoned her or any of the others. Eiko and Mitsuo felt betrayed, even discarded (*suterareta*), by their mother. Mitsuo pointed out that his mother had always declared that the children were equal, boys and girls, first born and last born, but in the end she took the traditional choice of the eldest son over the others. Eiko felt let down by her mother, who had promised to look after her. And Mieko had not seen her new great-grandchild, the grandchild of the deceased Tomoko, even though Tomoko's family lived in the area and visited frequently with family members. Mieko's siblings or friends had not been to visit her either.

That year and in the next few years, I arranged to meet Mieko at the Okura Hotel while I was in Tokyo. She was always escorted in a wheelchair by a *tsukisoi* and the daughter-in-law, and I was treated to a good lunch and pleasant conversation, albeit rather superficial. Mieko spoke little, and what she said was hard for me to understand since she spoke softly with a toothless mouth. The daughter-in-law told me about some the TV programs the grandmother liked to watch and reported on her own daughter, who was graduating from college. As we sat together, Mieko would clasp my hand tightly in hers, perhaps the only way she could express her feelings. I often felt like crying.

In the spring of the fourth year after Mieko moved to Susumu's place, I received news that she had died and the funeral was to be in two days. I sent flowers and a greeting of condolences, with appreciation for the long friend-ship with Mieko and her family. Later that year, I went with Akiko to Susu-mu's home to pay my respects. We were met cordially by the daughter-in-law, who explained that Susumu was in the hospital with a broken leg. She took us to the *butsudan*, where there were pictures of Mieko, the grandmoth-er, and Takashi, the grandfather. There was also a picture of the funeral and another of Mieko with me at the Okura Hotel. We lit incense, made our bows, and said our prayers. The daughter-in-law told us how comfortable and happy Mieko had been with them, what scenes she had liked to watch, which flowers she liked, how she had looked forward to her meetings with me. When I said it must have been quite a burden looking after her all those years, she denied that, saying that Mieko was easy to care for, always con-tent. She commented that she would ask Mieko if she wanted to phone any of the family, but Mieko would say no. Akiko and I thanked her for her hospi-tality, went to a coffee shop, and talked for much of the afternoon.

Akiko reported that her mother had died of cancer, but that she and the others were not told of the cancer or of her worsening condition until she was taken to the hospital. Akiko rushed to the hospital, as did the others, but found that her mother had just died. There was then a viewing (*otsuya*) two evenings later at the family home and then the funeral the next day at a funeral home near where Susumu and family lived in central Tokyo. The children and spouses, grandchildren, Mieko's siblings, and friends from the neighborhood attended. Takashi's relatives did not attend, since they too had had a falling out with Susumu about the business. As I recalled her popularity and the activity of Mieko's home, the very proper funeral seemed to me to express the loneliness of her later years.

Akiko recounted how her mother had continued living in her own house for two years after Takashi died, but that all that time she was upset about the children's fighting and in turmoil about what she should do. Then she was sick in the hospital for many months, and up until two days before leaving the hospital, she was planning to return to her house, with the three children looking after her. But then Susumu came and talked her into going to his place. Once she decided, she stuck to that decision, as she usually held to any decision.

Akiko and the others were certain that Mieko felt that she had to help and support Susumu, that this was probably the deciding factor. Susumu, after being a sickly child, was always in need of special care. I wondered to myself if Susumu had missed the later "weaning," the determined push toward inde-pendence that the girls had experienced. The care he needed at that time was access to his mother's money, since his business was going badly. He had many debts that had to be paid. If Mieko came to live with him, he would control her money. Earlier during the hospitalization, Susumu had offered to let Eiko care for Mieko if Eiko would send him money from Mieko's funds when he needed it for the business. Eiko, however, had refused. Akiko further suggested that the business had been going badly for quite some time, partly due to the economic recession, but also due to Susumu's inept handling. Akiko believed that her father was a good businessman, but that Susumu was too indecisive to be a business manager. Susumu should have taken Takashi's advice. Mieko made a mistake in protecting Susumu from Takashi so long. Takashi respected Mieko's advice about the children, so he listened to her in this instance, even though he knew more about business. In this one instance, Mieko and Takashi did not keep a firm boundary between their respective realms. They argued about Susumu in relation to the business. Mieko would not let any other person, even their father, influence how she cared for her children, even grown children. Her silent "no" won out, this time to everyone's misfortune.

Just as there had been fighting after Takashi's funeral, there was continual arguing between Susumu and the other three living children, with some input from Tomoko's husband. They were not talking to Susumu directly, but working through three lawyers. Susumu was demanding most of what was left of Mieko's money, plus some of the money the others inherited from Takashi because he needed it to pay business debts. If Susumu had his way, Akiko feared that she and her husband might even have to sell their house and move, while Eiko and Mitsuo would be disadvantaged since they were each alone with no outside support. When I wondered why her mother had not insisted that her other children could visit her freely, Akiko responded that her mother probably did not want to make trouble for Susumu and his wife. Once her mother decided which direction to go, she went all the way and wanted no more fighting, a trait we have seen before. Akiko, Eiko, and Mitsuo were furious at Susumu, whom they saw as selfish. I was surprised by the extent of this family battle and saddened to think of Mieko, whose main fulfillment in life was her children, spending her dying years cut off from most of her children and grandchildren. Mieko had achieved harmony via total submission to her eldest son and his wife.

Although I spoke with Akiko in the interim, I met with Eiko, Mitsuo, and Akiko together at the Okura Hotel two years later. They reported that they had settled the financial issues, negotiated via their lawyers. While Takashi had not left a will, Mieko had left one, saying to divide all her property five ways equally between the children. Susumu, however, had already used all of Mieko's money to pay business debts. His company had failed completely, and was now closed. He had wanted his siblings to give him some of their inheritance from their father to help with the business debts, but he lost that demand in the negotiations. He and his family had moved to a smaller condo (*manshon*) in Tokyo. Then all that was left to divide were the three houses—two vacation houses plus the main family house. Susumu was given one vacation house; the main house went to Eiko and Mitsuo; and the second vacation house was to be shared or divided by all five children (with Tomoko's husband and children receiving one share).

They were relieved that all was settled, but they were still angry with Susumu, and never spoke with him or his wife or daughter. All the other children and their families, including Tomoko's husband, who never remarried, remained close and friendly with each other. Akiko felt sorry for Susumu because he was all alone. Susumu's wife, the *oyomesan*, did not understand why Akiko and the others were so cool to her.

I asked again why Mieko did not have the tumor removed until much too late and why she never went to the dentist; they answered with the same reasons Mieko had given me: Mieko declared herself to be a believer in nature (*shizen shugi*) who disliked artificiality and believed in letting nature take its course. She refused to use makeup, and did not want to own too many kimonos. And while they were angry at what they saw as hypocrisy, stating her belief in equality but actually favoring the eldest son, they understood her clear-cut follow-through once she made a decision. Some years back, the children had all expected Mieko to go out for fun or to travel after the children grew up and Takashi retired, and they were surprised that she never did so. I shared with them my explanation: that their mother and father did indeed have some traits in common. Both of them were only comfortable where they did not have to worry about appearances and could simply be themselves.

Mitsuo still sang chanson in Tokyo, Eiko was living by herself and working in the pharmacy, and Tomoko's children had graduated from good schools and one was already married with children. Akiko and her husband led separate lives, one sleeping upstairs and one downstairs. He was retired, busy with gardening, and she enjoyed taking painting lessons. Her two children were basically well educated and happy, although Akiko and her husband did not quite approve of their son's political career and were disappointed for their daughter, who was unhappy with her love marriage.

While I thanked them for sharing with me what they had all gone through, my repeated refrain was how much our family's friendship with the Suzuki family had meant to all the Vogels, how much we learned from them, how much I appreciated meeting with them even now, and especially how much I always admired and loved their mother.

REFLECTIONS

As I left them that day, I continued to ponder how such a vibrant and joyful life had come to such a tragic ending. During the long years of child rearing, Mieko had developed a satisfactory balance between letting her husband control his area while she controlled the household, the children, and her life. During her husband's retirement years, however, she was less able to control the home life; she had to spend most of her days addressing her husband's wishes, or rather submitting to her own superego (conscience), which told her that she must care for him full-time. Feeling less in control of the household situation, she clung all the harder to control over her body. Calling herself a natural person, she held onto that tumor almost as though she were nourishing it. Others remarked that she seemed to enjoy caring for her husband and laughing with him, but she never talked to me about this being pleasurable. Rather she told me how he was childish and could do nothing for himself, and her days were taken up doing every little thing for him. When she was no longer able to control the situation, her silent "no" took over.

She implied that she wanted to die first, perhaps to show everyone how helpless her husband would be without her and how much trouble he would be to others. She must have hoped that he and others would finally appreciate all she did. Consciously or unconsciously, she decided not to seek medical or dental care and let herself grow old and decrepit. Accordingly, her teeth fell out and the uterine tumor grew larger. Perhaps it was her unconscious wish for revenge? Revenge at him, at her mother, and at the world that decreed that she had to subordinate herself to the wishes of persons she considered less wise and more self-centered than she?

While she resented having to do her husband's bidding about every little thing, she and he were really quite tied together. She felt a strong sense of duty that she must stay with him and care for all his needs; no one else could do it. And he stayed with her and provided for her. She did almost nothing for herself all those years. The one way she did resist her husband was to protect her oldest son from his father. But this was the one case in which she was not so wise, because without utilizing his father's well-earned business knowledge, the son's business gradually went bankrupt.

My sense is that her decision at the end of her first week of marriage was life-determining. She stuck to that decision forever, even in her later years with amazing determination and fortitude. Recall the trauma of her wedding night and her not letting her husband approach her physically. All that week she was undoubtedly experiencing an internal turmoil. Her abrupt decision at the end of the week was to obey her husband's commands and meet his requests, but to preserve control over the house and children. She must have decided not to go out of her way to make herself attractive to him. Thus her large abdomen, her refusal to see doctors, and her declaring herself to be *shizen shugi*, a nature devotee, was probably her way of taking control of her body, even while she would never refuse her husband.

This pattern continued for all her married life, with its satisfactions in the beginning and its frustrations in her later life. It broke suddenly when her husband died unexpectedly. Her defenses seemed to crack, and all the suppressed dependent and angry feelings came forth. Her world and her definition of herself were turned upside down, never to recover. She who most valued her independence found herself dependent, unable to care for herself. She, the decisive and stubborn one, found herself in a state of indecision. She, who had guided her children well, found she could not manage them and could not tolerate their continuing arguments. She then could not feel at peace until she gave up her struggles to "fix" the problem and submitted totally to her eldest son's will, thereby ending the argument between him and the other children. Was this similar to her giving into her husband's needs at the beginning of their marriage? She achieved this "peace" at great cost to herself: losing contact with all her other children and grandchildren, and most of her friends. A self-sacrifice for the well-being of her oldest son?

Looking back, I wondered if I could have done something to prevent this downward slide. Perhaps she needed a talking to, a confrontation like the ones she had given some of her children? Did she need to be told to grow up (yes, even at her age), to give up the childish and unrealistic expectation that she should and could do it all, that she should not need anyone? Although I had never been in a therapist role with her, she did ask me for a diagnosis that once. Perhaps then I should have insisted on arranging a psychiatric consult for her with Takeo Doi. At the time, however, I did not think seriously about doing that. Not only would I have expected her famous stubbornness to resist any such referral; I would not be in Japan long enough to follow through on such a recommendation. Also I thought her depression might be short-lived, as is often the case with an acute depression after a death. Perhaps I remembered her strength and her determination all too well. I had been so impressed with her enormous vitality while raising five wonderful children. I did not realize how thoroughly her defenses were crumbling. In any case, I never expected such a sad turn of events. My heart aches for Mieko!

NOTE

1. Takeo Doi, *The Anatomy of Dependence: The Key Analysis of Japanese Behavior* (Tokyo: Kodansha International, 1973).

Chapter Five

New Strains

The era of the professional housewife presented here in the stories of our three women is coming to an end as a result of profound social changes. Japan has gradually evolved from an insular, ethnocentric, self-styled homogeneous society emphasizing common values, stable family structure, and social cohesion into a diversified, international society, with varying moral guidelines and family patterns and more volatile economic and work conditions. This ongoing transition has pushed individuals to find satisfactory ways to live in moral and social circumstances never experienced by their forebears.

In the immediate postwar period, the woman's role was part of the traditional *ie* system of the hierarchical extended family, with generations living together and a strict division of labor between the sexes. Middle-class housewives were responsible for all household and family care, subservient to husbands and/or mothers-in-law. When we arrived in Tokyo in 1958 and first encountered our professional housewives—Tanaka-san, Itou-san, and Suzuki-san—we did not at first realize that a profound transformation was under way. With rapid economic growth and greater job stability, a new middle class had gradually emerged, with salaried husbands and full-time housewives. By the time of the Tokyo Olympics in 1964, we were startled to see that the pattern of having a young live-in maid from the countryside learning domestic and mothering skills began to disappear as factory work took over. Middle-class daughters were giving up bridal training (*hanayome shugyou*) in favor of college education. As many Japanese today begin to look back with nostalgia on the professional housewives of that era, I have tried in this book to describe realistically and in detail the lifestyles I observed at that time.

In this chapter, I seek to portray social changes in two distinct periods, the 1960s through the early 1990s and then from the late 1990s to the present. I contend that the professional housewife ideal continues to cast a shadow over Japanese society, even as it has faded over these two eras of change. Government policies, professional practices, and social norms have all reflected this ideal, and they have not seamlessly adapted to changing circumstances. This means, for example, that women are still constrained in their choices by government policies that presuppose a male breadwinner model. Social services and therapists are not sufficiently equipped to help women navigate their wider range of choices in this new social context. And women are plagued by their own underlying sense of failure at not being able to attain the professional housewife ideal, even if they know they do not really want it for themselves or their families.

Moreover, I contend that these social changes have had *psychological* effects: that is, they have affected the manifestations of psychological disorders. Japanese women are less tormented by rigid authority figures, such as mothers-in-law, and more burdened by overly dependent children. They are less bound by rigid social codes, and more anxious about how to manage choices.

PROGRESS AND PROBLEMS, 1960S–1990S

From the 1960s through the 1990s, Japanese pushed even harder for success, with men working long hours in companies and wives shouldering the responsibility for housework and childcare. The wives, like Itou-san, guided their children to study hard and succeed on school entrance exams with the goal of getting into the best high schools and universities and therefore into the most successful companies or ministries. During these years, Japan was successful economically and the family and social systems were relatively stable, even as they were evolving.

The professional housewife ideal for Japan's new middle-class women gradually gave way to greater diversity and complexity. From 1970 to 2005, multigenerational households decreased from 16.1 percent of households to 6.9 percent; one-person households increased from 20.3 percent to 29.5 percent; and nuclear households held relatively steady between 56 and 61 percent.[1] Arranged marriages (*omiai*) dwindled, and almost disappeared by the end of the century. Tanaka-san reported in 2000 that she never heard the term *sengyou shufu* anymore. More women were getting jobs, and marrying later or not at all. Many refused to marry men whose mothers lived with them. And they were having fewer or no children. The average age of marriage for women increased from 23 in 1950 to 25.9 in 1990, then to 27.0 in 2000 and 28.8 in 2010.[2] Meanwhile, the fertility rate dropped from 3.65 children in 1950 to 1.54 in 1990, 1.36 in 2000, and to a low of 1.26 in 2005.[3]

By the 1990s, women had achieved equality in education, and a majority were working outside the home. As in the United States, women were still struggling for admission to the highest ranks of government, business, and the professions, and they were grappling to balance career with family. Most women looked for work or activities that enhanced rather than conflicted with their family roles, suggesting that the professional housewife ideal still lingered. Their efforts to take on new roles while fulfilling old ones generated strains as well as successes, sometimes showing up in new kinds of mental health problems.

The high school girls we saw on the streets in 1958 generally wore generic, conservative uniforms; forty years later they were romping around Shibuya and other parts of Tokyo in tiny miniskirts, high heels, loose and high socks, and colored hair, following the latest teenage styles. I found this contrast jarring. Was it simply self-indulgence, or were they reveling in the freedom to do things their mothers could never have done? Merry White writes about how the passion for brand-name clothes led some high school girls to hook up with middle-aged married men and provide sexual favors for money.[4] If they could keep their parents or other adults from knowing about these activities, as many did, they might go on later to proper, fully acceptable marriages. When they did marry, however, some young women were unprepared for anything resembling a housewife role, certainly not in the traditional mold. I was surprised to meet among the wives of Japanese scholars studying at Harvard in 1990 one woman who had been so indulged that she hardly knew how to keep house; she was always looking for entertainment, completely dependent on her husband.

Looking at the Japan of the late 1990s, I wondered whether this was a nation suspicious of radical change, determined to preserve its "homogeneous" culture. Was it still a male-dominated society that demanded conformity, a society that "hammers down the nail that sticks out," as the old saying goes? Michael Zielenziger presents this view in *Shutting out the Sun: How Japan Created Its Own Lost Generation*.[5] He sees a clue to understanding Japanese society in the *hikikomori* phenomenon that became well known in the 1990s: growing numbers of young Japanese, mostly men, who withdraw from the world of rigid judgmentalism and stay for years within the safety of their (usually) maternal homes. Or does Veronica Chambers tell us more about Japanese society with her more positive spin in *Kickboxing Geishas: How Modern Japanese Women Are Changing Their Nation*?[6] She reports on women who are making progress, generation by generation, toward greater individuation, initiative, gender equality, and better relationships at home.

She describes innovative and successful women who are gradually influencing the larger society to change in more forward-looking ways.

Zielenziger and Chambers present accurate yet contrasting portrayals of Japanese society at the turn of the century. Rapid social change, even positive change, inevitably poses problems for the society as a whole and for individuals. It creates new choices and generates conflict about how much to hold on to the old values, how much to embrace innovation, or how to combine the two. For women and their families, the ideal of the professional housewife, though rarely articulated anymore, casts a shadow on their decision making. For example, Susan Holloway and Ofra Goldstein-Gidoni's recent studies on young Japanese mothers demonstrate that many are still attracted by historic models of parenting. Holloway finds, for instance, that these mothers generally believe in parenting that allows the child to learn from life experience while monitoring the child for emotional self-regulation.[7] Based on her fieldwork in the 2000s, Goldstein-Gidoni concludes that Japanese society is still largely oriented toward demarcated gender roles, and state agencies such as the media and the consumer market reproduce traditional roles for women.[8] Whatever their eventual choices, all Japanese women still have to deal at some level with the continuing, though weakening, influence of this ideal. Over the past twenty years, I have encountered many women who are making satisfying lives for themselves and embracing values that suit their own goals, even though they might differ from previous generations. I have also seen a range of problems arising for women who go to either extreme, hanging on too much to the caretaking role or avoiding it altogether.

MORE OPTIONS

We discovered very different patterns of social and psychiatric symptoms in the 1970s–1990s than we had before. In the early years after the war, Tokyo clinics most commonly reported cases of women suffering from depression or from psychosomatic illnesses, but also some cases of neurotic children who seemed caught in the conflict between mother and grandmother. The apparent cause was often suppressed anger and hurt due to mistreatment and exploitation by the husband's family. No wonder such women were depressed! They were caught in a pattern of abuse from which there was no escape, without anyone to whom to appeal for help. Sometimes their own relatives would take them in if they fled, but generally they would be pressed to return to their husbands after a brief respite, as there was really no other place for them to go. Wife abuse was generally considered a family issue not requiring interference from the outside. Only in the 1990s did wife abuse become recognized as a social problem and brought into the open, with the construction of shelters and the development of specialized counseling.

With the passing years, women gradually secured a stronger place and a more audible voice in Japanese society. As some of the extreme forms of oppression began to disappear, a frequent saying was that stockings and women had gotten stronger after the war. We heard fewer complaints about the cruel oppression of women or conflicts with domineering in-laws. Instead, we discovered the social isolation of young wives in *danchi* (large apartment complexes). They were alone all day and so concerned about keeping up appearances with their neighbors that they could not be comfortable and confidential with anyone. By the 1970s, many young women began refusing to live with their in-laws, and separate housing became more common. The divorce rate increased, albeit slowly and not approaching the U.S. level (figure 5.1). A divorced woman most often retained custody of her children, whereas previously the children had generally remained the property of the father and his family.

Women's options in life have greatly increased from the days when marriage was a necessity. Many have become freer than their brothers to study or travel because they are less pressured to get a prestigious permanent job right away. They are as loved and as spoiled as their brothers. In fact, some are so

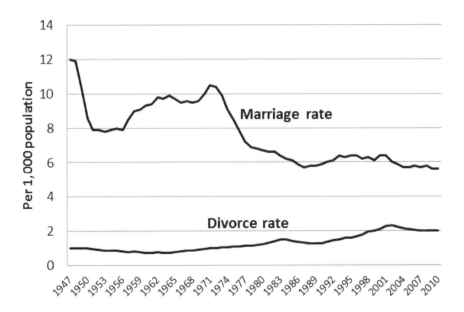

Figure 5.1.   Marriage and Divorce Rate. *Source:* Ministry of Health, Labor, and Welfare, *Jinkou doutai toukei* (Vital Statistics), 1947–2010.

spoiled that they do not know how to cook, clean the house, or care for children.

Despite increasing opportunities since the late 1970s, women have continued to struggle to find a secure and satisfying place in the working world while experiencing satisfaction and success as a mother and wife at the same time. Job opportunities for women increased during the "bubble" years of the 1980s, including some positions in the upper track of lifetime employment, but the obstacles for working women have diminished only slowly. Mary Brinton argues that labor markets, the education system, and the family, as well as social norms, combine to produce strong gender inequality in Japan. Parents have much lower aspirations for daughters than for sons, and once women enter the labor market they are constrained by highly sex-segregated work roles.[9] Many women have had to stop working when they married or gave birth. Those who returned to work later often found nothing available except temporary jobs with long hours, lower pay, no benefits, and little chance of promotion. Most women have felt compelled to choose right after college whether to pursue a full-time working career or marry and have children. Moreover, once a woman chose a lower track, perhaps because she planned to have a family, she could not easily change her mind later and move to a higher track, even in the same company. A woman seriously pursuing a career but not ruling out marriage might find her best chance in professions that offer some flexibility, such as dentists or doctors in private practice, writers, journalists, possibly college teaching, or independent entrepreneurs. She might also search for the highly desired but rare man who would share in housework and childcare. Most helpful of all, perhaps, was a nearby grandmother who could help with children.

Men, employers, and the society have become more tolerant of working women, partly because in the post-bubble economy many families needed the added income. Yet the feeling that employees should be totally devoted to the company and that mothers should be home taking care of children and catering to their hardworking husbands has been slow to die. As recently as 2007, Hakuo Yanagisawa, the Minister of Health, Labor, and Welfare, called women "birth-giving machines" in a badly miscalculated attempt to encourage women to have more children to reverse the declining birthrate.[10] He apologized after the predictable outrage, but such residual attitudes help explain why neither the government nor employers have done much to make it easier for women to combine work and family. Day care facilities are often criticized as insufficient and the hours too short, and women still resist using baby-sitters who are not relatives. Many elementary school children become *kagikko*, children who carry a key to let themselves into their houses after school and are alone until suppertime when Mother returns. This was unimaginable in the Japan of 1958, of course, and less common in middle-class America where mothers were more accustomed to baby-sitters.

NEW STYLES OF RELATIONSHIPS

With the decline in arranged marriages, Japanese men and women needed to cultivate the art of courtship, yet they were not prepared with the requisite social skills or experience. The traditional family pattern with clear gender roles had discouraged socializing and encouraged people to form relationships only in the context of the accepted gendered segregation. Both men and women had little experience in forming or sustaining the give-and-take of mutual relationships. Many were unskilled in coping with horizontal relationships: cross-sex friendships, dating, couples in nuclear families. Young people were slow to cultivate new ways to get to know potential partners through dating.

Meanwhile, the changing family structure and new values necessitated greater cooperation and intimacy between husband and wife. The strength of a family began to depend less on a prescribed structure, and more on the strength of the marital bond. Women more than men pressed for change. Wives were eager for role modification and for an interactive, communicative relationship, while husbands tended to feel more secure and satisfied with their traditional role. Women pushed for equality at home and work faster than men could accept or adapt. Wives complained of having to do all the housework and childcare, even while holding down jobs needed to earn money for the family, and husbands lamented that their wives neglected them. These differences in views have been described as Japan's gender "gap." Many couples foundered; they needed to reformulate the relationship but were unable to do so.

In the 1980s, the media popularized the term "Narita divorce," describing couples who would embark upon their honeymoon and determine that their marriage was a mistake by the time they returned to Narita Airport. Having gone through the expected time-honored rituals surrounding the wedding, they discovered they did not really know each other and perhaps did not even like each other. They did not wish to uphold outward proprieties (*tatemae*) in the absence of a good relationship. Around the same time, an older age group of Japanese was experiencing a new and different kind of marital problem. Some husbands who retired, expecting to be comfortably cared for by their wives for the rest of their lives, were instead greeted by a demand for a divorce (commonly referred to as *jukunen rikon*, or late-life divorce). Such a wife, who had been pursuing her own activities during her husband's long working hours, was not inclined to start staying home with a man she had never really gotten to know. These unfortunate husbands were called *nureochiba* (wet leaves clinging to one's shoes), or even *sodaigomi* (large trash).

My most direct encounter with this gap in consciousness occurred during the 1980s and 1990s at Harvard University's Mental Health Clinic, where I consulted with Japanese graduate students, scholars, and researchers who came for a few years with their families. These couples might never have come to the attention of clinicians if they were not facing the anxieties of living and working overseas. The husbands were under great stress, studying or conducting research in a foreign language and culture. A few husbands came to the clinic by themselves, usually with symptoms of depression or anxiety. But mostly the wives came first, with symptoms of depression, anorexia, or bulimia—or even shoplifting. Typically they were aware of their husbands' stresses and they were trying very hard to be supportive caretakers, but they found their own needs unrecognized. At home in Japan, they could care for their households, even with a job, as they knew the stores and streets and had friends or family nearby. But as new arrivals in Cambridge, they found themselves newly dependent on their husbands. This was usually because their husbands had greater command of English and could better navigate the necessities of daily life: banking, shopping, and driving lessons or licenses. The wives were often lonely, finding it hard to make friends in a strange place, having had to give up jobs in Japan, or perhaps being stuck at home alone with small children. Not wanting to bother their busy husbands, they did not complain but suffered alone. The wife who was caught shoplifting first awakened me to the general problem. She had never been a shoplifter before; rather her shoplifting seemed to be a cry for help. When we invited her husband in for a joint consultation, he was surprised to hear how miserable she felt. It never occurred to him that she was in need of support; he only looked to her for support. After that he made an effort to be more understanding, as did many of the other husbands once they were made aware of their wives' suffering.

"TOO-GOOD" MOTHERS (AND WIVES)

While Japanese mothers are generally praised and admired for their mothering skills, Amy Borovoy makes it clear that there can be too much of a good thing. She sees hazards as well as strengths rooted in the nature of the caretaking role. Her research explores a major problem in recent decades: the challenges faced by the wives of alcoholic men. For a year or more, she met with a group of these wives in their regular group meetings at a public clinic. American mental health professionals would label these women as codependents or enablers. They did not cause the husbands' alcoholism, but they were complicit with it. They were indulging their husbands too much, could not say "no" to them. They tended to assume responsibility for any problem in the family.[11]

Although the treatment at that clinic was based on Alcoholics Anonymous as developed in the United States, Borovoy found that the response of Japanese wives to their husband's alcoholism was quite different from that of

American wives. Specifically, she heard no wives declaring their right to a separate, independent life, none rebelling against the housewife role or demanding a divorce. Rather, after talking about the pain of their struggles and searching for ways to help their husbands and their families, some women began to listen to what the social workers were telling them. They recognized that alcoholism was a disease and that giving their husbands whatever they wanted, including liquor, did more long-term harm than good. They also came to sense that they were too intertwined emotionally with their husbands. They found greater peace for themselves as they learned to refrain from meeting all of the husbands' wishes, to feel less guilty for the husbands' problems, and to put some degree of emotional distance between themselves and their husbands. Borovoy found they resisted change mostly because of the *strengths* inherent in their housewife role: the importance of maintaining the family's stability, the wife's own social status, and the husband's income. Still they seemed to realize that the optimal fulfillment of their role at times required doing less, not more. As they learned to say "no" occasionally, some even learned to leave a drunken husband where he collapsed on the sidewalk, so he might begin to see the need to take more responsibility for himself.[12]

Borovoy takes up another example of the too-good mother in discussing disturbed adolescents who refuse to go to school (*toukou kyohi*), stay in the house all day without going outside (*hikikomori*), or sometimes become violent to their parents, particularly the mother (*kateinai bouryoku*). She notes that these mothers are much more resistant to change than the wives of alcoholics because they are so strongly identified with their children and blame themselves for the child's abusive behavior. Seeing a problem with the child makes them give *more*, as they interpret any problem as indicating unfulfilled *amae*. The child, finding that his demands are met by compliance, becomes like a dictator in the house. He may demand that the mother fulfill all his requests and strike her if thwarted. He often sleeps during the day but stays awake at night. Increasingly afraid of being hit, the mother becomes even more cowed and does whatever the child says.[13]

Hasegawa Hospital, where I supervised social workers for four to six weeks a year from 1989 to 2006, had many such cases, mostly hospitalized children in their teens or twenties, but a few in outpatient treatment or day care. The underlying diagnosis was usually borderline personality disorder, although the upfront diagnosis might be depression, anxiety, eating disorders, or antisocial behavior. Hasegawa probably had more than its share of such adolescents, as many other hospitals were reluctant to take them because of the extraordinary and long-term difficulties in their therapy.

PSYCHOLOGICAL EFFECTS

Mental health professionals only began giving the diagnosis of borderline personality disorder after the war, but it has boomed ever since. Perhaps this reflects developments in society as well as changes in the profession. Both the United States and Japan have experienced more rebelliousness and internal turmoil among young people in recent decades, conditions that suggest such a diagnosis. As these societies made the transition from more rigid and moralistic societies to more open, flexible, and less punitive ones, they encountered all the messy contradictions inherent in this transition, and this seemed to be particularly indicative of borderline personality disorders. The more rigid but clearly structured traditional societies fostered more clear-cut neuroses or psychoses. Borderline personality disorder cases, a quite diverse wastebasket category, tended to emerge from inconsistencies in society and in family upbringing. Could it be that when a society solves one problem, a new and different one arises? Perhaps a new social structure, even a preferred one, produces a different set of difficulties?

For several decades, Hasegawa Hospital employed a larger number of social workers than is common in Japan, and hospital teams planned containment, medication, and psychotherapy for the patient and the family, including the social worker's family therapy. In the 1990s, I often encountered the following pattern. A patient, more often a male, who was docile, shy, and close to his mother as a child, becomes a school refuser when he hits a social or academic difficulty in junior high. No one insists that he go to school, even though education through ninth grade is nationally mandated. Instead, the mother, feeling her previous caretaking was insufficient, becomes totally solicitous and helps the child feel comfortable at home, while the school offers the resources of the school counselor and the nurse's office but makes no demands on the child. If the child does not get better fairly soon, the problem continues and escalates, often into violence toward his mother. Even without going to school, the child officially graduates from middle school. The mother may go to a local clinic for counseling, but the child refuses. The parents are reluctant to define the child as a psychiatric problem because of the stigma, so they cooperate with the child while hiding him at home. The child does not come to the attention of the hospital until the problem has become rather extreme and the child begins hitting the father as well as the mother. At that point, the patient is hospitalized. Then he is controlled at least temporarily, probably with medication and/or restraints.

Social workers reported in the 1990s that they would initially see only the patient and the mother together, since the father was too busy at work. The assumption that the child's care was the sole responsibility of the mother initially went unquestioned. After some time without improvement, and perhaps after the mother had expressed anger about the father's not taking responsibility, the father might agree to join the family sessions at the hospital. That is the point, the social workers stress, at which the patient and the family would begin to improve.

This demonstrates one of the most serious failings of the "too-good mother": that she cannot set limits and feels she has to meet her child's every request. This capitulation of the mother to the child's wishes is also evident in cases of *hikikomori* when the child does not become violent but continues to stay enclosed at home, out of sight, not studying or working, sometimes well into adulthood. Some of these indulgent mothers might have been *kyouiku mama*, catering full-time to children while pressuring them to study for entrance exams. That tendency is often intensified by an "absent" father, an overworked father who spends hardly more than a few hours on Sunday with his family. Many fathers have in effect relinquished their authority in the family, partly because of the demands of their jobs. Male authority in the home is thus undermined by the gender division of labor. When the father can be brought back into active participation in family life, however, the family benefits.

I have often wondered whether a distortion of the principle of *amae* contributed to the feeling on the part of late-twentieth-century Japanese parents, teachers, and counselors that a child should be allowed to do as he pleases and given what he wants. Formerly, the only children who were given such latitude were preschool age, under seven. It may be that the greater affluence of economic growth in Japan contributed to a rejection of discipline and austerity in favor of a new extreme of permissiveness. I know of counselors in the 1980s who advised parents to let their children do as they wish. They did not encourage limit setting.

Certainly Japanese parents have become less authoritarian since the 1950s, more inclined to let children be "free" to grow up without so many rules, with the only pressure being to study. Doi, however, stresses that such spoiling is not *amae*, nor is it healthy nurturing on the part of the mother. In Doi's view, when a mother spoils her child, she is acting on her overidentification with the child and projecting her own wishes onto the child. In other words, the mother may act to appease the child as a way to obtain peace and approval for herself rather than to respond to the real needs of the child.[14] Likewise, some of the "education mothers" may have pushed their children to study so that the *mother* could feel successful.

When the mother fails to respond to the child's genuine *amae*, the child is likely to escalate his demands and attacks on his mother. The child's innermost needs, his real *amae*, may be covered up by some overt request. He may want something that is lacking, genuine emotional closeness and understanding from his mother, and he may need the limits and structure that could give him protection. His mother's compliance is not nearly as important to him as the strength and wisdom he needs to prevent a misdeed he may regret. He also needs her to be a real person, so he can learn to differentiate between her feelings and his own. He does not need her to be an extension of himself, nor does the mother need him to be an extension of herself.

PSYCHOLOGICAL DISORDERS, UNITED STATES VERSUS JAPAN

Different historical periods and cultures beget different patterns of strengths and vulnerabilities for individuals and society. For instance, how do disturbed teenagers in Japan compare with those in the United States? We observe major differences in behavior, even though the underlying problems may be similar. Unhappy Japanese teenagers tend to stay inside the house, keeping to their own room in a solitary existence. American teenagers will go out, and may get involved with delinquent activities and companions. We might say that American teenagers act *out* while Japanese teenagers act *in*. Whereas the American teenager hides his dependent feelings and struts his independence, the Japanese teenager lays bare his dependence and his demand for total family care. Both are rebelling in infantile ways. While one tries to deny the *amae* urge, the other drowns himself in it.

Likewise, as Borovoy notes, Japanese wives tend to efface themselves in service to their family to an extent that Americans would deem excessive. American wives might find the Japanese housewife role too confining, while Japanese wives might view an American wife's attention to personal care as selfish. Yet Borovoy stresses that no matter how limiting it might seem, the Japanese housewife role provides stability, status, and self-respect for women and gives them freedom from worry about holding on to a husband. Many do not feel anxious about such things as their physical attractiveness, but are secure in their status. It is the American, not the Japanese, who says apologetically, "I am *just* a housewife."[15]

Doi sees a denial of dependent feelings (*amae*) in the behavior of many Americans and even in many Western psychological theories.[16] Americans do not like to see themselves as dependent, and often resist acknowledging their dependence. Americans do not idealize childhood as much as Japanese do and are typically eager to grow up or at least to take on the privileges of adulthood. American men, perhaps even more than women, are likely to go into vigorous denial if their independence is questioned. The masculine ideal is to be a strong, rugged individual, leaning on no one, beholden to no one, fighting if necessary for independence. The American glorification of the Western cowboy is no accident. Americans want to be totally free to make their own choices. Doi would point out that this is unrealistic, that no one is that free. All of us are unavoidably dependent on other people, groups, and institutions. And in recent years, American psychologists have begun to point out that male violence, verbal or physical, particularly within the family, comes from the man's unwillingness to admit and deal with his dependency needs. Terrence Real argues that a man's violence and depression are closely related, and often stem from a man's unmet dependency need that he will not acknowledge to himself. Women may succumb to this as well, but they are less reluctant to admit to some dependency. [17]

The United States has more violence overall than Japan, yet less school refusal, withdrawing inside the house for long periods, and violence to parents. Americans have less of the excessive caretaking and long-term dependence on parents evident in Japan. An American child who is unhappy with school would probably switch to another school or a different group of friends or get into a fight with classmates. Once during the late 1980s, two psychologists, one American and one Japanese, were collegially chatting for a half hour about family violence before they discovered that the American was referring to *child* abuse while the Japanese was referring to *parent* abuse. Perhaps we could say that *over-dependence* is more of a problem in Japan while *over-independence* is more of a problem in the United States.

Even as the professional housewife ideal eroded, it remained as an obstacle for women who wanted to combine marriage and career. Young women in the 1990s often talked of struggling with the career versus marriage decision. Many women were reluctant to compromise with the ideal, worried about social disapproval. Those women who pursued careers often felt guilty because they worried that they had neglected their children. Other career women gave up wishes for marriage and/or children because they just could not see how they could meet that high ideal. Many men, even while adjusting to women's work schedules if it helped family finances, longed for wives like their mothers who took care of everything. At the same time, some women who were hoping for marriage sacrificed their ambitions and settled for low-paying jobs or became "parasite singles"—living rent-free with their parents and using their salaries to travel, shop for expensive clothes, and enjoy nightlife—until they could find a man to support them.

Japanese young women have gained the freedom of choice, but are often filled with conflicted feelings. The wives I talked with in 1958 experienced little internal conflict since they knew their only option was to marry. Americans hold tightly to the idea of individual choice, but they tend to forget that having choices carries its own complexities. The prevalence of divorce in the United States is a testament to the problems associated with free choice and high expectations. Americans see marriage as based on the emotional relationship and the satisfaction of the two parties involved, not as a job of making a family. Americans have a marriage ideal that leaves them vulnerable to disillusionment. Americans with problematic marital relationships are less inclined to be patient and tolerant and are not interested in Japanese-style "divorce inside marriage." Maybe we should rethink the old Japanese saying that marriage is too important to be based on romantic love.

Borovoy discusses the importance of a Japanese wife choosing where to draw the line between how much care or nurturing is enough and how much may be too much or not necessary.[18] Despite this almost universal struggle, many are learning how to find an acceptable place to draw the line. They are recognizing that they can take better care of their families if they also take care of themselves. They see that self-sacrifice can breed inner resentment, which then inhibits empathy. Self-sacrifice can be noble and even essential, but it can also be counterproductive. Many women still make sure their home responsibilities are taken care of before they take on an outside hobby or job. Many women seek an outlet for themselves that will also benefit their families, such as community or school volunteering. And a few are starting to look for ways to more comfortably combine work and family.

NEW PROBLEMS, 1990S–PRESENT

By the late 1990s a quite different era was under way, with accelerated social change and new patterns of psychological disorders. The collapse of the bubble economy in 1991 and the ensuing long recession had presented new challenges, as diminished financial and employment security translated into greater personal insecurity. Faltering lifetime employment and seniority systems reduced the number of permanent, full-time employees (*seishain*), and the numbers of freelancers and part-timers surged. The share of nonregular workers (temporary workers and others without job security) increased from 20.2 percent of the workforce in 1990 to 33.7 percent in 2010.[19] Some of the nonregular employees are referred to as "freeters," for "free workers." Usually males under thirty-five and without full-time jobs, they freelance without benefits or job security, and often live with their parents. They have trouble finding partners or starting a family, and their failure to lock into a career early jeopardizes their chances to do so later in life. Another type is known as "NEETs," an acronym coined in Britain for "no employment, education, or training." Some of the NEETs deliberately remain unemployed when they fall off their desired career track and are unwilling to take a job that does not measure up to their standards. I have known several young people with all the right family and education credentials who became long-term unemployed because they did not get the job they wanted after college, or they quit their first job when it did not fit their expectations. Some quit for rather opaque reasons, seemingly due to a misfit between the individual's personality and the social patterns on the job. Overall unemployment rose from 2.1 percent in 1990 to a high of 5.4 percent in 2002, declining to 3.9 percent in 2007 and then rebounding to 5.1 percent in 2009 and 2010. For the fifteen- to twenty-four-year-old cohort, unemployment surged from 4.3 percent in 1990 to 10.1 in 2003, then 7.2 percent in 2008, and 9.4 percent in 2010.[20]

Many mental health professionals believe that the social strains of this era are fostering new types of psychological problems. Japan has experienced a marked rise in psychological disorders and reported suicides since the 1990s (figures 5.2–5.6). While some of the overall rise in psychological disorders may reflect an increasing willingness to report and/or treat these disorders, the scale of the rise is considerable (figure 5.3). Moreover, we find a more rapid increase in the more socially conditioned mood/affective disorders (figure 5.4) compared to schizophrenia and other delusional disorders (figure 5.5), and we also see a substantial gap between men and women.

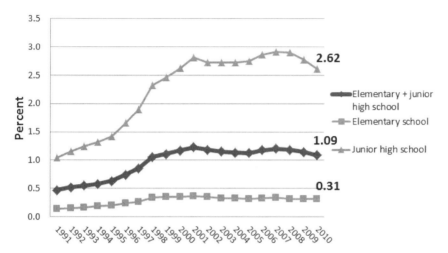

Figure 5.2. Proportion of School-Age Children Taking a Long-Term Absence from School. *Source:* Ministry of Education, Culture, Sports, Science, and Technology, *Gakkou kihon chousa* (Basic Survey of Schools), 1991–2010.

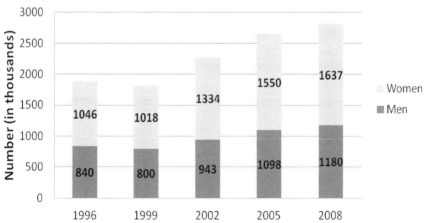

Figure 5.3. Increase in Mental and Behavioral Disorders. *Source:* Ministry of Health, Labor, and Welfare, *Kanja chousa* (Patient Survey), 1996–2008.

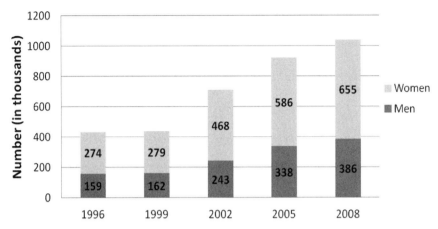

Figure 5.4.   Increase in Mood (Affective) Disorders. *Source:* Ministry of Health, Labor and Welfare, *Kanja chousa* (Patient Survey), 1996–2008.

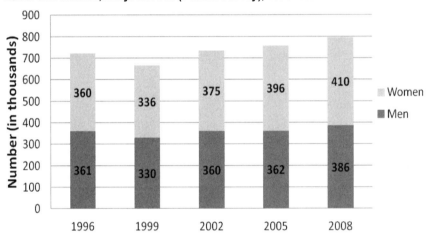

Figure 5.5.   Increase in Schizophrenia and Schizotypal and Delusional Disorders. *Source:* Ministry of Health, Labor, and Welfare, *Kanja chousa* (Patient Survey), 1996–2008.

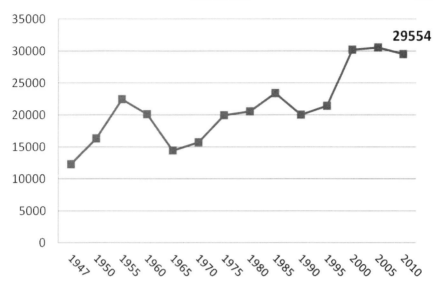

Figure 5.6.   **Number of Suicides.** *Source:* **Ministry of Health, Labor, and Welfare,** *Jinkou doutai toukei* **(Vital Statistics), 1947–2010.**

The depth and magnitude of these changes came home to me when I learned of the recent rise in "sexless" young couples (figure 5.7). I heard about this from psychiatrists doing marriage counseling, but there were also write-ups in professional journals and popular magazines. Clinicians also told me of increasing referrals of children who just could not get along with other children at school, or of mothers who gave their children no guidance. What a difference between these mothers and the devoted professional housewives with well-trained children I knew in 1958–1960! A prominent psychiatrist reported to me in 2008 about cases of patients who seemed "empty," as if they had no self and did not understand their own feelings, much less the feelings of others. This was consistent with what I was hearing from some young people about the new phenomenon of "K.Y." (*kuuki o yomenai,* or the inability to "read" the mood or atmosphere or the vibes between people). This suggested to me that the skill of *sassuru,* which had so impressed me fifty years ago, was dwindling among younger people. All counselors reported more people having trouble solving arguments or conflicts among themselves, and individuals having trouble making decisions. Some individuals would wander back and forth trying to decide on a life course, while others were too paralyzed by anxiety even to begin the process.

Mental health problems grew as unemployment and underemployment increased. The movie *Tokyo Sonata* centers on the anguish and humiliation of a Japanese salaryman who is laid off and feels compelled to create a charade of working rather than tell his wife. A report by sociologist Matthew Marr comparing homelessness in Tokyo and in Los Angeles found that social

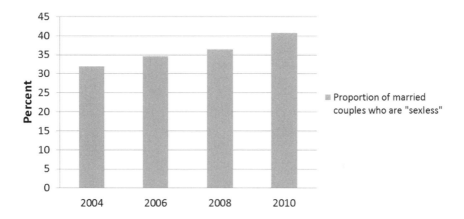

Figure 5.7.   Figure 5.7. Increase in Sexless Couples in Japan. *Note:* Couples are counted as "sexless" if they report not having sex within the last month. *Source:* Japan Family Planning Association, *Danjo no seikatsu to ishiki ni kansuru chousa* (Survey of Men's and Women's Lifestyles and Attitudes), 2004–2010.

workers in Tokyo focused exclusively on finding jobs for homeless men, while social workers in Los Angeles sought to reconnect them with relatives or to find a stable living situation for them as well as helping them find work. Marr points out that without a job and steady wages, a Japanese man feels as though he has no home, no place in the family; he cannot fulfill his role in the family, and sometimes he chooses to leave it. That is why the social workers put sole priority on finding work for homeless men.[21] For men in particular, being jobless decimates one's pride and social status and can lead to isolation, depression, or suicide.

So how might social trends contribute to the increase in psychological stress and the emergence of new types of disorders? Emiko Ochiai interprets recent developments as a collapse of the modern family and other social institutions that had been stable for many years.[22] Individuals had gained freedom to choose their path in life, and the goal of self-fulfillment was no longer shameful or "selfish." Yet without the stability of the employment system and the family system, what was there to guide or support people as they tried to navigate the new options?

Relationships became problematic, as many people did not know how to relate to others, or even how to make friends. They did not understand themselves, much less others. In such circumstances, intimacy was difficult or impossible. The numerous instances of "sexless couples" was ample testimony, but that was corroborated by the appearance of more cases of "2-D" (two-dimensional) lovers who turned to the "*otaku*" subculture and virtual reality and avoided the demands of 3-D relationships with real human beings.

Psychiatrists who treat sexless couples relate that many are afraid of intimacy, even afraid of touching. Women sometimes fear pain, and elite men, established in prestigious employment, may be unable to have an erection (*bokki shougai*), often unconsciously worrying about critical, overprotective mothers. One therapist relates that he occasionally tells couples to "get their parents out of the bed!" The trouble many have in navigating modern romantic life or even close friendships show up in government survey statistics: A quarter of men and women between ages thirty and thirty-four are virgins, and 50 percent of men and women in Japan do not have friends of the opposite sex. [23]

Such problems were not seen in the 1950s or 1960s when structures for the family, for marriage, and for employment, and rules for social interaction were clear and widely accepted. Even during the bubble years of the 1980s, when some flexibility (and anxiety) had entered the employment and social systems, they remained stable for the most part. That stability has now been shaken by two decades of economic stagnation. As established structures become less dependable, there is more freedom, more choice, and fewer rules. Today, the *ie* system is moribund; husband and wife roles have become more fluid and subject to invention; and a child can no longer assume that study and success in school entrance exams will guarantee secure lifetime employment in business or government. Grown children cannot expect parents to make decisions or find spouses for them. Young couples do not expect to live with their parents, nor do the elderly expect to live with their children. Time-honored skills in the use of language (uses of polite and honorific speech, for example), for so long a universal means of acknowledging a relationship, are now spotty or forgotten.

More Japanese seek adaptability, flexibility, and spontaneity in this new environment, but they do not know to attain these goals. Even young people from successful families may loll into chronic unemployment a few years after graduating from excellent universities. I have known sons of famous fathers who leave a job or two and then stay home for years. Some have spent all their spare time studying for entrance exams, may not know how to make friends, much less how to relate to the opposite sex on a date, or they may find it impossible to relax and be spontaneous in bed with a spouse. For previous generations, there was little dating, just formal introductions, and young wives (like the young Suzuki-san) were told to let their husbands be their guides in bed. Today, those strictures are gone, but young people have trouble building emotional or sexual intimacy without the old social props. Learning of such cases in Japan, I am reminded of Japanese students in the United States, who consulting for less serious matters, ask me how to talk to a doctor, a professor, or even a friend. Some are frightened by the expectation that they should size up the situation on their own, decide how to deal with it, and then take action. They grope for external guidelines, American codes of behavior that largely do not exist.

Some young people feel liberated by the easing of pressures to conform to defined social patterns, and thrive on the new freedoms. They welcome the chance for greater spontaneity, and they find no difficulty in making the most of social relationships and less structured employment opportunities. Such individuals are able to create and enjoy new relationships, new activities, new institutions, and new enterprises. Veronica Chambers describes the way women in Japan today are breaking traditions and reformulating the rules of their society as they make choices about work and family based on their own skills, preferences, and fulfillment.[24] Some pursue careers but others decide to stay home with children because they feel that that lifestyle is most personally satisfying. Several women in the second and third generations of our families (chapters 2–4) exemplify this. One woman whom I know well, after some overseas exposure, established her own international consulting business for various Japanese and American corporations. Another, while raising three children with her hardworking but cooperative husband, has changed jobs frequently according to family needs, always moving up in the offices of various businesses. Men also have more opportunities to go into a job or vocation based on what interests them and the kind of life they prefer to lead. One young man of my acquaintance, with all As from an elite U.S. university, easily found employment, first in a prestigious engineering firm and then in banking. But within a few years he had left both jobs because he found them too confining and demanding, with long hours so he had no time for a personal life. Giving up the large salary he once had, he opened a risky but personally more rewarding consulting business of his own.

While both men and women experience the anxieties of making decisions when the social guidelines are no longer clear, I find that men are having a harder time adjusting to the loss of the old structures. The most perplexing questions for women are whether to marry or pursue employment or how to combine the two. Frequently they vacillate trying to make decisions. In some cases, they end up with an unhappy marriage, a low-paying or unsatisfying job, or wishing they had children, feeling lonely and dissatisfied with work and family. But women have been working to advance their cause since the 1970s. They have been pushing for more freedom and wider choices, as well as a more equal and cooperative relationship with a spouse, and therefore they have developed slightly more ability to be assertive and to relate. They are somewhat less likely to fall into the *hikikomori*, the passive, stay-at-home-with-mother stance of the young men about whom Satoshi Kotani writes.[25] But when it comes to dating and marriage, they say it is hard nowadays to find men who are self-confident, are active in relationships, and can become reciprocating partners. Men more than women lived easily for decades with the salaryman system that gave them status and self-respect, provided a stable income and good benefits, and gave employees the security and companionship of the company community. Hence the "gap" (discussed above) arose between men and women: While women pushed for change, men were content with the status quo. When the status quo began to crumble, men were more confused about how to redirect their goals.

With such pervasive uncertainty and indecision in these changing times, the views of scholars like Ochiai might be alarming. According to her, enduring and stable social and economic institutions are in the process of collapse, leaving Japanese with neither a strong family system nor a dependable employment structure.[26] But her collapse does not mean the collapse of Japanese society in general. Rather it signifies a search for and a movement toward a new system or systems. In this case, it seems to be a more individualistic, more diversified society. No one group is pushing for particular changes, and no clear political cleavages between groups are evident. Changes are coming about gradually as individuals make a variety of decisions that their parents or grandparents would not have made. These adaptations give us clues about coming trends and raise provocative questions about how to encourage healthy, positive developments.

COPING WITH CHANGE

Certain postwar institutions served a purpose. The "lifetime" employment (*shuushin koyou*) system worked well while the economy continued its steady, rapid growth until 1990. Under those conditions, it helped both businesses and individuals to prosper. The family system, modeled on the *ie*, was essentially stable, and provided support, guidance, and social cohesion for families and individuals. The underlying, often unconscious, principle of social life was to identify with one's group, follow its rules of behavior, and further the group's interests while the group took care of its members.

Japanese society has transformed, however, and the Japanese government, mental health professionals, and individuals must join forces to adapt to this transformation. The government could help people adjust to new social and economic circumstances by doing more to enact family-friendly policies: support working mothers, facilitate job mobility, and strengthen the social safety net. This could nudge people to adjust their values by removing the stigma of onetime failure or time off for childcare or psychological healing. Policy measures could give positive valuation to the lifetime experience people accumulate and encourage them to continue working in various kinds of productive endeavor instead of retreating to inactivity to save face. Successful economic reforms could bring stronger financial security, which for most young couples is the prime consideration in the decision to marry and have children.

Meanwhile, Japanese individuals themselves would do well to embrace this new era rather than shun it. They may need to develop personal skills in decision making and assertiveness to thrive in this environment. They must be creative and adventurous, willing to take risks. They need to be aware of their own best interests and able to think through issues and decide when change is needed at work or at home. A new individualism is increasingly in evidence, as more and more people feel the need for greater freedom of choice. But along with that freedom, constructive individualism demands individual responsibility. We can see now that my friend Itou-san was ahead of her time, showing natural adventurousness in the 1960s and sustaining criticism for it.

Scholars such as Ayumi Sasagawa are calling this era individualistic, having observed individuals making their own decisions based on their own best judgments for themselves and for those they care about. Sasagawa's account describes women who no longer follow the earlier rules that women should devote themselves totally to the care of their children, husband, or other family members, even to the point of considerable self-sacrifice. Rather, they think in terms of their own self-fulfillment—what lifestyle they prefer and how they want to enhance their important relationships. Some decide to marry, have children, and stay home full-time, but not because they feel socially pressured or morally obligated. Instead, they see their self-fulfillment in enjoying more flexible time at home with children and husband while pursuing their own outside activities or hobbies and avoiding the complications of combining family and career. Others decide that pursuing an interesting career is most important, and they choose to forgo marriage and children. Still others want both family and career, and search out acceptable ways to combine them. These women, who in previous years were considered deviants, today are models for the healthy future development of Japanese society. They represent a change in social norms and in their own attitudes toward themselves.[27]

While the above principles apply to both men and women, there are some issues peculiar to the feminine role, including those arising from the professional housewife ideal. I thoroughly absorbed Takeo Doi's teaching about the necessity for a child to be able to *amaeru* on his mother during the first few years. And I greatly respected the excellent child rearing of the professional housewives I observed during our first stay in Japan. Today, however, not only is this impractical, but I see other ways—besides total obedience to the professional housewife way—to achieve the same goals for the child's healthy development.

Doi points out the importance of the intimate communication between child and parent, with the mother always near her baby and often carrying the baby (*dakko* or *ombu*), always sensing her child's needs.[28] This kind of close communication and awareness of and responsiveness to the baby's needs are crucial to a child's healthy development for at least the first three years, and preferably much longer. However, most experience shows that it does not have to be the one and same person all the time. Japanese families today are reluctant to have strangers in their house, wanting to keep them outside (*soto*) and protecting the inside (*naka*) from intrusion. This surprised me at first because I remember so well when most middle-class families had live-in well-trusted maids (*jochuusan*), but I realize that these maids were like members of the family.

The rigid application of the one-on-one professional housewife ideal has also fostered the insistence that the mother should not only be the main caretaker but should stay home full-time to care for the child and family. This has greatly contributed to housewife malaise, and unhappy mothers have contributed to unhappy or even problematic children. Overprotection (*kahogo*) has sometimes been pathological, probably contributing to producing individuals who do not know how to relate to a spouse emotionally or sexually. As Ochiai explains in detail, mothers need outside friends and activities, whether from employment or community activities.[29]

PROFESSIONAL SUPPORT

How to support this new individualism? In the past, Japanese could rely on proper etiquette and established social forms to maintain relationships, but now they require a deeper, conscious knowledge of both self and others. It is not surprising that they are showing more interest in the benefits of psychology.

Consider the conventional way of handling psychological problems in companies. As long as priorities were on loyalty and dedication to one's job, combined with the organizations' imperative to appear as perfect as possible, companies tolerated psychological problems occurring in regular, full-time employees and discreetly cared for the employee. Similar problems occurring prior to employment usually disqualified the job applicant. In one case, an employee of a prestigious banking firm developed severe neurotic symptoms while on assignment abroad for a few years. He was given a year off for "rest" (with salary) and improved enough to continue at the firm for the remainder of his working life with reduced responsibilities. He could not have done this if he were not already secure in a lifetime employment position. Job maintenance not only sustains good performance but also preserves "face," hiding problems from the outside world.

Doi many years ago elaborated on the difference between true feelings, desires, and intentions (*honne*) and the exterior presented to the outside (*tatemae*).[30] Nowadays, however, people are beginning to understand that the unwillingness to reveal inner difficulties becomes an obstacle to healing and growth. Being unable to confront one's true situation and express one's true feelings makes it nearly impossible to utilize outside resources, much less mobilize one's own internal resources. The concern for face is static. In dynamic changing societies, what keeps them moving is not appearances but individual responsibility, initiative, and the courage to take risks, the strength to recover from a failure, learn from it, and try again.

Japanese have long demonstrated a profound awareness of and sensitivity to the feelings of others. It was usually unarticulated but it has been a two-way shared awareness. This nonverbal sensing of another's feelings or state of mind, *sassuru*, is deeply embedded in relationships. However, the way many younger people these days are having relationship problems makes one wonder if the skill of "*sassuru*" is diminishing. What Western-style psychology can offer is verbal explanation and discussion to understand one's self and others better. Empathy (*kyoukan*), for example, comes from putting oneself in the shoes of another person and taking an interest in how he or she might feel. When we talk with someone while noting the nonverbal clues, we gain a deeper understanding of that person. Even if we do not agree with that person, we will be more likely to understand his or her *honne*. That can become the basis for conflict resolution, or for a more genuine relationship.

Professional assistance and/or group support is not only helpful, but often essential, in guiding people to make constructive decisions and to handle relationship problems. In previous eras, the family took the largest responsibility for nurturance and protection, for assigning tasks or roles within the group and within society, and for managing intra-family conflict. If individuals are to carry out those responsibilities, they need social resources and supports to enable them to do so competently. The United States has developed these resources over many years; we have had a longer struggle with individualism and decision making. But Japan in recent years has also been cultivating its own array of resources.

Many schools now have counselors and more are being added. Japanese psychologists have learned to start early working with children to help them to express themselves, to listen to others, and to make everyday decisions. School counselors consult with parents and teachers as well as with children who are experiencing social or academic problems. I have been impressed with the methods of the school counselor I know best, Kazuko Hayakawa, who works in connection with school counseling departments in Tokyo and runs a "Friendship Support Program." Hayakawa-san, who had substantial experience with counseling women, has more recently focused on conflict resolution. She does not lecture either children or adults, but rather helps them have broadening experiences that are productive of emotional and social growth. With young schoolchildren, for instance, she starts simply by having each child speak up, introducing himself or herself and telling something about his or her interests and activities. Meanwhile, each child learns to listen to other children speaking about themselves. This becomes the basis for nurturing the ability to express and understand self and others, to make decisions, and to solve classroom conflicts in ways that are comfortable for each child. She also organizes experiential workshops for the professional development of the counselors and teachers.

Many counselors have been trained in psychology graduate programs in universities in Tokyo, Kyoto, or other cities, and have received master's degrees or even doctorates. These programs are excellent in terms of teaching the basics of how to listen to and understand individual clients, most often using the well-tested theories of Carl Rogers. All too often both psychiatry (MD) and social work (MS) programs include surprisingly little about psychological understanding. The limitation of Rogerian theory is that while it teaches understanding via careful listening it often does not explain when and how to take a more active role; nor does it teach much about families. Nowadays psychology training is broadening, but what is most essential is that social workers be brought in to work with the families of troubled children. Japan has many skilled therapists among the various mental health professions, but more are needed. Japanese professionals need more clinical training, not textbook learning: working with clients or patients directly under the supervision of an experienced professional, learning how to interview, how to understand clients' lives, and how to develop therapeutic relationships.

For adult clients trying to make difficult decisions or deal with difficult problems, there are counselors in community agencies, in clinics, or in private practice. The best ones do not just listen and then offer an opinion, but rather help the client make his or her own decision. For example, a counselor talking with a college student trying to decide whether to aim primarily for a career or for marriage would undoubtedly listen to her pros and cons. But the counselor would also look for clues as to what style of life is most deeply satisfying to this woman, and lead her to explore that inside herself. A woman needs to explore her inner self, her *honne*, to discover what activities come naturally to her and which are most fulfilling, rather than always thinking of what she *should* be doing.

An American counselor reported to me her work with a Japanese woman having multiple difficulties making decisions. A very attractive and intelligent graduate student in a prestigious university, she was overwhelmed with her struggles to decide, perhaps all the more so because she had only recently come to this foreign land to study. Her decisions included selecting an apartment among many available, choosing which professional course to follow after receiving her graduate degree, whether to stay in this country or return to Japan, and whether to stay with her boyfriend. She seemed to want the counselor to decide for her. She could clearly list the issues: One apartment was too far from her school, for instance, and another was close but too expensive. She was very much in love with the boyfriend whom she was seeing every night, but he was much younger and not interested in marriage or children anytime soon, while she wanted to start a family. Unable to decide until she found just what she wanted in an apartment, she wasted study time to some detriment of her test scores. Unable to give up either the boyfriend or an early marriage, she pressed him to prove his devotion to her over all other priorities until finally he withdrew from her demands. This loss began to open her eyes to the pitfalls in her rather perfectionistic strivings and her need to search her soul for what she most cared about. Then as she gradually understood her own needs more fully through talking with the counselor, she was able to prioritize, deciding to stay in this country for now working in a hospital partly for her own interest and partly because she figured she was more likely to meet an available man her age in such a setting.

THE CULTURAL CONTEXT OF MENTAL HEALTH

Cultural attitudes are difficult to quantify or categorize, but they are embedded in any mental health approach and are important in facilitating the understanding and treatment of social and psychiatric problems. In times of social transition, for example, problems often arise as a new pattern of behavior conflicts with an older value system. The struggle that ensues can be seen as a battle between new and old cultural values. For example, a very depressed young woman told of going to work in a large and prestigious firm in her field, but within a couple of years she found herself getting harassed, tormented, criticized, and in her terms, "teased" (*ijimeraremashita*). She had grown up in an achievement-oriented family, with two hardworking, independent professional parents, but the company she entered was a rather traditional organization, with strong groups of mostly men, all working together for the common goal. Evidently her independence and her striving to learn new things, to improve herself and move up the status ladder, were unacceptable to colleagues who valued group rapport and cohesiveness. Today in Japan such a collision of values is not uncommon.

Two scholars have recently written about how the Japanese high valuation of family and group solidarity impedes the understanding and resolution of individual problems. Amy Borovoy describes how efforts to help *hikikomori* have focused on soothing and comforting them. These withdrawn young people are allowed to stay at home from school under Mother's care, away from all pressures, and avoid social opprobrium. There they are comforted and then gradually encouraged to become part of a group where they can blend in comfortably. Typically no individual diagnosis is made and no individualized treatment given, even though the causes of *hikikomori* are quite varied. *Hikikomori* may hide away for years, shielded from stress and pressures. Borovoy calls this a "kind of warehousing of the nonfunctional in hopes that, over time, they will eventually rehabilitate and rejoin society."[31]

This contrasts with American mental health practices, which, coming from a culture with strong individualistic values from the start, focus on diagnosing individual symptoms and searching for individual cures. American attitudes regarding school nonattendance also contrast with Japanese perspectives. While Japanese school dropouts are permitted to stay out of school, although they graduate in due time anyway, American children are required to attend until age sixteen or seventeen and to fulfill state-mandated academic requirements. Dropping out of school is immediately seen as a problem and the American child and family are referred to counseling where they are helped to address the particular stresses the child is experiencing. By confronting the issues, they seek, together with the counselor, to find ways of dealing with them so the child does not have to miss school. These children may object, but they do not hide. Those who legally drop out at age sixteen or seventeen usually find work, or they may become caught up in unproductive and sometimes hazardous street life. Some may finish their education later, but they do not become *hikikomori.*

Yuko Kawanishi emphasizes what she views as a serious lack of communication skills, "both verbal and non-verbal expression of honest feelings and emotions."[32] The longing for silent oneness with those one is close to, the wish to be understood without words, expressed in words like *ittaikan* (belonging or oneness) or *sassuru*, still have a powerful sway in Japan. Kawanishi goes on to note that "people in a culture that has never emphasized the articulate communication of feelings, because it is assumed that understanding will occur without such effort, will be lost when such communication fails."[33] The greatest danger to present-day society, she suggests, is socially isolated individuals, often alone and fearful because they expect silent understanding, which they seldom get, who put too much emphasis on social approval. Shy individuals who are bent on saving face and unskilled at making relationships are inclined to spend all their time on computers or computer games, or with fantasized lovers, or as *hikikomori.* Both Borovoy and Kawanishi are suggesting that the samurai-type cultural standard of maintaining a perfect *tatemae*, of oneness with one's group and never showing one's individual self (*honne*), impedes good mental health and healthy social relationships. People who strive for such perfectionistic standards and experience mental health problems need group interaction, or individual therapy, or both.

Anne Allison, in lectures and in a forthcoming book, raises alarms about individuals who are more extreme in their desolation, who feel totally "lost," much as Kawanishi warns. A much more painful extreme than *hikikomori*, they have lost any sense of belonging, any faith in the future or in themselves. Some are net café refugees, others homeless, maybe sleeping in a cubicle or, worse, the "drifting poor." She asserts that this existential emptiness is the biggest threat facing young Japanese today. Such individuals are liable to suicide or other sudden violent behavior, like Tomohiro Kato with the Akihabara rampage in 2007. While describing this social emptiness, Allison emphasizes that there is a "care deficit spiraling across the country." Whereas earlier individuals could rely on the family or on corporations to care for many problems, this is no longer possible due to economic changes and to the new emphasis on individual responsibility.[34]

Allison's recent research, however, brings some encouraging news. She finds several spots around Japan where groups are gathering, often spontaneously, in drop-in centers where anyone is welcome, where there is open-ended "being and belonging," recognition and acceptance for all. Rules are limited to such as the following:

- Don't talk about people in their absence.
- Don't stare and ask "Who is that?"
- Come and go as you wish.
- Ask for help when you need it but help others when you can.
- Spend time here as you like.
- Make no distinction between those caring and those being cared for.

The names of some of these groups speak of their comfortable homeyness: *uchi no jikka* (my home), *chiiki no chanoma* (community living room), or *fureai ibasho* (a space to interact with others). The openness of individuals just being themselves without pretense makes for genuine from-the-heart communication. For lonely, lost souls to find a place where they can allow themselves to be known is the beginning of self-acceptance and the start of healthy relating. From this beginning, one can hope for developing relationships and groups built on realistic understanding and cooperation.[35]

Uncertainty and instability have increased in recent years in Japan, especially in the aftermath of the economic downturn. Many see today's issues as a social or cultural crisis. There is no one simple way to deal with such deep and broad problems, but Japanese society has enormous strengths, strong individuals capable of finding new avenues for health and growth and institutions to support them. With an improving employment situation, and with ongoing public and professional supports like the examples discussed above, the Japanese people can allow outgrown laws and social patterns to fade, while preserving those that are still effective and developing creative new approaches.

This book has focused mainly on women in Japan, people I have known well and whose joys and hardships I have shared. I have been closely involved with women from three generations, and I have been fully engaged in the issues that concerned them the most. I began in 1958 by trying to understand the professional housewife ideal, and I find myself hopeful more than fifty years later that the unsurpassed mothering embodied in that role will endure, even as women are freed from the rigidities that compelled them to seek alternatives. In the end, it may be less a matter of finding alternatives than a matter of adjusting the essential values of the professional housewife to a new era and new circumstances.

NOTES

Portions of this chapter were originally published in a slightly different form in *Asian Survey*, Vol. 52 No. 4, pp. 687–713. © 2012 by The Regents of the University of California. Reprinted by permission of the Regents.

1. Ministry of Internal Affairs and Communications, *Kokusei chousa "nihon no jinkou"* [Population Census] (2005).

2. Ministry of Health, Labor, and Welfare, *Jinkou doutai chousa* [Vital Statistics Survey] (2010).

3. Ministry of Health, Labor, and Welfare, *Jinkou doutai chousa* [Vital Statistics Survey] (2009).

4. Merry I. White, *Perfectly Japanese: Making Families in an Era of Upheaval* (Berkeley: University of California Press, 2002), 113–15.

5. Michael Zielenziger, *Shutting Out the Sun: How Japan Created Its Own Lost Generation* (New York: Nan A. Talese, 2006).

6. Veronica Chambers, *Kickboxing Geishas: How Modern Japanese Women Are Changing Their Nation* (New York: Free Press, 2007).

7. Susan D. Holloway, *Women and Family in Contemporary Japan* (Cambridge: Cambridge University Press, 2010).

8. Ofra Goldstein-Gidoni, *Housewives of Japan: An Ethnography of Real Lives and Consumerized Domesticity* (New York: Palgrave Macmillan, 2012).

9. Mary C. Brinton, *Women and the Economic Miracle: Gender and Work in Postwar Japan* (Berkeley: University of California Press, 1994).

10. *New York Times*, January 30, 2007, A4.

11. Amy Borovoy, *The Too-Good Wife: Alcohol, Codependency, and the Politics of Nurturance in Postwar Japan* (Berkeley: University of California Press, 2005).

12. Borovoy, *The Too-Good Wife*.

13. Borovoy, *The Too-Good Wife*.

14. Takeo Doi, *Zoku "amae" no kouzou* [The Anatomy of Dependence, Continued] (Tokyo: Kobundo, 2001).

15. Borovoy, *The Too-Good Wife*.

16. Takeo Doi, *The Anatomy of Dependence* (Tokyo: Kodansha USA, 2002).

17. Terrence Real, *I Don't Want to Talk About It: Overcoming the Secret Legacy of Male Depression* (New York: Scribner, 1997).

18. Borovoy, *The Too-Good Wife*.

19. Ministry of Internal Affairs and Communications, *Roudouryoku chousa* [Labor Force Survey], multiple years.

20. Ministry of Internal Affairs and Communications, *Roudouryoku chousa* [Labor Force Survey], multiple years.

21. Matthew Marr, *Better Must Come: Exiting Homelessness in Two Global Cities, Los Angeles and Tokyo* (doctoral dissertation, University of California–Los Angeles, 2007).

22. Emiko Ochiai, *The Japanese Family System in Transition: A Sociological Analysis of Family Change in Postwar Japan* (Tokyo: LTCB International Library Foundation, 1997).

23. National Institute of Population and Social Security Research, *Dai 13-kai shussei doukou kihon chousa: kekkon to shussan ni kansuru zenkoku chousa dokushinsha chousa no kekka*

gaiyou [The 13th Annual Population and Social Security Surveys: Summary of Unmarried Survey], 2006.

24. Chambers, *Kickboxing Geishas*.

25. Satoshi Kotani, *Kodomotachi wa kawatta ka* [Have Children Changed?] (Kyoto: Sekai Shisousha, 2008).

26. Ochiai, *The Japanese Family System in Transition*.

27. Ayumi Sasagawa, "Changing Middle-Class Mothers in Japan," paper for the Association of Asian Studies Annual Meeting, March 22–25, 2007, Boston.

28. Doi, *The Anatomy of Dependence*.

29. Ochiai, *The Japanese Family System in Transition*.

30. Doi, *The Anatomy of Dependence*.

31. Amy Borovoy, "Japan's Hidden Youths: Mainstreaming the Emotionally Distressed in Japan," *Culture, Medicine and Psychiatry* 32, no. 4 (December 2008): 566.

32. Yuko Kawanishi, *Mental Health Challenges Facing Contemporary Japanese Society: The "Lonely People"* (Kent, UK: BRILL/Global Oriental, 2009), 139.

33. Kawanishi, *Mental Health Challenges*, 146.

34. Anne Allison, "Ordinary Refugees: The Loss (and Re-making) of 'Homeism' in Post-Fordist Japan," paper presented at the Sawyer Seminar—Precarious Work in Asia, University of North Carolina, 2011.

35. Allison, "Ordinary Refugees."

Index

abortion and birth control, 26, 71, 120; Mieko Suzuki, 120

abuse. *See* violence and abuse

Agora magazine, 16

Akihabara rampage (2007), 176. *See also* violence and abuse

alcoholism, 111, 156–157; and Yaeko Itou, 64, 88

Allison, Anne, 175–176

amae: distortion or denial of, 159, 160; empathy, 11; mother-child relationship, 10, 11, 13, 170

The Anatomy of Dependence (Takeo Doi), 10

The Anatomy of Self (Takeo Doi), 10

Aoki, Tokuzou. *See* Itou, Tokuzou

Aoki, Yayoi, 14, 17

assertiveness and deference, 168, 170; Hanae Tanaka, 21–23, 25, 28–29, 38–39, 40; *uchibenkei* (quiet with outsiders but loud within family), 33; Yaeko Itou, 61–62, 69, 105, 112

baby-sitters, 15, 154. *See also* child-raising

birth control. *See* abortion and birth control

Borovoy, Amy: on group solidarity and individual expression, 175; on *hikikomori* (social withdrawal), 174; on housewife role, 160; on mothering skills, 156–157, 162

breast-feeding and weaning, 11, 41; Mieko Suzuki, 121, 122–123; Tanaka family, 29; Yaeko Itou, 72. *See also* child-raising

Brinton, Mary, 154

bubble economy (1980s), 154, 167

capitalist industrial society, 17

Chambers, Veronica, 151–152, 168

chiiki no chanoma group (community living room), 176

childbirth, 119

child-raising: *ai no muchi* (love-spanking), 24; baby-sitters, 15, 154; breast-feeding and weaning, 11, 29, 41, 72, 121, 122–123; day care, 16, 154; Japan and America, 11, 12, 112n4, 123; Katsuko Itou (Mrs. Matsunami), 100–101; Mieko Suzuki, 115–116, 118–128, 132–134; modern era, 156–157, 158–159, 162, 170–171; physical contact and *ombu*, 5, 11, 41, 72, 121; postwar, 41, 58, 71, 96, 116; prewar, 116; weaning as metaphor for independence push, 123–124, 125, 136, 145; Yaeko Itou, 71–75. *See also* education

chounan (eldest son), 55. *See also* eldest son relationship

Christianity: Hanae Tanaka, 26, 59; Yoshiko Tanaka, 43–44, 57

marital relationship, 21–23, 49–50; as mother-in-law, 49; work outside the home, 22, 27, 40, 51–53

Tanaka, Kazuko: marriage, 47–48; parental relationship, 46–47; work outside the home, 41, 47–48

Tanaka, Mamoru: birth, 26; education, 36–37; later life, 41; marriage, 50

Tanaka, Masako: birth, 26; education, 34; later life, 42–43; social development, 35

Tanaka, Masami: birth, 26; career, 40–41; early rebelliousness, 33; education, 33

Tanaka, Michiko: birth, 26; education, 35; independence, 46; later life, 45–46; social development, 35; working outside the home, 41

Tanaka, Takao: children, 33; death, 39; early life, 23–24; during and after war, 26–27

Tanaka, Yoshiko: birth, 26; and Christianity, 57; education, 34; independence, 43–44; later life, 43–44; social development, 35

tatemae (outward proprieties), 155, 171, 175. *See also* face-saving

Tokyo Sonata (2008), 165

tsukisoi (traditional caretaker), 143

Tsunoda family, 62

uchibenkei (quiet with outsiders but loud within family), 33. *See also* assertiveness and deference

Uchimura, Kanzou, 26

uchi no jikka group (my home), 176

Ueno, Chizuko, 14, 17

vertical society (*tateshakai*), 7

violence and abuse: Akihabara rampage (2007), 176; American independence ideal, 160–161; and dependent child relationship, 19, 157, 158; *ijime* (teasing or bullying), 64, 104, 174; and son-in-law relationship, 64; wife abuse, 9, 152

Vogel, David, x, 6

Vogel, Eve, x

Vogel, Ezra F., ix, 4, 187

Vogel, Suzanne Hall, 187; death and memorial, x; divorce, 49, 54, 140; *The Japanese Family in Transition*, x, xi; *Japan's New Middle Class*, ix; psychotherapy and sociological research methods, ix

wagamama (selfishness), 8

weaning. *See* breast-feeding and weaning; child-raising

women's activity outside the home, 17; employment, 2, 16, 41, 154, 162, 168, 171; feminist movement on, 17; flower arranging, 6, 22, 23, 27, 40, 51–53; and government policy, 2, 16, 150, 154; Hanae Tanaka, 22, 23, 27, 40, 51–53; and housewife role, 161; Katsuko Itou (Mrs. Matsunami), 90, 103; Kazuko Tanaka, 41, 47–48; Masami Tanaka, 40–41; Michiko Tanaka, 41; problems of, 14–15, 16; PTA (Parent-Teacher Association), 6, 23, 75, 76, 80, 82; Yaeko Itou, 75, 76, 80, 82–84, 109

Yanagisawa, Hakuo, 154

Yasuko (Yoshiko Tanaka's daughter), 53, 57–58

Zielenziger, Michael, 151–152

About the Author

Suzanne Hall Vogel was a psychotherapist at the Massachusetts Mental Health Center, McLean Hospital, and the Harvard University Health Services, who conducted research on Japanese women, family, and mental health issues for more than fifty years. She first engaged in fieldwork in Japan in 1958–1960 with her former husband, Ezra Vogel, resulting in the publication of his classic work on Japanese society, *Japan's New Middle Class* (1963). She also published a highly influential article "Professional Housewife" (1978), as well as many other works. She received a Fulbright Fellowship in 1988–1989 to consult with the Social Work and Psychiatry Departments of St. Luke's International Hospital in Tokyo and to research family life and mental health in Japan. Subsequently, she spent about six weeks every year supervising social workers at Hasegawa Hospital in Tokyo from 1989 to 2006. After her retirement from Harvard, she continued a private practice focusing on helping Japanese in the Boston area struggling with mental health and cultural adjustment.